Getting the Best from CAT

A Practical Guide for Secondary Schools

Steve Strand

nferNelson
understanding potential

Published by nferNelson Publishing Company Ltd
The Chiswick Centre, 414 Chiswick High Road,
LONDON W4 5TF, UK
Tel: +44 (0) 845 602 1937
Fax: +44 (0) 845 601 5351
www.nfer-nelson.co.uk
nferNelson is a division of Granada Learning Limited

Designed by Oxford Designers & Illustrators

Printed and bound in Great Britain

Code 0090008818   ISBN 0-7087-0376-3   3(10.06)

Contents

Contents

List of figures and tables

Contents

Introduction

The *Cognitive Abilities Test* (*CAT*) is the most widely used test of reasoning ability employed in schools in the UK. In the academic year 2001–02, nearly one million pupils in the UK were assessed using *CAT*. The complete series, from Levels A to H, provides a continuous scale for appraising cognitive development – from age seven years six months, right through to post compulsory education. Levels G and H were published in September 2003: these extend the upper age range of *CAT* to 17 years and above and are discussed further in Chapter 8, page 162.

Using this book

This guide is based on the popular nferNelson course 'Getting the best from *CAT*'. Its approach is practical and the focus is on:

- interpreting and using the reports from the *CAT* Computer Scoring and Analysis Service;
- independently analysing your own *CAT* data;
- using the results within your school.

It also contains case studies of effective *CAT* practice in secondary schools. The intended audience for the book is wide ranging, including classroom teachers, Special Educational Needs Coordinators (SENCOs), middle and senior managers within schools and local authority staff concerned with pupil assessment and school improvement.

Components

This book

The guide provides all the relevant information needed to interpret *CAT* scores. Where appropriate, cross-references are made to the *CAT3 Administration Manual*, the *CAT3 Technical Manual* and various technical reports and material contained on the *CAT* website (www.nfer-nelson.co.uk/cat).

Please note that any text referring to material on the accompanying CD, which is described below, is marked by this logo:

The CD

The book is accompanied by a CD, which contains two types of information:

- sample school and pupil data, which will be used to illustrate the analyses and give practical 'hands-on' experience of working with *CAT* scores and results;
- Microsoft Excel workbooks to assist in analysing your *CAT* data.

A summary of the contents of the CD is contained in Appendix 1.

Please note that the Microsoft Excel tools provided on the CD are based on *CAT3* data. You cannot use these workbooks with *CAT2E* scores. However, you can download similar workbooks for *CAT2E,* together with annual updates of the *CAT* Excel tools, from the nferNelson *CAT* website (see www.nfer-nelson.co.uk/cat).

It is assumed that users will have experience of using Excel in order to access and manipulate the worksheets contained on the CD: the specific skills needed are listed in Chapter 2, page 21. Most UK teachers should have been able to develop these skills through the New Opportunities Fund (NOF) ICT training.

Summary of contents

Chapter 1 gives general background information on the content of *CAT,* and the main uses of the test. It also includes a discussion of the ways in which performance on *CAT* is expressed – that is, using raw scores, standardised scores, stanines and percentiles – and how these scores should be interpreted.

Chapter 2 considers some analyses to establish the accuracy of your *CAT* data. It includes guidance on how to check your pupil listing to ensure correct interpretation of results, and how to use the *CAT* data disk to complete such checks for all your pupils should you choose to do so.

Chapter 3 considers the *CAT3* Individual Pupil Profile in detail. The Profile provides a rich source of information, allowing you to identify a pupil's cognitive strengths and weaknesses in reasoning with verbal, quantitative and non-verbal concepts. It provides a categorisation of profiles so that these can be grouped and analysed in a meaningful and structured way; for each type identified, there is guidance on the implications of the profile for teaching and learning. This chapter is likely to be of particular interest to classroom teachers concerned with pupils' learning styles.

Chapter 4 considers how *CAT* can be used to compare the results for different groups of pupils against national averages and to judge whether any score differences between groups are significant. The *CAT* Computer Scoring and Analysis Service group profiles and gender difference reports are reviewed. Examples of the range of possible differences are discussed. Practical tools are presented to allow you to compare and contrast the results for a class or group, to consider the spread of visual and verbal preferences across the group and to compare results by gender, ethnicity or teaching groups. You should be able to judge the significance of the change in a pupil's scores over time, and to understand the implications for retesting. An automated procedure is available to convert *CAT2E* to *CAT3* scores using Microsoft Excel worksheets.

Chapter 5 describes briefly how the Key Stage 3, GCSE and Scottish Standard Grade indicators are calculated, and discusses the Key Stage 3, GCSE and Standard Grade indicator reports provided by the *CAT* Computer Scoring and Analysis Service. It considers the range of factors impinging on pupils' performance and shows how *CAT-GCSE* Progress Charts can be used in pupil target setting.

Chapter 6 provides case studies that demonstrate successful practice in whole-school pupil tracking and progress monitoring.

Chapter 7 explains how you can calculate a measure of the 'value added' for your class, subject, department or school, by comparing pupils' actual national test or examination results against the indicators provided by *CAT*. 'Value-added' analyses are essential if schools and teachers are to obtain an indication of the *progress* made by their pupils, rather than simply considering their absolute level of attainment. A Microsoft Excel workbook is included on the accompanying CD to support such analyses. The chapter considers some of the questions that can arise from a detailed consideration of value added.

Chapter 8 considers some wider issues, including the relationship between *CAT* scores and thinking skills, the extent to which *CAT* scores can be improved through high-quality teaching and challenging learning activities and the relationship between *CAT* and Key Stage 2 test scores, particularly in relation to target setting. Detailed suggestions are given for reporting *CAT* results to parents, including examples of practice in a number of schools. Further developments of *CAT* are described, particularly the online version and *CAT3* Levels G and H, which extend the upper age range of *CAT* through to 17 years and above.

It is not necessary to read the complete guide from start to finish. For example, if you are already familiar with the content of *CAT*, and with the concept of standard age scores, you may want to proceed directly to Chapter 2. Classroom teachers may be most interested in Chapter 3, which explores the implication for teaching and learning of the individual pupil profiles, and in the section in Chapter 5 on target setting. Colleagues with responsibility for school-wide analysis of *CAT* and other pupil performance data may be most interested in Chapters 2, 4, 5, 6 and 7, while senior managers may be particularly interested in Chapter 7 on value added (page 130).

What is *CAT*?

While many readers will be well acquainted with *CAT*, a description of the key features of the test is provided below. More detail can be found in the separate *CAT3 Technical Manual* (pages 1 to 9).

Symbolic reasoning

CAT assesses an individual's ability to reason with and manipulate different types of symbols. Three main types of symbol play a substantial role in human thought. These symbols represent:

■ words;

■ quantities;

■ spatial, geometric or figural patterns.

In *CAT*, separate batteries of subtests are provided to assess competence in working with each of these three types of symbol:

- Verbal Battery;
- Quantitative Battery;
- Non-verbal Battery.

Where possible, parallel question types have been incorporated in two or all three batteries, so that the influence of the differing media can be identified more clearly. For example, tests of reasoning through analogies are included in all three batteries. The set of three scores will give a profile showing the level and pattern of each pupil's abilities. Knowledge of areas of relative strength and weakness should help both the individual and the school to use strengths most effectively, and to compensate for areas of weakness (see Chapter 3).

Perceiving relationships

CAT3 emphasises *relational thinking* – the perceiving of relationships among elements. Throughout each of the subtests the basic elements have been kept relatively simple, clear, familiar and appropriate to the ages of the pupils who will take the test. All pupils educated in UK schools and exposed to modern cultural influences should have had an opportunity to acquire the background knowledge needed to answer the questions. All questions in the subtests were pre-trialled with random samples of pupils of different ages, and only those questions that were of the desired difficulty and clarity were included in the final test. Questions were also closely evaluated to minimise or eliminate sex or ethnic bias. Thus questions that proved to be exceptionally difficult or easy for one or other sex or ethnic group were omitted or counterbalanced in the final test (see the *CAT3 Technical Manual*, pages 15 to 24).

Developed abilities

CAT measures *developed* rather than *innate* abilities. The development of these abilities begins at birth and continues through early adulthood. It is influenced by both in-school and out-of-school experiences. Although test scores are based on experience, this does not negate the value of the test in helping to understand the individual as he or she is at the present time. Because these abilities are closely related to an individual's success in school in virtually all subjects, *CAT* scores, together with other relevant information, can be used to devise the types of learning experiences that will help pupils to improve their current levels of performance.

The three *CAT* test batteries

Verbal Battery – thinking with words

The Verbal Battery comprises three subtests:

- Verbal Classification;
- Sentence Completion;
- Verbal Analogies.

Although performance in these subtests depends upon the pupil's store of verbal concepts, the questions included in the Verbal Battery have been written with a view to making demands primarily upon the individual's flexibility in using his or her concepts.

The Verbal Battery is designed to assess relational thinking when the relationships are formulated in verbal terms. Since the greater part of education is presented through verbal symbols, the relevance of a verbal test for educational prognosis and diagnosis is clear. Tests of verbal reasoning have always been among the best ways of predicting educational progress.

Quantitative Battery – thinking with numbers

The Quantitative Battery comprises three subtests:

- Number Analogies;
- Number Series;
- Equation Building.

The solution of the problems in each question requires that the pupil has a basic store of quantitative concepts, but all the questions call for *perception of relationships* among concepts and for *flexibility in using* quantitative concepts. None of the questions in the subtests require reading, so reading skills will not affect performance.

Next to verbal reasoning, the ability to reason with quantitative symbols is the one most frequently required in an educational setting. Subjects such as mathematics, science, geography and economics make heavy demands on quantitative abilities. Quantitative reasoning together with verbal reasoning constitutes what some theorists have called 'academic ability'.

Non-verbal Battery – thinking with shape and space

The Non-verbal Battery comprises three subtests:

- Figure Classification;
- Figure Analogies;
- Figure Analysis.

The questions in this battery involve neither words nor numbers, and the shapes or figures used bear little direct relationship to the formal school curriculum. The first two subtests emphasise discovery of, and flexibility in manipulating relationships expressed in figures. The third subtest, Figure Analysis, assesses 'spatial ability': that is, the ability to create, maintain and manipulate visual–spatial images.

Despite the lack of overlap with formal schooling, non-verbal reasoning tests have been found to relate significantly to school achievement, providing a useful addition to verbal tests. Among pupils with similar levels of verbal ability, the level of non-verbal ability may well identify those with the greater aptitude for the visual–spatial academic disciplines, such as mathematics, physics, art and design and technology. Tests of spatial ability are used in employment settings to identify those with aptitude for such careers as design, engineering and architecture.

The Non-verbal Battery measures what has been termed 'fluid intelligence': that is, an ability to reason that is not strongly influenced by cultural and educational background. Where performance on this battery is superior to that on the other two batteries, it may suggest potential that is not fully expressed in performance on school-related tasks, for one reason or another. Scores on this battery may be particularly valuable in assessing the reasoning ability of pupils with poor English language skills, pupils with specific problems in language-based work, or disaffected pupils who may have failed to achieve in academic work for motivational reasons.

Using *CAT* scores in secondary schools

The main uses of *CAT* scores in secondary schools are:
- to identify an *individual pupil's cognitive strengths and weaknesses* in order to inform teaching and learning;
- to *compare the performance of groups* of pupils, in order to better identify needs and to target resources;
- to *identify pupils, or groups of pupils, who may be underachieving*;
- to monitor *trends or changes* in the ability profile of the intake over time;
- to inform *target setting* with regard to national tests and public examinations;
- to set a baseline against which to *assess the 'value added'* by the school.

The guide will address each of these issues.

Understanding the scores from *CAT*

Raw score
The raw score is simply the total number of correct answers obtained by the pupil. The raw score is calculated for each battery. These raw scores can be converted to three

types of normative scores called standard age scores (SAS), stanines and percentiles. These scores are described below.

Standard age score (SAS)

One way to make a raw score more readily understandable would be to convert it to a percentage: for example, '33 out of 50' becomes 66 per cent. However, the percentage on its own does *not* tell us the average score of all the pupils or how 'spread out' the scores are, whereas standard age scores do relate to these statistics.

In order to provide a standard age (or standard score) scale, some tests are standardised so that the average standard age score for any age group is always 100: this makes it easy to tell whether a pupil is above or below the national average. The spread of scores (the 'standard deviation') is also set to plus or minus 15 points, so that for any age group about two-thirds of the pupils in the national sample will have a standardised score of between 85 and 115. *CAT3* was nationally standardised in October/November 2000 with a representative sample of 16,000 pupils from 556 schools in England, Scotland, Wales and Northern Ireland. Full details on the development process and the standardisation are contained in the *CAT3 Technical Manual*, pages 7 to 9. Raw scores are converted to standard age scores using tables of norms: for the *CAT3* conversion tables, see the *CAT3 Administration Manual*, pages 61 to 107.

Standard age scores allow you to compare the level of cognitive development of an individual with the levels of other pupils in the same age group. The properties of standard age scores mean that approximately two-thirds of pupils in the age group score between 85 and 115, approximately 95 per cent score between 70 and 130, and over 99 per cent score between 60 and 140. Figure 1.1 shows the frequency distribution, known as the normal distribution, for standard age scores, stanines and percentiles.

Figure 1.1: The normal curve of distribution showing the relationships of stanines, national percentile ranks (PR) and standard age scores (SAS)

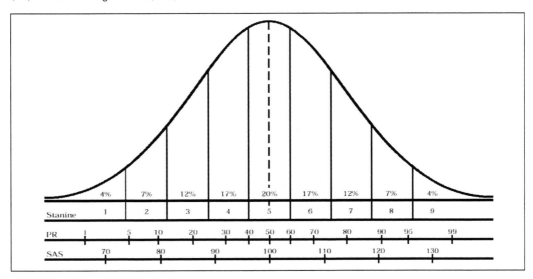

Standard age scores have three particular benefits, as described below.

■ *They place a pupil's performance on a readily understandable scale.* As we have seen above, standard age scores allow a pupil's performance to be readily interpreted. It is immediately deducible from the score itself that a verbal reasoning score of 95 indicates a level of performance just below the national average, but well within the average range.

■ *An allowance can be made for the different ages of the pupils.* In a typical class in England and Wales, it is usual that most pupils are born between 1 September of one year and 31 August of the following year, which means that the oldest pupils are very nearly 12 months older than the youngest. Almost invariably, older pupils achieve slightly higher raw scores in tests and examinations than younger pupils. However, standard age scores are derived in such a way that the ages of the pupils are taken into account by comparing a pupil *only* with others of the *same age*. An older pupil may in fact gain a higher raw score than a younger pupil, but have a lower standardised score. This is because the older pupil is being compared with other older pupils in the norm group. Pupils of different ages who gain the same standard age score have done equally well, with each being judged in relation to their standing among pupils of their own age.

■ *Scores from different tests can be meaningfully added or compared.* Standardised scores for most tests cover the same range, from 60– to 140+. Hence a pupil's standing in, say, mathematics and English can be compared directly using standardised scores. It is not meaningful to add together *raw* scores from tests of different length or difficulty. However, should you wish to add *standardised* scores from more than one test – for example, in order to obtain a single overall measure of performance – they can be meaningfully combined.

Stanines

Standard scores run from 60– to 140+ and give differentiated, finely-graded information on the performance of each pupil. However sometimes a shorthand summary is more useful. Stanines, short for 'standard nines', are just nine summary score bands calculated directly from the standard scores, as shown in Table 1.1. Based on the national standardisation, we can say what proportion of pupils are expected within each stanine, and these are also given in the table. The broad nature of stanines minimises over-interpretation of small, insignificant differences among test scores. Stanines are therefore particularly useful in reporting test information to pupils and to parents, as they are relatively easy to understand and interpret.

Table 1.1: Stanines score bands for *CAT3*

Description	Stanine	*Percentage of pupils	Corresponding percentiles (NPR)	Corresponding SAS
Very high	9	4	97 and above	127 and above
Above average	8	7	90–96	119–126
	7	12	78–89	112–118
Average	6	17	59–77	104–111
	5	20	41–58	97–103
	4	17	23–40	89–96
Below average	3	12	12–22	82–88
	2	7	5–11	74–81
Very low	1	4	4 and below	73 and below

*The 'Percentage of pupils' figures have been rounded to the nearest whole number.

National percentile rank (NPR)

This indicates the percentage of pupils in the national sample who obtain a standard age score at or below a particular score. For example, a pupil with a standard age score of 108 has a National Percentile Rank (NPR) of 70: he or she has performed as well as, or better than, 70 per cent of pupils of his or her age group. An NPR of 50 is average for an age group. Table 1.2 on page 10 shows the conversion from standard age score to NPR.

The nferNelson *CAT3* Computer Scoring and Analysis Service dataset

At several points in this guide, in Chapters 2, 3 and 4 in particular, reference is made to typical patterns of errors on *CAT*, to the relative frequency of different types of individual pupil score profiles or to the balance of visual and verbal abilities. These data are drawn from an analysis of the *CAT3* results for over half a million pupils who completed *CAT3* between September 2001 and January 2003. Data of this scale and depth are unprecedented, and allow this guide to provide a rich and detailed insight into the performance of your pupils.

Table 1.2: Conversion of standard age scores to national percentile ranks

Conversion of standard age scores (SAS) to national percentile ranks (NPR)					
SAS	NPR	SAS	NPR	SAS	NPR
133 or more	99	109	72	90	26
130–132	98	108	70	89	24
128–129	97	107	68	88	22
126–127	96	106	66	87	20
125	95	105	63	86	18
123–124	94	104	60	85	16
122	93	103	58	84	14
121	92	102	55	83	13
120	91	101	52	82	12
119	90	100	50	81	11
118	89	99	48	80	9
117	87	98	45	79	8
116	86	97	42	78	7
115	84	96	40	76–77	6
114	82	95	37	75	5
113	80	94	34	73–74	4
112	78	93	32	71–72	3
111	77	92	30	68–70	2
110	74	91	28	67 or less	1

Review

In this chapter we have considered the purpose of *CAT*, the content and structure of the test, and the different types of standardised scores. You should now understand the range of abilities assessed by *CAT* and feel confident in interpreting different kinds of standardised scores. In Chapter 2 we shall consider some *CAT* results for actual pupils, and describe some analyses that you can carry out with the results for your own pupils.

2 Establishing the accuracy of your data

AIMS

In this chapter, we will:

■ examine the *standard outputs* from the *CAT* Computer Scoring and Analysis Service, specifically the *Group Summary of Results*;

■ learn *how to check the pupil listing* to ensure *correct interpretation of pupils' results*, including checking for error flags, chance level raw scores, the number of attempts etc.;

■ consider *how to complete the above checks for all pupils* using the *CAT* data disk;

■ analyse *particular patterns of errors or omissions* within pupils' results, and the possible implications for interpreting the score.

Introduction to the *CAT* Computer Scoring and Analysis Service reports

Three standard reports are produced by nferNelson's *CAT* Computer Scoring and Analysis Service:

■ the Group Summary of Results;

■ the Individual Pupil Profile;

■ the Group Distribution of Standardised Scores (also referred to as the group profile).

For full details, please refer to the current nferNelson education catalogue, or telephone Customer Services on 0845 602 1937.

This chapter looks at the Group Summary of Results, which lists pupils' results in detail. The Individual Pupil Profiles will be considered in Chapter 3 and the group profiles in Chapter 4. Other optional *CAT* Computer Scoring and Analysis Service reports, such as national test and examinations indicators, are considered in Chapter 5.

Understanding the Group Summary of Results

The Group Summary of Results gives you a summary of the results for all the pupils in your class, with 25 pupils listed on each page. This gives, for all the pupils separately, their:

■ identification number (if you asked pupils to complete this field);

- name;
- age at the time of testing;
- sex;
- scores on each battery (raw score, standard age score, stanine, national percentile rank and rank order within the group being tested);
- mean standard age score (which is the arithmetic mean of the pupil's standard age scores across *all the batteries they completed*);
- group rank based upon the mean standard age score.

An example of a Group Summary of Results is given in Figure 2.1. This is the first page of the report for a group of 30 pupils from Year 7 who completed Level D of *CAT* in March 2002. The types of scores given in the listing were described in detail in Chapter 1 (see pages 6 to 10) and are briefly summarised below. Where appropriate, an example is given from the pupils listed in Figure 2.1.

Raw score (RS)
The raw score is the total number of correct answers obtained by the pupil on each battery (see page 6). For example, in the group listed in Figure 2.1, **David Smithers** has a raw score of 35 on the Verbal Battery.

Standard age score (SAS)
These scores allow you to evaluate a pupil's performance in relation to other pupils of the same age, and have a mean of 100 and a standard deviation (SD) of 15 (see page 7). For example, **Charlotte Barnet** has a verbal reasoning standard age score of 70, indicating that her abilities are very low in this area, compared to other pupils of her age; **Gemma Greenwood** has a verbal reasoning standard age score of 122, indicating very well-developed verbal reasoning abilities in relation to other pupils of her age.

Stanines (ST)
These are a shorthand summary of the standard age scores in nine score bands, ranging from 1 (low) to 9 (high) (see page 8). Based on the national standardisation, we can say what proportion of pupils are expected in each stanine: these figures were given in Table 1.2 (see page 9). For example, **Stephen Bradie** obtained a standard age score of 102 on the verbal battery, placing him in stanine 5. This score band may be described as average, and includes the middle 20 per cent of pupils in the standardisation sample.

National percentile rank (NPR)
This indicates the percentage of pupils in the national sample who obtain standard age scores *at or below* a particular score (see page 9). For example, in the Group Summary of Results shown in Figure 2.1, **Kirsty Barnsley**, who has a verbal reasoning standard age score of 108, has performed as well as, or better than, 70 per cent of pupils who are aged 12:0 to 12:2.

Group rank (GR)

This indicates a pupil's rank within the group. For example, **Kirsty Barnsley** had the fifth highest score for verbal reasoning in this group of 30 pupils, and the eighth highest for both quantitative reasoning and non-verbal reasoning. Where several pupils in the group have the *same* standard age score, this is indicated with an equals sign. For example, **Ronald Barson** and **Emma Murphy** both have a verbal reasoning standard age score of 95, making them =11th in group rank.

Figure 2.1: Example Group Summary of Results report

CAT 3

Group Summary of Results (alphabetical) Section A Page 2 of 5

School: **Neltest School**
Class/Group: **Y7 /7A**
No. of Pupils: **30**   CAT Level: **D**   Date of Test: **15/Mar/2002**

ID Number	Name Of Pupil	Age	Sex	VERBAL					QUANTITATIVE					NON-VERBAL					MEANS	
				RS	SAS	ST	NPR	GR	RS	SAS	ST	NPR	GR	RS	SAS	ST	NPR	GR	SAS	GR
	BARNET, CHARLOTTE	11:11	F	!15	70	1	2	=23rd	18	79	2	8	17th	35	92	4	30	=11th	80	17th
	BARNSLEY, KIRSTY	12:0	F	66	108	6	70	5th	47	105	6	63	8th	41	97	5	42	8th	103	6th
	BARSON, RONALD	12:1	M	52	95	4	37	=11th	38	95	4	37	=9th	39	95	4	37	9th	95	=11th
	BRADIE, STEPHEN	12:4	M	62	102	5	55	=8th	55	118	7	89	4th	56	114	7	82	3rd	111	4th
	CLELAND, LOUISE	11:10	F	56	100	5	50	10th	37	95	4	37	=9th	44	100	5	50	6th	98	=7th
	GOWERLY, STEVEN	11:10	M	67	111	6	77	3rd	55	120	8	91	3rd	48	105	6	63	4th	112	3rd
	GREENWOOD, GEMMA	12:2	F	74	122	8	93	1st	56	122	8	93	2nd	58	118	7	89	2nd	121	2nd
	HALE, DARREN	11:10	M	37	86	3	18	15th	@					@					86	=15th
	HARDE, BRUCE A	12:5	M	65	105	6	63	6th	36	91	4	28	12th	34	91	4	28	14th	96	10th
	HARTLEY, EMMA	12:2	F	71	115	7	84	2nd	57	126	8	96	1st	64	137	9	99	1st	126	1st
	HEPWORTH, LIAM	11:8	M	!14	71	1	3	22nd	13	76	2	6	=19th	!13	78	2	7	=18th	75	=22nd
	IVES, JOANNE	11:8	F	24	79	2	8	18th	26	87	3	20	13th	35	93	4	32	10th	86	=15th
	KIRKHAM, CLAIRE	11:9	F	!15	70	1	2	=23rd	!12	75	2	5	=21st	!11	77	2	6	20th	74	24th
	LANE, JADE	12:0¹	F	21	74	2	4	20th	29	86	3	18	14th	!9	76	2	6	=21st	79	18th
	MAILING, LIAM	11:9	M	!1	60-	1	1	=29th	!10	74	2	4	=23rd	!6	73	1	4	=24th	69	=28th
	MALCOLM, ANGUS	12:5	M	69	110	6	74	4th	!0	60-	1	1	=27th	!0	60-	1	1	=27th	76	=20th
	MURPHY, EMMA	12:11	F	58	95	4	37	=11th	@					@					95	=11th
	OAKLEY, LOUISE	12:0¹	F	27	78	2	7	19th	23	81	2	11	16th	!10	76	2	6	=21st	78	19th
	RENNIE, SCOTT	12:3	M	45	89	4	24	14th	!0	60-	1	1	=27th	!0	60-	1	1	=27th	69	=28th
	SMITH, DEAN	12:0¹	M	52	95	4	37	=11th	48	106	6	66	7th	35	92	4	30	=11th	98	=7th
	SMITHERS, DAVID	12:4	M	35	82	3	12	17th	40	95	4	37	=9th	24	84	3	14	17th	87	14th
	TOMPSON, FRANK T	12:3	M	!12	64	1	1	28th	17	77	2	6	18th	!6	73	1	4	=24th	71	27th
	TOWLER, LEAH	12:2	F	!14	68	1	2	26th	14	76	2	6	=19th	24	85	3	16	=15th	76	=20th
	WATFORD, MICHAELA	11:7	F	!15	72	1	3	21st	!10	74	2	4	=23rd	!13	78	2	7	=18th	75	=22nd
	WIFFLEY, IAN	12:7	M	!6	60-	1	1	=29th	!9	71	1	3	25th	25	85	3	16	=15th	72	26th

Key:
> Letter unreadable in name.
1 Unclear date of birth. Estimated age used.
2 Age unknown. Average age used.
3 Age out of range. Youngest allowed used.
4 Age out of range. Oldest allowed used.
@ Insufficient data for battery.
! Chance level raw score
* 5 or more unclear responses.
= Used if several pupils have the same Group Rank.

Checking the accuracy of your pupil data

Before beginning to interpret the Group Summary of Results and associated reports, you should first carry out a few simple checks on the integrity of your results. These checks are summarised as a flowchart in Figure 2.2 on page 14.

Figure 2.2: Pre checks on your *CAT* Group Summary of Results pupil listing

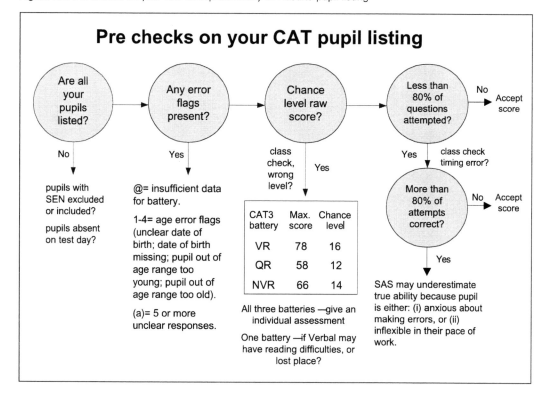

There are five checks in total. Each check is described in detail below.

1. Are all pupils listed?

It is not uncommon for users to look first at the average standardised score for their whole class or school, *before* checking whether all their pupils are included, and then to wonder why the average score looks higher or lower than they expected. For example, if pupils with special educational needs (SEN) were not included in the testing, the average score for the group might appear higher than would be expected. As a first check, therefore, you should determine whether the listing includes *all* the pupils from the relevant group. Are any groups of pupils excluded? Are any individuals absent from the list?

2. Are there any error flags?

During computer scoring, any irregularities in a pupil's results are highlighted by an error flag. These symbols will appear in the relevant position in the pupil listing and are described in detail in Table 2.1. You should determine whether any of your pupils have an error flag and, if so, the action you will take. This might include recalculating the pupil's standard age score, or administering missing subtests or batteries. Full details are given in Table 2.1.

Table 2.1: Interpreting the error flags on the *CAT* Group Summary of Results pupil listing

Symbol	Location	Description and suggested action
1–4	Age column	The numbers 1 to 4 appearing as superscripts against the pupil's age indicate a problem with the recording by the pupil of their date of birth (DOB). The four errors are: • 1: the DOB is unclear because *one of the elements* (day, month or year) is *missing*; • 2: the pupil has *not completed any of the DOB details*; • 3: the DOB may be deemed incorrect because the resulting *age of the pupil* is *below* that specified for the level of *CAT* being administered; • 4: as above, the DOB may be deemed incorrect – this time, because the resulting *age of the pupil* is *above* that specified for the level of *CAT* being administered. In these cases an estimated age is used in order to generate a standard age score. This may be acceptable where there is only a small variation between the pupil's *true* age as calculated from their actual DOB and the *estimated* age displayed in the age column. However, if the variation between the pupil's *actual* age at the time they took the test and the *estimated* age used would place them in a different age band, you should recalculate the standard age score. The age bands are shown in the tables of norms given in the *CAT3 Administration Manual* (pages 62 to 109).
@	Raw Score (RS) column	The pupil has not completed the battery. This may indicate that he or she: • *was absent through illness* on the day of the missing battery: consider whether you want to test the pupil on the missing battery to ensure the completeness of the profile; • *has failed to answer any questions* in one of the 3 subtests within the relevant battery: if there are no marks for one of the subtests, then the Computer Scoring Service cannot tell whether or not the pupil was present for it; to allocate a total score to a pupil who had missed one of the subtests would be misleading, therefore such cases are flagged (although they occur relatively rarely). If one of your pupils has this error flag, you should consult the pupil's record in the data disk. If he or she has a raw score of zero in any of the 3 subtests, you may want to consider administering the missing subtest.

a	Raw Score (RS) column	The pupil made *5 or more unclear responses*. An unclear response means that 2 or more answers were given for a question. This may occur where a pupil changes his or her mind on an answer but fails to erase the first response, or fails to erase it clearly. If this has happened on 5 or more questions, it may be wise to disregard the test outcome. The pupil may not have understood the response requirements, or may not have been provided with an eraser. This outcome is very infrequent, fewer than around 1 in 2,000 scripts.
!	Raw Score (RS) column	Chance level score (see pages 16 to 17).

3. Are any pupils performing at the chance level?

CAT is a multiple-choice test with five option choices per question. As with any multiple-choice assessment, a certain level of performance could be achieved by chance alone. If a pupil were to make a random choice among the five options for each question then they would get one question in five, or 20 per cent, correct by chance. Table 2.2 shows the number of questions and the chance level raw scores for each of the three *CAT* batteries.

Where performance is at or below the chance level, this is indicated on the pupil listing by an exclamation mark ('!') against the pupil's score in the raw score (RS) column. For example, in Figure 2.1, **Charlotte Barnet** has a chance level raw score on the Verbal Battery, while **Claire Kirkham** has chance level raw scores on all three batteries.

Table 2.2: Chance level raw scores for each of the three *CAT* batteries

CAT battery	Number of questions in battery	Chance level number correct
Verbal	78	16
Quantitative	58	12
Non-verbal	66	14

Very few pupils achieve chance level scores, because when the tests were constructed care was taken to include an appropriate number of easy items to assess even those pupils whose abilities were low for their age. The *CAT3* results of around 500,000 pupils were analysed when preparing this guide (see page 32). On each battery only around 5 per cent of pupils were found to obtain scores at or below the chance level.

In interpreting chance level scores, a sensible approach is to work systematically through possible explanations for poor performance, starting with the most superficial and ending with the more fundamental:

■ *Review the test session*. Did the pupil fully understand what had to be done? Did he or she complete the practice questions correctly? Were there any reasons why the pupil might have been distracted, worried or insufficiently motivated?

■ *Consider the pupil's overall experience of formal timed testing*. Was this a new and stressful experience? Did the pupil understand the need to work quickly?

■ *Look at the pupil's performance across all three batteries*. Is the pupil performing at or below chance level across all three?
  – if *yes*: any pupils whose achievement is markedly below expectations for their age should be checked for other problems, such as poor vision or hearing, learning difficulties, behaviour or attention difficulties or severely disrupted education;
  – if *no*: the pupil may have a chance level score on only one battery. If the chance level raw score is on the *Verbal Battery*, this often reflects poor reading skills, a bilingual pupil's lack of fluency in English or specific language processing disabilities. A chance level score on the *Non-verbal Battery* may indicate a pupil with a lack of confidence in working with novel or unfamiliar materials.

A pupil who is answering around the chance level probably has a low level of skill in the cognitive area tested, or the low score could arise from other causes, as discussed above. Other possibilities are that the pupil could have lost his or her place on the answer sheet (although the letter coding of the answer options on the answer sheet mitigates against this) or even decided not to cooperate with testing on that day. While the score probably reflects the pupil's true level of ability in that area at the time of testing, it cannot be relied upon with total confidence. For such pupils an individual administration of *CAT*, or one of the separate nferNelson verbal, non-verbal or spatial reasoning tests, might be appropriate to obtain a better view of their abilities.

Class check
If more than half the pupils in your class are performing at or below the chance level, check that you have administered the correct level of *CAT*. It may be that the level used was too hard and that you should use a lower level.

4. How many questions were attempted?

The fourth check involves considering the number of questions that the pupil has attempted on each battery. This information is *not* contained in the Group Summary of Results. You can find the number of questions the pupil attempted on the pupil's Individual Pupil Profile (see Chapter 3, page 31, for an example). For the moment, we will assume that you are making this check only for pupils whose results surprise you, possibly because they are lower than you expected. Accessing and using a second source of information on each pupil's number of attempts – the *CAT* data disk – is described later in this chapter (see page 21).

More than 80 per cent of questions attempted

The majority of pupils attempt all or nearly all of the questions in each battery. Some pupils may omit answers to one or two questions, but this very rarely affects their overall standard scores. Indeed, the vast majority of pupils answer over 80 per cent of the questions for each battery. Where pupils have attempted this many questions, it is rare for any omissions to make a substantial change to their overall score. This is because the omitted questions are almost always the most difficult questions towards the end of the tests. For these pupils their scores are probably secure and no further investigation is warranted.

Less than 50 per cent of questions attempted

A very small proportion of pupils, around 1 per cent, answer fewer than half the questions for each battery, although the figure is slightly higher for the Quantitative Battery at around 3 per cent.[1] It is probably as well to discount the scores for these pupils. It may be that the test is too difficult for them, or they may have decided not to cooperate with the testing on that day. Whatever the reason, the score is based on so few attempts as to be unreliable for further interpretation. You may wish to consider an individual assessment for these pupils (see page 17).

Between 50 per cent and 80 per cent of questions attempted

A small proportion of pupils (around 6 per cent) attempt only 50 to 80 per cent of the questions. For pupils with question attempts in this range, the omitted questions may, but will not necessarily, alter the interpretation of the pupil's obtained scores. To determine whether the results of these pupils might be affected, we need to consider them in more detail. The pupils you need to focus on will be those who made:

■ between 39 and 62 attempts on the Verbal Battery;
■ between 29 and 46 attempts on the Quantitative Battery;
■ between 33 and 52 attempts on the Non-verbal Battery.

For these pupils, proceed to check 5 opposite.

Class check

You should consider a class check on the number of questions attempted. If more than half your class have attempted only 80 per cent of the questions or less, it is possible that there has been an error in the administration of the test.

---

[1] These figures are averages across all CAT levels. They tend to be slightly higher for CAT Levels A and B, which are taken by younger pupils.

The most likely error is *an error in timing*. For example, if pupils were given eight minutes rather than 10 minutes for the Sentence Completion subtest, this might have a significant impact on the number of questions they could answer. Errors in timing are most likely to occur in the Quantitative Battery, where each subtest has a different time allocation (12, 10 and 14 minutes respectively for each subtest, see Table 2.3).

Alternatively, but more rarely, it could mean that *one of the three subtests in a battery has been omitted*. If, for example, the majority of the class are showing 40 attempts for the Quantitative Battery, this could mean the Equation Building subtest, composed of 18 items, has been omitted (see Table 2.3 for the number of questions in each subtest).

Table 2.3. Number of questions and time allocation for each *CAT3* subtest (A–F)

Battery	**Test**	**Number of questions**	***CAT* levels A–F Time allocation (in minutes)**
Verbal	Verbal Classification	24	8
	Sentence Completion	24	10
	Verbal Analogies	30	10
Quantitative	Number Analogies	20	12
	Number Series	20	10
	Equation Building	18	14
Non-verbal	Figure Classification	24	10
	Figure Analogies	24	10
	Figure Analysis	18	10

5. How many of the questions attempted were answered correctly?

This check is necessary only for those pupils who *attempt only 50 to 80 per cent of the questions* on a battery. In interpreting the number of attempts that were answered correctly, we can again apply an '80 per cent' decision rule.

Less than 80 per cent of attempts answered correctly
If the pupil gets *less than 80 per cent* of the questions they attempted correct, it is likely that the obtained score *reflects the pupil's current level of performance* in the cognitive area assessed. The pupil probably marked answers to the easier questions, but not to the more difficult questions on the test. Given the low score on the easier items, it is unlikely that the pupil's score would differ greatly if they had answered the more difficult questions.

80 per cent or more of attempts answered correctly
If the pupil gets *80 per cent or more* of the questions they attempted correct, then their

achieved score may be *an underestimate of their ability*. In these cases, there are two common patterns of unanswered questions:

■ *Pattern A: they are spaced in an apparently random fashion within each subtest.* For example, within any particular subtest the pupil may have answered questions 1, 2, 3, 5, 9, 11, 12 and 15 but omitted all others. This typically indicates a pupil who is very *anxious about making errors* and avoids guessing. He or she does not answer the question at all unless certain of the correct answer.

■ *Pattern B: they are positioned towards the end of each subtest.* The pupil may have answered questions 1 to 12 in the Verbal Classification subtest, but not questions 13 to 24, and so on throughout all the subtests. This indicates a pupil who works at his or her own pace, irrespective of the demands of the task. When told that they have 10 minutes for a task, such pupils *do not adapt their pace* accordingly.

You can determine which of these two patterns might be occurring by looking closely at the pupil's answer sheet. The pattern you find is important because it may reveal something about the pupil's approach to learning in general, not just his or her test-taking skills. You can help pupils whose results fall into the two categories described above by adopting the following strategies:

■ *Pattern A (unanswered questions randomly spaced / pupil anxious about making errors):* These pupils need to learn to take chances and make 'best guesses', since these are strategies we often need to use in a learning environment. Classrooms should provide a supportive environment where pupils feel free to explore and possibly make mistakes. Does your classroom provide an environment of this kind? Small group work on active problem solving and group discussion of various solutions might support these anxious pupils as they learn to build their confidence in guessing and hypothesising.

■ *Pattern B (unanswered questions all at the end / pupil unable to adapt pace):* These pupils need to be flexible in adapting their time to the fluctuating nature of the tasks that they are set, or which they set themselves. There are 90 minutes allocated for a game of football, not 95 or 100; similarly, if a piece of homework needs to be completed by the end of *this* week, it is not appropriate for the pupil to hand it in *next* week! Discuss with the students these and other examples, such as making a speech or presentation. Consider strategies such as task analysis and allocating time to task elements: when writing an essay, for example, how much time should be allocated to preparation, planning and production? Draw examples from a range of academic and non-academic activities. The emphasis needs to be on the pupil developing an awareness of task constraints and self-regulating skills.

Completing the attempts check on a whole class or group

The section above suggested that the check on the number of attempts was probably only necessary where a pupil's results surprise you, possibly because they are lower than you expected. However, for screening purposes, you may want to check the number of attempts for all your pupils.

This can be done easily using the *CAT3* data disk and a spreadsheet (or 'worksheet') package such as Microsoft Excel. The process is illustrated below for the Verbal Battery using an example data file. You would use your own school data file but, to demonstrate the process, an example data file (named **dataset1.csv**) is included on the attached CD. The example file used for this demonstration is for a class of 46 pupils from P6 in Scotland (equivalent to Year 5 in England and Wales, P6 in Northern Ireland), who completed Level B of *CAT3*.

The following example assumes that you have Microsoft Excel, Version 95 or higher, loaded onto your computer. It also assumes that you are conversant with Excel, at least to the level expected following NOF training. The specific skills assumed include being able to:

- insert columns;
- enter formulae in cells;
- define cell formats;
- copy cell formulae to other cells;
- highlight and sort data.

1. Opening the data file

If you requested a *CAT3* data disk as one of your *CAT* Computer Scoring and Analysis Service options, your *CAT* data file will have been sent to you on a disk. It will have the prefix 'kit' followed by a four-digit number and a final letter, like **kit1510H.csv**. All *CAT3* data files have the prefix 'kit'. If your data file has the prefix 'cat', this indicates that you are working with a *CAT2E* data file. The same checks as described here can be completed with *CAT2E* files, but the specific field names and file layout will differ. The specific directions and examples in this guide deal only with *CAT3* data files.

- To open the file, double-click on it. The file should open in Excel and the screen should appear as in Figure 2.3 on page 22.

Figure 2.3: *CAT3* data file disk – the 'select spreadsheet' cell marked with a white cross

	A	B	C	D	E	F	G	H	I	J	K	L	M	N	O
1	CAT Versi	CAT3 LEV	YearGroup	ClassName	ClassNum	Family_Name	First_Nam	iD	Gender	DOT	DOB	True_Age	Test_Age	DobFlag	Manua
2	CAT3E	B	P6	6	1	ADAM ALLUM	ARABELL		F	#######	#######		10:07		
3	CAT3E	B	P6	6	1	ANDERSON	RACHAEL		F	#######	#######		10:02		
4	CAT3E	B	P6	6	1	ARMITAGE	SARAH		F	#######	#######		09:11		
5	CAT3E	B	P6	6	1	BAIRD	KIRSTY		F	#######	#######		09:09		
6	CAT3E	B	P6	6	1	BELL	VICKY		F	#######	#######		10:04		
7	CAT3E	B	P6	6	1	BROWN	ROSS		M	#######	#######		11:00		
8	CAT3E	B	P6	6	1	BURNSIDE	FERN		F	#######	#######		10:06		
9	CAT3E	B	P6	6	1	CAMPBELL	ALEX		M	#######	#######		10:05		
10	CAT3E	B	P6	6	1	CONWAN	FIONA		F	#######	#######		10:06		
11	CAT3E	B	P6	6	1	DALGLEISH	ABBY		F	#######	#######		10:00		
12	CAT3E	B	P6	6	1	DALLAR	CHRIS		M	#######	#######		09:08		
13	CAT3E	B	P6	6	1	EARNSHAW	CHARLIE		M	#######	#######		09:11		
14	CAT3E	B	P6	6	1	EASTLAND	DARREN		M	#######	#######		10:05		
15	CAT3E	B	P6	6	1	ELDER	JAMES		M	#######	#######		10:04		
16	CAT3E	B	P6	6	1	ENTWISTLE	JAMIE		M	#######	#######		11:00	4	
17	CAT3E	B	P6	6	1	FORREST	JOSH		M	#######	#######		11:00	4	
18	CAT3E	B	P6	6	1	FORSYTH	GEMMA		F	#######	#######		09:11		
19	CAT3E	B	P6	6	1	FORSYTH	MICHAEL		M	#######	#######		10:08		
20	CAT3E	B	P6	6	1	FORSYTH	KATE		F	#######	#######		10:03		
21	CAT3E	B	P6	6	1	FRENCH	SARAH		F	#######	#######		09:11		
22	CAT3E	B	P6	6	1	HARDWICK	ARIANNA		F	#######	#######		09:11		
23	CAT3E	B	P6	6	1	HARKNESS	CRAIG		M	#######	#######		10:06		
24	CAT3E	B	P6	6	1	HENDERSON	RYAN		M	#######	#######		10:03		
25	CAT3E	B	P6	6	1	KING	IAIN		M	#######	#######		10:07		
26	CAT3E	B	P6	6	1	KNOWLES	JAMES		M	#######	#######		10:06		
27	CAT3E	B	P6	6	1	MACINTYRE	DAVID		M	#######	#######		10:02		
28	CAT3E	B	P6	6	1	MACKAY	MICHEL>		F	#######	#######		10:00		
29	CAT3E	B	P6	6	1	MACLEOD	MORAY		M	#######	#######		09:10		
30	CAT3E	B	P6	6	1	MAXWELL	JADE		F	#######	#######		09:09		
31	CAT3E	B	P6	6	1	MCALLISTER	LAURA		F	#######	#######		09:10		
32	CAT3E	B	P6	6	1	MCKAY	CAMERO?		M	#######	#######		10:03		
33	CAT3E	B	P6	6	1	MCNAUGHTON	RU> AIDH		M	#######	#######		09:09		
34	CAT3E	B	P6	6	1	MORRIS	KENDRA		F	#######	#######		10:01		

2. Preparing the file

The first step is to expand the column widths so that you can see all the column labels contained in row 1. Select the whole worksheet by clicking in the top left outer cell, above the number 1 and to the left of column A, as indicated by the white cross in Figure 2.3. Now move the cursor over the boundary between columns A and B, until the cursor changes to the cross-and-arrow symbol, as shown in Figure 2.4.

Figure 2.4: *CAT3* data file disk – positioning the cursor between columns A and B

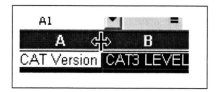

■ Now double-click the mouse. All the columns should expand so that you can read the full contents of the first row headings.

■ Click on the right arrow on the bottom cursor bar until the column headed 'Family_Name' is the column appearing on the far left of the screen.

■ Position the cursor in the cell H2, to the right of 'First_Name' and under the column heading 'iD'. From the menu select Window/Freeze Panes and press return. This will keep 'Family_Name' and 'First_Name' fixed as the two columns on the far left of the screen.

■ Now click on the right arrow on the bottom cursor bar until you get to the column headed 'Verbal_Attempts'. The screen should now appear as in Figure 2.5.

Figure 2.5: *CAT3* data file disk – showing pupils' names and Verbal Battery scores

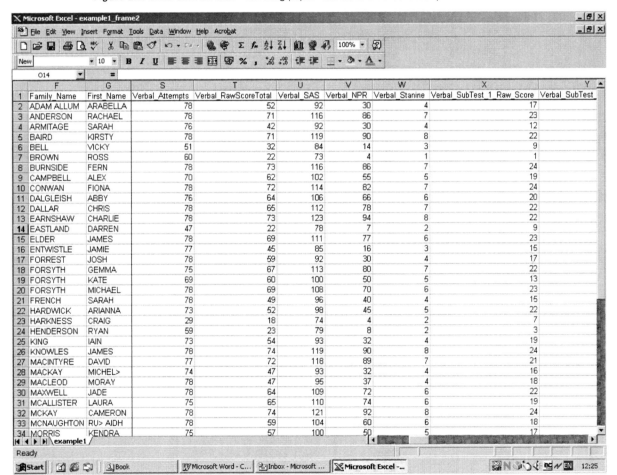

3. Calculating the percentage of questions attempted

■ Insert a new column to the right of 'Verbal_Attempts', and name the column '%Vattempts' to indicate that this is the column that will hold the percentage of the Verbal Battery questions that each pupil has attempted.

■ Now you need to enter a formula into the new column to calculate the percentage of attempts. This will mean dividing the number of attempts for each pupil by the total number of questions in the battery (78 questions for the Verbal Battery). Type +S2/78 in the second row of your new column and press return. Use Format/Cells to set the format to percentage with no decimal places.

▪ Copy the contents of cell T2 down to all pupils. When you have done so, the screen should be as shown in Figure 2.6.

Figure 2.6: *CAT3* data file disk – calculating the percentage of questions attempted

	Family_Name	First_Name	Verbal_Attempts	%Vattempts	Verbal_RawScoreTotal	Verbal_SAS	Verbal_NPR	Verbal_Stanine	Verbal_SubTest_1_Raw_Score	Ve
2	ADAM ALLUM	ARABELLA	78	100%	52	92	30	4	17	
3	ANDERSON	RACHAEL	78	100%	71	116	86	7	23	
4	ARMITAGE	SARAH	76	97%	42	92	30	4	12	
5	BAIRD	KIRSTY	78	100%	71	119	90	8	22	
6	BELL	VICKY	51	65%	32	84	14	3	9	
7	BROWN	ROSS	60	77%	22	73	4	1	1	
8	BURNSIDE	FERN	78	100%	73	116	86	7	24	
9	CAMPBELL	ALEX	70	90%	62	102	55	5	19	
10	CONWAN	FIONA	78	100%	72	114	82	7	24	
11	DALGLEISH	ABBY	76	97%	64	106	66	6	20	
12	DALLAR	CHRIS	78	100%	65	112	78	7	22	
13	EARNSHAW	CHARLIE	78	100%	73	123	94	8	22	
14	EASTLAND	DARREN	47	60%	22	78	7	2	9	
15	ELDER	JAMES	78	100%	69	111	77	6	23	
16	ENTWISTLE	JAMIE	77	99%	45	85	16	3	15	
17	FORREST	JOSH	78	100%	59	92	30	4	17	
18	FORSYTH	GEMMA	75	96%	67	113	80	7	22	
19	FORSYTH	KATE	69	88%	60	100	50	5	13	
20	FORSYTH	MICHAEL	78	100%	69	108	70	6	23	
21	FRENCH	SARAH	78	100%	49	96	40	4	15	
22	HARDWICK	ARIANNA	73	94%	52	98	45	5	22	
23	HARKNESS	CRAIG	29	37%	18	74	4	2	7	
24	HENDERSON	RYAN	59	76%	23	79	8	2	3	
25	KING	IAIN	73	94%	54	93	32	4	19	
26	KNOWLES	JAMES	78	100%	74	119	90	8	24	
27	MACINTYRE	DAVID	77	99%	72	118	89	7	21	
28	MACKAY	MICHEL>	74	95%	47	93	32	4	16	
29	MACLEOD	MORAY	78	100%	47	95	37	4	18	
30	MAXWELL	JADE	78	100%	64	109	72	6	22	
31	MCALLISTER	LAURA	75	96%	65	110	74	6	19	
32	MCKAY	CAMERON	78	100%	74	121	92	8	24	
33	MCNAUGHTON	RU> AIDH	78	100%	59	104	60	6	18	
34	MORRIS	KENDRA	75	96%	57	100	50	5	17	

4. Sorting the data sheet

You now need to sort the results in order of the percentage of attempts, putting the pupil with the *lowest* percentage of attempts at the top of the list and the pupil with the *highest* percentage of attempts at the bottom. First, highlight all the cells in the data file. These extend from cell A1 at the top left to cell CK47 at the bottom right.

▪ Select Data/Sort. In the drop-down menu select '%Vattempts'. Press return.

▪ The file should now be sorted so that the pupil with the lowest percentage of attempts appears first in the list. The screen should appear as in Figure 2.7.

■ This operation has identified seven pupils in the class of 46 pupils who have attempted 80 per cent or less of the questions on the Verbal Battery. We now need to look at the results for these pupils in more detail.

Figure 2.7: *CAT3* data file disk – results in order of percentage of attempts

	F	G	S	T	U	V	W	X	Y	
1	Family_Name	First_Name	Verbal_Attempts	%Vattempts	Verbal_RawScoreTotal	Verbal_SAS	Verbal_NPR	Verbal_Stanine	Verbal_SubTest_1_Raw_Score	Ve
2	HARKNESS	CRAIG	29	37%	18	74	4	2	7	
3	EASTLAND	DARREN	47	60%	22	78	7	2	9	
4	STEWART	CALLUM	49	63%	36	86	18	3	10	
5	BELL	VICKY	51	65%	32	84	14	3	9	
6	TOMLIN	AD>	56	72%	35	80	9	2	17	
7	HENDERSON	RYAN	59	76%	23	79	8	2	3	
8	BROWN	ROSS	60	77%	22	73	4	1	1	
9	FORSYTH	KATE	69	88%	60	100	50	5	13	
10	CAMPBELL	ALEX	70	90%	62	102	55	5	19	
11	SHOREED	CHRIS	72	92%	61	103	58	5	19	
12	MORRISON	EM>	72	92%	10	71	3	1	3	
13	HARDWICK	ARIANNA	73	94%	52	98	45	5	22	
14	KING	IAIN	73	94%	54	93	32	4	19	
15	MACKAY	MICHEL>	74	95%	47	93	32	4	16	
16	FORSYTH	GEMMA	75	96%	67	113	80	7	22	
17	MORRIS	KENDRA	75	96%	57	100	50	5	17	
18	MCALLISTER	LAURA	75	96%	65	110	74	6	19	
19	DALGLEISH	ABBY	76	97%	64	106	66	6	20	
20	O RAWE	RACHEL	76	97%	64	101	52	5	20	
21	ARMITAGE	SARAH	76	97%	42	92	30	4	12	
22	MACINTYRE	DAVID	77	99%	72	118	89	7	21	
23	O DONNELL	DAVID	77	99%	67	110	74	6	19	
24	ENTWISTLE	JAMIE	77	99%	45	85	16	3	15	
25	ADAM ALLUM	ARABELLA	78	100%	52	92	30	4	17	
26	WATSON	CAITLIN	78	100%	59	101	52	5	22	
27	STANFIELD	CALLUM	78	100%	65	103	58	5	23	
28	MCKAY	CAMERON	78	100%	74	121	92	8	24	
29	EARNSHAW	CHARLIE	78	100%	73	123	94	8	22	
30	DALLAR	CHRIS	78	100%	65	112	78	7	22	
31	BURNSIDE	FERN	78	100%	73	116	86	7	24	
32	CONWAN	FIONA	78	100%	72	114	82	7	24	
33	MAXWELL	JADE	78	100%	64	109	72	6	22	
34	ELDER	JAMES	78	100%	69	111	77	6	23	

5. Calculating the percentage of attempts that are answered correctly

■ Insert a column to the right of 'Verbal_RawScore' and name the column '%Vcorrect'.

■ You should now enter a formula into the column to calculate the percentage of attempts that are answered correctly for each pupil. This will mean dividing the number of correct answers (raw score) by the total number of questions the pupil attempted. Type **+U2/S2** in the second row of the newly created column and then press return. Use Format/Cells to set the format to percentage with no decimal places.

■ Copy the formula down to all cells in the column so that you have the percentage of attempts answered correctly for each pupil. The screen should appear as in Figure 2.8 on page 26.

Figure 2.8: *CAT3* data file disk – calculating the percentage of attempts answered correctly

	F	G	S	T	U	V	W	X	Y	Z
1	Family_Name	First_Name	Verbal_Attempts	%Vattempts	Verbal_RawScoreTotal	%Vcorrect	Verbal_SAS	Verbal_NPR	Verbal_Stanine	Verbal_SubTest_1_Raw
2	HARKNESS	CRAIG	29	37%	18	62%	74	4	2	
3	EASTLAND	DARREN	47	60%	22	47%	78	7	2	
4	STEWART	CALLUM	49	63%	36	73%	86	18	3	
5	BELL	VICKY	51	65%	32	63%	84	14	3	
6	TOMLIN	AD>	56	72%	35	63%	80	9	2	
7	HENDERSON	RYAN	59	76%	23	39%	79	8	2	
8	BROWN	ROSS	60	77%	22	37%	73	4	1	
9	FORSYTH	KATE	69	88%	60	87%	100	50	5	
10	CAMPBELL	ALEX	70	90%	62	89%	102	55	5	
11	SHOREED	CHRIS	72	92%	61	85%	103	58	5	
12	MORRISON	EM>	72	92%	10	14%	71	3	1	
13	HARDWICK	ARIANNA	73	94%	52	71%	98	45	5	
14	KING	IAIN	73	94%	54	74%	93	32	4	
15	MACKAY	MICHEL>	74	95%	47	64%	93	32	4	
16	FORSYTH	GEMMA	75	96%	67	89%	113	80	7	
17	MORRIS	KENDRA	75	96%	57	76%	100	50	5	
18	MCALLISTER	LAURA	75	96%	65	87%	110	74	6	
19	DALGLEISH	ABBY	76	97%	64	84%	106	66	6	
20	O RAWE	RACHEL	76	97%	64	84%	101	52	5	
21	ARMITAGE	SARAH	76	97%	42	55%	92	30	4	
22	MACINTYRE	DAVID	77	99%	72	94%	118	89	7	
23	O DONNELL	DAVID	77	99%	67	87%	110	74	6	
24	ENTWISTLE	JAMIE	77	99%	45	58%	85	16	3	
25	ADAM ALLUM	ARABELLA	78	100%	52	67%	92	30	4	
26	WATSON	CAITLIN	78	100%	59	76%	101	52	5	
27	STANFIELD	CALLUM	78	100%	65	83%	103	58	5	
28	MCKAY	CAMERON	78	100%	74	95%	121	92	8	
29	EARNSHAW	CHARLIE	78	100%	73	94%	123	94	8	
30	DALLAR	CHRIS	78	100%	65	83%	112	78	7	
31	BURNSIDE	FERN	78	100%	73	94%	116	86	7	
32	CONWAN	FIONA	78	100%	72	92%	114	82	7	
33	MAXWELL	JADE	78	100%	64	82%	109	72	6	
34	ELDER	JAMES	78	100%	69	88%	111	77	6	

6. Interpreting the results of the analysis

Less than 50 per cent of questions attempted

Our analysis of the example data file has identified that **Craig Harkness** attempted only 29 (37 per cent) of the questions in the Verbal Battery. Craig's raw score of 18, and standard age score of 74, on the Verbal Battery is therefore likely to be unreliable.

If we complete the same analysis of the number of attempts for the other two batteries, we see that Craig attempted 72 per cent of the questions on the Quantitative Battery, and 95 per cent of the questions on the Non-verbal Battery, giving standard age scores of 86 and 100 respectively. The high level of attempts on the Quantitative and Non-verbal batteries suggests that there was no problem with Craig's general cooperation with testing, but that he had particular difficulties in accessing the verbal materials.

If Craig had attempted the additional 49 Verbal Battery questions he omitted, and had got 20 per cent of these correct (as might be expected had he guessed his answers at random), the additional 10 marks would have raised his raw score to 28. His verbal standard age score would therefore have increased from 74 to 80. His Verbal Battery standard age score would then be more in line with his Quantitative Battery standard age score, but both would still be significantly below his Non-verbal Battery standard age score of 100. The term 'significantly' is being used here in a statistical sense. Detailed discussion on evaluating the size of a difference between batteries may be found in Chapter 3 (pages 31 to 32).

Craig's non-verbal reasoning skills are average for his age, but he may well have particular problems with reading and with verbal materials. Further assessment of Craig's work in English – and his reading skills in particular – may be warranted.

Between 50 and 80 per cent of questions attempted

We also find from our analysis that there are six pupils in the class who attempted only 50 to 80 per cent of the questions. We needed to look at the results for these pupils in more detail, and so we also calculated the percentage of the questions attempted that they answered correctly. None of the six pupils answered 80 per cent or more of their attempts correctly; therefore, we accept these pupils' standard age scores as an estimate of their current level of functioning in the verbal area.

Callum Stewart is something of a borderline case, with 73 per cent of his attempts on the Verbal Battery correct. To be thorough, we further examine his attempts on the other two batteries. This examination suggests that Callum's low level of attempts is a consistent feature across all batteries. In addition to only attempting 63 per cent of the verbal questions, he also attempted only 59 per cent of the quantitative and 77 per cent of the non-verbal questions. In all cases, the percentage of attempts answered correctly is below 80 per cent (73 per cent, 62 per cent and 25 per cent for verbal, quantitative and non-verbal reasoning respectively). We therefore accept Callum's standard age scores of 86, 82 and 72 for verbal, quantitative and non-verbal reasoning as accurate indicators of his current level of developed ability, although with a lower degree of certainty in the verbal area.

We remain concerned, however, about Callum's low number of attempts. Callum does not appear to be reluctant to make errors, as he has attempted 77 per cent of the non-verbal questions despite getting only 25 per cent correct. His scores, particularly on the Verbal Battery, may instead be affected by a slow pace of work. This is an issue we would want to explore further through observation, evaluation and discussion. Does he often leave work incomplete or unfinished? Is he poorly organised, for example in planning tasks or activities? Does he appear motivated or is he disinterested in lessons?

Review

Before interpreting your data, carry out the five checks:

- 1: Are all pupils listed?
- 2: Are there any error flags?
- 3: Are any pupils performing at the chance level?
- 4: How many questions were attempted?
- 5: If the number of attempts is low, how many of the questions attempted were answered correctly?

You may choose to carry out the latter two checks only for pupils whose results are unexpected for some reason – maybe they are lower than anticipated. Alternatively, you can complete them as a screening process for the whole class or group: use the *CAT3* data disk to do so.

Having completed these checks, you will be better informed about the reliability and accuracy of the *CAT* results for your pupils. You will also feel more confident in manipulating and interpreting, and therefore understanding, your *CAT* data.

With these basic checks completed, we can move on to consider the interpretation of the *CAT3* Individual Pupil Profile and its implications for teaching and learning.

3 Differentiation in the classroom

AIMS

The aims of this chapter are to:

■ *describe and explain* the information contained in the *CAT3* Individual Pupil Profile;

■ present a *classification* of *CAT3* Individual Pupil Profiles;

■ describe how the *CAT3* Individual Pupil Profile can be used to *identify strengths and weaknesses* in pupils' cognitive abilities;

■ consider the *implications* of *CAT3* Individual Pupil Profiles for *teaching and learning*.

Adapting teaching to meet pupils' needs

An important use of *CAT* scores is to help teachers adapt teaching methods, materials, emphasis and pace to the needs of individual pupils. Successful differentiation requires an understanding of the interactions that occur between aspects or qualities of the *pupil* (such as their abilities) and aspects or qualities of the *environment* (such as the degree of structure or support offered). For example, learning is generally enhanced where pupils are interested and engaged, but impaired where pupils are anxious. Yet the same task that engages one pupil (for example, a spoken presentation to the class) may make another pupil anxious. It is the interaction between pupil characteristics and the demands of the task or classroom that will influence learning outcomes.

Variation among pupils

Success in school depends on many personal and social factors. For example, pupils vary in their motivation: some may be motivated by an interest in the subject matter, others by a need for achievement or competition, and others by a fear of failure. Pupils may differ in their self-esteem, the amount of effort they are willing to make, their confidence or social skills and whether they are prepared to persevere with tasks. All of these factors can affect their success.

Cognitive factors, such as the abilities to reason with words, quantitative concepts and spatial images, are also important. Pupils can differ in their overall reasoning ability, and in the pattern of strengths in each of these three different areas. For example, some pupils are strong in, and therefore prefer, visual modes of thinking. These pupils may not achieve their full potential in contexts where knowledge is mostly communicated through the spoken or written word, or evaluated solely through assessments relying on reading and writing.

Demands of the learning activity

Learning activities also differ along many dimensions: for example, in the amount of structure they provide, or in the opportunities they present for active or collaborative learning. They also differ in the extent to which they require pupils to process information in verbal, quantitative or visual forms. In lessons, pupils are likely to be presented with written texts, graphs or diagrams, videos, tabulated data, maps or other forms of information. They may be asked to take notes, to record numerically, to discuss their sources, to translate their results as charts, to make written reports or oral presentations. Pupils' abilities to interpret, analyse and reason in these different media may vary greatly. One way to adapt teaching is to attend closely to these demands and, when possible, to allow pupils to use their better-developed abilities in one area to support or scaffold their learning in another. For example, a pupil with strong verbal but poor quantitative reasoning ability might improve the latter through group discussion about mathematical concepts or problems, rather than just working silently on worksheets or a computer.

The sections that follow provide detailed analyses of pupils' reasoning abilities as illustrated by their *CAT3* Individual Pupil Profiles. The profiles are discussed in terms of the pupil's strengths and weaknesses, what these might reveal about the pupil's preferred learning style and their implications for teaching and learning. When teachers have an awareness both of the strengths of the individual and the abilities demanded by a particular task, learning will be most successful.

Understanding *CAT3* Individual Pupil Profiles

When thinking about differentiation, it is particularly important to focus on pupils' scores on the three *CAT* batteries rather than on their mean *CAT* score. The Individual Pupil Profile shows the level of scores on each battery and also whether some scores are significantly higher or lower than other scores.

Example profile – Amy

An example of a *CAT3* Individual Pupil Profile is shown in Figure 3.1. If you have selected the Key Stage 2, Key Stage 3, GCSE or Standard Grade indicator options, and have asked for the indicators to be included in the profile, these will also be shown. The example profiles shown in this chapter include GCSE indicators. The GCSE and other indicators are considered separately, in Chapters 5 to 7; for the moment our discussion will focus only on interpreting the *CAT* scores.

Figure 3.1: *CAT3* Individual Pupil Profile with GCSE indicators – Amy

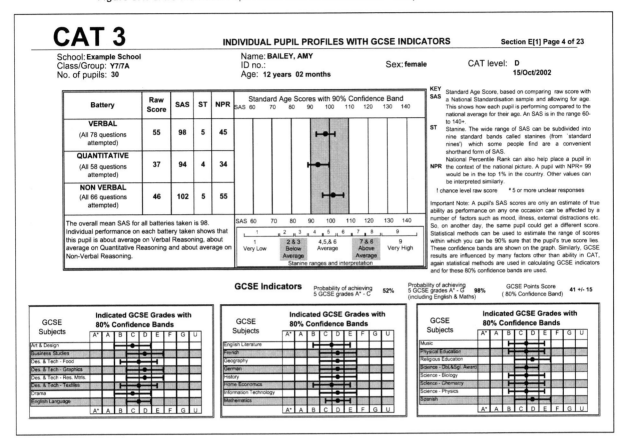

Test scores

The Individual Pupil Profile for **Amy Bailey** shows her raw score, standard age score, stanine and percentile on each battery. Amy's standard age scores are 98, 94 and 102 respectively for each battery, placing her in stanines 5, 4 and 5, and at the 45th, 34th and 55th percentiles respectively. The profile also shows the number of questions attempted on each battery (see the 'Battery' column on the left). Amy attempted all of the 78 verbal questions, 57 of the 58 quantitative questions and all of the 66 non-verbal questions. This information may be important if you have reason to question the accuracy of the scores for Amy, as we discussed in Chapter 2 (see pages 17 to 20).

Standard age score plot and confidence bands

The Individual Pupil Profile also presents the standard age scores in a graphical format on a scale ranging from 60 to 140: this appears to the right of the 'NPR' column. The pupil's actual standard age score is indicated by a dot.

There is a horizontal line either side of the standard age score dot, which indicates the 90 per cent *confidence band*. Any test score is generated from a particular performance on a particular day. We know that the *CAT* is a highly reliable test (see the *CAT3 Technical Manual*, pages 10 to 13), but nevertheless we can expect scores to fluctuate or change to some extent due to chance factors. The confidence band indicates the range in which a pupil's score would be expected to fall on nine out of 10 test occasions.

For *CAT3*, the confidence bands are typically plus or minus five standard score points around the pupil's actual standard age score. These confidence bands are important in order to prevent us over-interpreting small differences in scores. For example, if a pupil scored 95, and was retested some months later and scored 98, the second score is well within the confidence band for the first score and so does not represent a significant change. The confidence bands are also important when it comes to identifying significant differences between a pupil's scores on the three batteries, as we shall see later. However, they vary depending on the *CAT* level taken, the particular battery and the absolute level of the score. For example, the confidence bands for high and low scores will tend to be wider on the side going towards the national mean (100).

'Average' range

You will notice on the same diagram that the area denoting standard age scores of between 90 and 110 has been shaded. This is the band containing the scores for the middle 50 per cent of pupils of the same age, and is included to give a visual guide to the 'average' range.

Mean CAT score

Finally, the text beneath the three sets of battery scores gives the pupil's mean *CAT* score: in this case, 98. This is derived by summing the pupil's scores over all three batteries taken and dividing by the number of batteries taken – that is, $(98 + 94 + 102) / 3 = 98$.

Analysing Individual Pupil Profiles

The four types of score profile

The data from over 500,000 pupils who completed *CAT3* in the period between September 2001 and January 2003 have been analysed. Using this information, four broad types of score profile have been identified: these types are described below.

▪ In an *even (E)* profile, the pupil's verbal, quantitative, and non-verbal scores do not differ significantly from each other. By 'even', we mean that all the standard age scores are within *nine or fewer* standard age score points of each other. There is only one general piece of information provided by the test, and that is the overall level, which will be well summarised by the mean *CAT* score. This is what we would expect if reasoning ability were a single dimension. Just over one third of pupils (36 per cent) have even profiles. (For examples, see pages 35 to 39.)

■ In a *distinct (D)* profile, one of the three battery scores is significantly different from the other two scores. The pupil shows a relative *strength* when one score is significantly above the other two, or a relative *weakness* when one score is significantly below the other two. In forming the classification of profiles, a difference of *10 or more* standard age score points is used to identify a significant score difference. There are a total of *six* possible distinct strength or weakness profiles depending on which of the three batteries is identified and whether we are seeing a strength or a weakness. As shorthand these are referred to as V+, Q+ and N+ (strengths) and V–, Q– and N– (weaknesses). For example, the verbal score may be significantly higher than the other two (V+), or the non-verbal score may be significantly lower than the other two (N–). Overall, approximately 40 per cent of pupils have distinct profiles. (For examples, see pages 40 to 57.)

■ In a *contrast (C)* profile, the pupil shows both a relative strength *and* a relative weakness. These differ from the distinct profile, since there is only one significant score difference, that between the *highest* score and the *lowest* score, with the third score in between the other two. For example, a pupil may have a verbal score significantly above his or her quantitative score (that is, by 10 or more standard age score points), with the non-verbal score in between the other two. This can be summarised as a 'verbal strength/quantitative weakness' (V+ Q–) profile. About 20 per cent of pupils have contrast profiles. (For examples, see pages 58 to 59.)

■ The profiles of a small proportion of pupils show a *complete contrast (CC)* across all three batteries. In these cases *all three scores* differ significantly from each other (that is, by 10 or more standard age score points). Thus the verbal score may be significantly lower than the quantitative score, which may in turn be significantly lower than the non-verbal score. Such a profile would be described as (V– N+). Around 5 per cent of all pupils have profiles showing a complete contrast across all three batteries. (For an example, see pages 59 to 61.)

Table 3.1, on page 34, summarises the different types of profiles described above.

The remainder of this chapter will describe the four types of profile in greater detail, giving illustrative examples: these are thumbnail sketches only, but nevertheless give a flavour of some of the typical characteristics of pupils with such profiles. The particular examples discussed relate to pupils assessed shortly after entering secondary school (Year 7 in England, Wales and Northern Ireland; S1 in Scotland). The issues are therefore discussed from the perspective of a receiving secondary school. However, most are general points that will apply throughout a pupil's educational career.

Table 3.1: Summary of *CAT3* Individual Pupil Profile types

Profile type	Description	Specific subtypes	Percentage of the population
Even (E)	No significant difference between any of the 3 batteries	None	36%
Distinct (D)	The score for one battery is significantly higher (+) or significantly lower (–) than the other 2	6 subtypes identifying the specific strength or weakness: V+, Q+, N+, V–, Q–, N–	40%
Contrast (C)	One significant score difference, between the highest (+) and lowest (–) batteries	6 subtypes contrasting the highest and lowest scores: (V+ N–), (V+ Q–), (Q+ N–), (Q+ V–), (N+ V–), (N+ Q–)	20%
Complete contrast (CC)	All 3 battery scores differ significantly from each other	6 subtypes contrasting the highest and lowest scores: (V+ N–), (V+ Q–), (Q+ N–), (Q+ V–), (N+ V–), (N+ Q–)	5%

Patterns and levels of scores

The implications for teaching and learning will depend on both the *pattern* of scores (strengths and weaknesses) and the *overall level* of the pupil's scores (high or low). An estimate of the overall level is captured by the mean *CAT* score. In general, the mean *CAT* score carries:

- the *most* information for *even* profiles;
- *less* information for *contrast* profiles (which contain one significant score difference);
- *still less* information for *distinct* strength or weakness profiles (which contain two significant score differences);
- the *least* information for profiles with a *complete contrast* between all three scores.

Therefore when you are asked to consider the overall level of scores, the mean *CAT* score will provide only a rough guide. For 'distinct' or 'complete contrast' profiles in particular, you should consider the level of the scores on the individual battery or batteries most relevant for the profile.

Even profiles

All scores above average (stanines 7 to 9)

The profile reproduced in Figure 3.2 shows that **Gemma Greenwood** has scores that are above average (stanines 7, 8 or 9) in all three batteries, and the overlapping confidence bands for the three batteries indicate an even profile of *above average* scores. It is important that pupils like Gemma are identified at the earliest possible opportunity on entering the school. These pupils are likely to become bored or disaffected if not given sufficiently stretching or engaging work. Expectations for their attainment across the curriculum need to be appropriately high.

DELIVER FAST-PACED INSTRUCTION AND NURTURE INDEPENDENT STUDY SKILLS
These pupils are usually self-motivated and independent learners. Encourage them to follow their interests. Help them to develop their independent study skills such as use of the library, the internet and other resources. They tend to learn very quickly and need very little practice to gain competence in a new skill. They benefit from a fast pace of instruction. They will be good at asking questions, forming hypotheses, predicting and

Figure 3.2: *CAT3* Individual Pupil Profile with GCSE indicators – Gemma

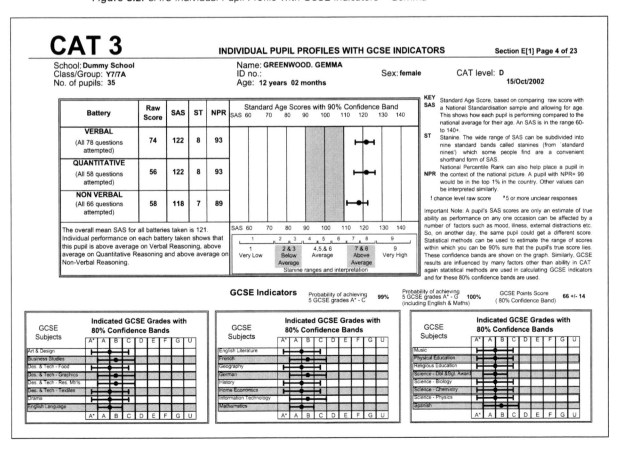

applying examples to new situations. They are most engaged when allowed to discover relationships themselves using 'guided discovery' approaches.

PROVIDE EXTENSION ACTIVITIES

They need to be challenged with materials, projects and problems that are somewhat more difficult than those used for the typical pupil. Tasks need to be differentiated, or extension work provided, to give opportunities for greater challenge. The reasoning skills of these pupils can be further improved by encouraging them to find modes of communication that most precisely describe the relationships among concepts or the rules that sequence them. For example, in writing, encourage pupils to find words that express ideas *exactly* rather than *approximately*. Also encourage them to monitor their own thinking and problem solving by recording the processes that they have gone through: a written record or concept/memory map may be useful.

ENCOURAGE GROUP WORK

Above-average pupils generally enjoy group work and are valuable group members. They can learn well both in groups with *other able peers*, through an additional element of challenge, and in *mixed ability groups*, where they can help to explain, summarise discussions and model higher-order thinking skills for other pupils.

'GIFTED AND TALENTED'?

Schools in England involved in the Excellence in Cities (EiC) initiative are required to identify 10 per cent of their cohort for the initiative's 'Gifted and Talented' strand. It is very likely that Gemma would be identified for this strand; indeed, many schools explicitly use *CAT* as part of their process for identifying gifted and talented pupils. *CAT* is frequently used because a focus on reasoning ability can identify pupils who may not be found through an analysis of purely curriculum-related attainments. *CAT* can also provide a measure of the pupil's abilities against a national sample, not just in relation to his or her peers within the school. For example, we can see that Gemma is in the top 7 per cent of her age group nationally on the Verbal and Quantitative batteries and in the top 11 per cent on the Non-verbal Battery.

For the extremely high scoring pupil, *CAT* is one of the tests recognised by the National Academy for Gifted and Talented Youth established at Warwick University in February 2002. The academy guidelines (see www.warwick.ac.uk/gifted/EZAMember.htm) indicate that a score in stanine 9 (standard age score of 127 or above and in the top 4 per cent of the age group) on any one of the three *CAT* batteries provides one relevant piece of evidence for membership of the Academy.

All scores below average (stanines 1 to 3)

The profile of **Liam Hepworth**, reproduced in Figure 3.3, shows a pupil where all three scores are *below average* (stanines 1, 2 or 3) and the overlapping confidence bands for the three batteries indicate an even profile of below average scores. Liam has standard

Figure 3.3: *CAT3* Individual Pupil Profile with GCSE indicators – Liam

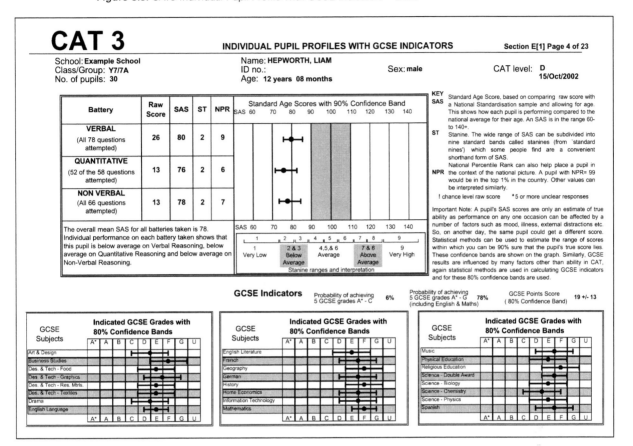

age scores of 80, 76 and 78 on the Verbal, Quantitative and Non-verbal batteries respectively, placing him in stanine 2 on each battery.

The profile for Liam is in some ways the opposite of the profile for Gemma: all his scores are consistent, but at the opposite end of the scale. However, both pupils are similar in that very careful attention needs to be paid to their learning environments. It is important to consider all the information that has been received from the primary school. Assuming typical liaison has occurred between SENCOs in feeder primaries and the receiving secondary school, pupils with very low *CAT* scores may have an identified special educational need or record of an Individual Education Plan. More generally, attainment is likely to be relatively low and basic literacy and numeracy skills may be a target for development. Are there detailed records of attainment in English and mathematics? It may be that the 'catch up' units of the Key Stage 3 strategy in literacy (DfEE, 2001a) and numeracy (DfEE, 2001b) are appropriate.

PROBLEMS IN UNDERSTANDING ABSTRACT CONCEPTS
Pupils with poorly developed reasoning abilities often have difficulty in learning abstract concepts. Few have effective strategies for learning and remembering. Therefore, they tend to approach learning tasks in a trial-and-error fashion and do not spend much time

planning before attempting to solve a problem. As a result, they tend not to transfer knowledge and skills learned in one context to another context – unless prompted to do so. Such pupils have difficulty detecting relationships, similarities and differences that go beyond appearances and are easily distracted by salient but irrelevant details in problems.

GIVE DIRECT GUIDANCE AND MEANINGFUL TASKS

Pupils with low scores are unlikely to benefit from unstructured approaches. They often have difficulty identifying what is important to learn and judging where they should focus their attention in a learning situation. Therefore, they need very specific directions before they start a task or start to study. In general they will benefit from direct guidance, coaching, and support, and a slower pace of instruction. They will work best when given a clear purpose for any activities they are asked to undertake. If writing, then for what purpose is the pupil being required to write? A meaningful task, such as writing a letter of complaint after receiving faulty goods, is more likely to be motivating than creative story writing. Later in secondary school, public examinations in vocational areas or work experience placements may be particularly motivating since they provide a 'real' context in which curriculum skills may be applied and therefore seen as relevant.

BUILD ON INTERESTS AND ACHIEVEMENTS

There are likely to be issues of low self-esteem and low motivation to address. Look for strengths in terms of specific interests and achievements. Even more than other pupils, those with less well-developed reasoning abilities will make greater effort and have greater engagement if you can discover and build on their interests. The 'Playing for Success' scheme in England, establishing study centres within national football and other sports clubs, has built very successfully on the interests of boys in particular. Football, rugby, cricket and basketball are used as a route to other knowledge, skills and understanding, not only in literacy and numeracy, but also in geography, history and ICT.

LEARNING THROUGH DOING

Active methods, such as the use of spreadsheets and games, can be powerful motivators, particularly for these pupils. Pupils with lower reasoning scores tend to have weak listening comprehension skills, so they will not necessarily learn effectively in highly verbal teaching situations. Teaching strategies that use teacher- or peer-modelling, concrete representation of abstract concepts, demonstrations, pictures or other types of illustrations, films, videotapes and hands-on activities are likely to be more effective than verbal strategies. Kinesthetic strategies may be particularly effective as 'doing' is preferred to 'talking about doing'. Regular breaks to get up, stretch, move and breathe deeply can be helpful during extended tasks that stretch across a double period.

IMPORTANCE OF INTERACTION

It can be counterproductive to teach solely in classes or groups of low-scoring pupils. Pupils who have difficulty reasoning when alone typically learn more effectively when they have many opportunities to interact with *more able peers*. Even if their level of participation is initially low, they can still learn much by observing and listening. They may record the group's discussion, lead a practical demonstration (for example, testing colour theory through mixing various paints) or take an active role in a drama. Allowing these pupils to be *participants* rather than *observers* builds their self-esteem by making explicit their valuable role within the group. More able peers can sometimes provide the guidance these pupils need in order to focus on relevant aspects of a task, keep track of what they are doing and avoid errors.

REDUCE DEMANDS ON WORKING MEMORY

Psychologists have identified 'working memory' as a key concept in learning. This refers to the amount of information (concepts, images, sound sequences, sentences etc.) that can be held, analysed and monitored in a person's memory at one time.

One way to improve learning is to reduce the number of things that must be held simultaneously in working memory. For example, some pupils will have difficulty coordinating what they *hear* with what they *see*, or what is on the *board* with what is on the *paper* in front of them. Eliminating the need to remember ideas, even temporarily, can greatly assist these pupils. Working memory burdens can also be reduced by using familiar concepts. For example, use a 12-inch ruler as a physical analogy to illustrate the measurement of mental qualities such as attitude scales, market research or democratic voting systems. This can also work at a more complex level by making concrete analogies to familiar physical systems, for example: thermostats; mechanical systems such as levers, balances, scales; hydraulic systems such as drip feeds and overflows. Finally 'overlearning' (and therefore making automatic) basic processes like writing or number facts will free the pupil to spend greater resources on the more demanding aspects of the learning activity or task.

Distinct strength or weakness profiles

In the three profiles considered so far, including Amy's on page 31, all three *CAT* battery scores have been consistent. We know this because the confidence bands around all three standard age scores overlap. This is true for just over one third of pupils: there is no significant difference in their ability to reason with words, numbers or shapes. However, the remaining two-thirds of pupils show more varied scores across the three *CAT* batteries.

For about 40 per cent of pupils there is a distinct strength or weakness in *one* of the batteries, compared to the other two. The pupil shows a relative *strength* (when one score is significantly *above* the other two) or a relative *weakness* (when one score is significantly *below* the other two).

There are six distinct strength or weakness profiles: V+, Q+, N+ and V–, Q–, N–. In the text below, an example pupil is shown for each of the six distinct profiles, although in each case the pupil is only one of a wide range of possible examples. The implications that each profile may have for teaching and learning are explored. If a pupil shows a particular cognitive strength, you should capitalise on the strength to enhance development in other areas. Where the profile identifies a specific weakness, consider how the relative strengths can be used to support pupil learning in the weaker area.

It is important to consider the *level* of the *CAT* scores as well as the *specific* area of strength or weakness. A V– profile – a significantly lower score on the Verbal Battery than on the other two batteries – may have different implications if the level of the verbal score is *low (say 85)* than if it is *high (say 115)*. For example, the former might suggest a focus on core aspects of literacy, while the latter might suggest a wider focus on extending verbal concepts and higher-order verbal thinking. Nevertheless, you should consider how the relative quantitative and non-verbal strengths of both pupils could be used to support their learning in the verbal area.

Finally, in a small proportion of cases the confidence bands on the Individual Pupil Profile may appear to overlap, even where there is a difference of 10 or more standard age score points between two batteries. This is because comparing confidence bands is a slightly more conservative method of evaluating the significance of score differences, as opposed to comparing the two scores directly. If in doubt, apply the 10 or more standard age score point difference rule.

Relative strength in verbal reasoning (V+)

The profile of **Bruce Harde** (see Figure 3.4) shows a relative strength in verbal reasoning (V+). He has a standard age score of 105 on verbal reasoning, with a standard age score of 90 on the Quantitative and 93 the Non-verbal batteries.

ADEPT WITH LANGUAGE

V+ pupils will generally do best when they talk and write about their learning. They are likely to enjoy group discussions, paired work, writing, word games, essays and creative writing. They tend to do relatively well in language-based subjects where verbal skills are to the fore (for example, English, history, modern languages and other humanities subjects). Where verbal scores are high, they will be quick to see links between verbal concepts and are adept at interpreting and understanding the nuances and ambiguities of language (for example, distinguishing between everyday uses of words and their subject-specific uses – *energy, resistance* and so on). They will be good at developing ideas and lines of thinking in continuous text and explaining a process logically. One of the best ways to build reasoning skills is to participate in real reasoning dialogues. Pupils with high verbal reasoning scores can further develop their skills, and play a prominent role in developing the skills of others, through group work. For example, they can lead discussion within the group, asking 'Why?' 'What?' and 'How?' questions, and modelling processes such as giving reasons for their ideas.

Figure 3.4: *CAT3* Individual Pupil Profile with GCSE indicators – Bruce

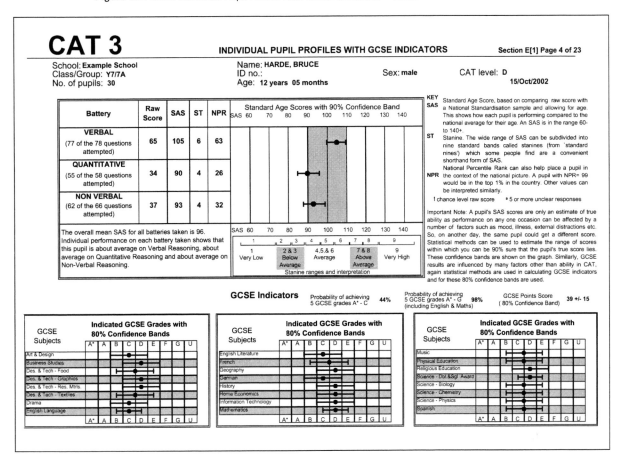

TALK IT THROUGH

Since their non-verbal scores are relatively low, V+ pupils may need some support in using visual modelling systems (in subjects such as science, geography or technology), where they are required to interpret diagrams, model ideas through pictures or translate verbal material into graphs, charts, tabular or other non-verbal forms. Encourage them to practise making visual models of the events in a text. It may be helpful at any points of difficulty in the curriculum to use strategies that build on their particularly well-developed language skills. For example, you may need to talk through, analyse and plan how to solve a mathematics problem (see bullet list on page 42). The oral and mental lesson starters from the *Framework for Teaching Mathematics* (DfEE, 2001b) can be very positive in building pupils' visualisation, thinking and communication skills.

SUPPORTING MATHEMATICS

V+ pupils tend to have higher national test and examination attainment than pupils with a similar mean *CAT* score who have their strength on the Quantitative or the Non-verbal batteries. Overall, therefore, a relative verbal strength can compensate for lower scores in the quantitative and non-verbal areas. However if the level of the scores is low (stanines 1 to 3), then pupils are still likely to experience problems, particularly in mathematics. For such pupils, the verbal strength can be used as follows:

- Translate mathematics problems that use numbers and symbols into *word problems*: give pupils practice in making such translations and in reading them aloud or explaining them to others – the benefits of auditory learning for such pupils are often overlooked.

- Practise storing facts as *verbal associations in exact sequences of words* (such as '7 plus 8 equals 15' or '6 times 8 is 48'), which can be accessed through rapid mental recall. Overlearning such facts can free the pupil to spend greater working memory resources on the mathematical aspects of the task. Again, practise saying these aloud.

- Guide pupils to *search for cue words* when interpreting and analysing mathematics problems: for example, *greater than, sum, double, halve, factor, round, divisor, prime, remainder, compute, sign, etc.* Talking in pairs might help them to better understand terms that have a more general or different meaning in day-to-day use: for example, *property, round, estimate, range, mean.* Encourage the pupils to distinguish between different meanings, for example 'in general, *round* means ... but in mathematics *round* means ...'

V+ profiles tend to be slightly more common for girls, while V– profiles (see page 47) tend to be more common for boys. This reflects the fact that girls, on average, score around two standard age score points higher than boys on the Verbal Battery (there is no significant sex difference in mean score on the Quantitative or Non-verbal batteries). Do not be surprised therefore if you identify different proportions of boys and girls with these profiles within your class.

Relative strength in quantitative reasoning (Q+)

Colin Winstanley (see Figure 3.5) shows a strong profile, with all scores at or above the national average score of 100. However Colin has a particular strength in quantitative reasoning, with a quantitative score of 120, significantly above both his verbal (107) and non-verbal (100) scores.

Pupils with Q+ profiles are strong in understanding relationships between numbers, in seeing patterns and order in numbers and in their flexibility in combining and recombining various quantitative elements in meaningful ways. Q+ profiles tend to be associated with relatively high achievement in mathematics, and in other subjects with a significant quantitative component (such as business studies, science, and statistics).

Figure 3.5: *CAT3* Individual Pupil Profile with GCSE indicators – Colin

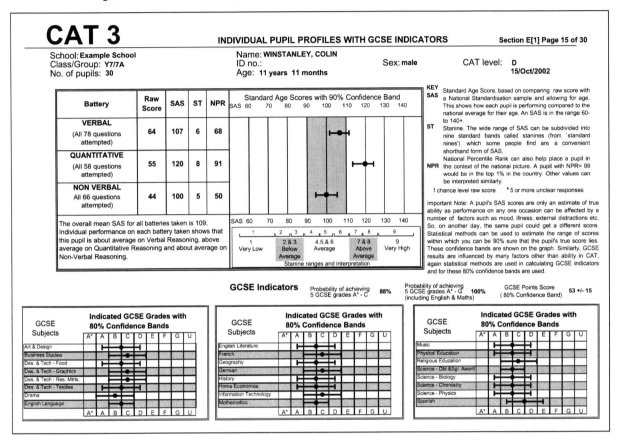

EXTRACTING AND REASONING WITH ABSTRACTIONS

Pupils with a strength in quantitative reasoning often learn computer skills more readily than their peers, especially procedures such as using text editors, spreadsheets or cut-and-paste facilities. Pupils with high quantitative reasoning scores are typically strong in extracting regularities from their experiences and then reasoning with these abstractions. Their abilities can be encouraged through mathematical tasks, games and puzzles. If focused on individual achievement, it is preferable that these games have a non-competitive focus, although in group work a competitive element can bring into focus the valuable asset of the quantitatively strong pupil. ICT offers good opportunities to support possibly weaker areas of mathematics such as geometric or spatial reasoning. For example, Q+ pupils can use dynamic geometry software to deduce formulae for the area of a parallelogram, or the area of a triangle from the formulae for the area of a rectangle.

CAPITALISE ON SPEED AND ACCURACY

At lower score levels, a quantitative strength tends to be most apparent in the acquisition of the simple *computational* aspects of mathematics rather than the *conceptual* or *semantic* aspects. Teaching could build on the quantitative strength by capitalising on the pupil's speed and accuracy in basic computation. This can provide a way for the pupil to make a valuable contribution in group work across the curriculum.

ENCOURAGE DEVELOPMENT OF EXPRESSIVE LANGUAGE

Q+ pupils may be able to present concise, reasoned arguments using mathematical notation, symbols or diagrams (in the area of algebra, for example) but struggle to explain and justify their inferences and deductions verbally. Again, this suggests careful grouping strategies to provide good models for expressive language skills. Some research has suggested that pupils who excel in learning rule-based mathematical knowledge can show better than expected knowledge of grammar. If this is the case, then the grammatical strength can be praised and used when asking pupils to give feedback on each other's writing. Such group work can, in turn, be an entry for helping these pupils acquire knowledge of higher-level writing skills such as principles of style or organisation.

PROVIDE EXTENSION OPPORTUNITIES IN MATHEMATICS

Pupils with high quantitative reasoning scores should also be encouraged to exploit and further develop this ability. Such pupils will deal with abstract mathematics much more readily than other pupils. They will progress more quickly through the yearly teaching programmes of the *Framework for Teaching Mathematics* (DfEE, 2001b) and they will need extension and enrichment opportunities to develop the breadth of their mathematics and the depth of their thinking. If quantitative scores are very high, pupils may be grouped into an 'express' set, as suggested in the *Framework*, where they can benefit from discussion with other pupils working at a similarly high level. They may also benefit from enrichment activities such as the London Mathematical Society's *UK Mathematical Challenge* and other competitions, although careful consideration of individual pupils' personal and social circumstances is important if introducing a competitive element.

Relative strength in non-verbal reasoning (N+)

James Denton has a non-verbal reasoning score at the national average for his age (see Figure 3.6). However his verbal and quantitative reasoning scores are low, in the bottom 14 per cent and 12 per cent of his age group respectively. It is likely that his curriculum attainment is low. At the end of Key Stage 2 (age 11) we know James was achieving Level 3 of the national curriculum (England) in English, mathematics and science.

Figure 3.6: *CAT3* Individual Pupil Profile with GCSE indicators – James

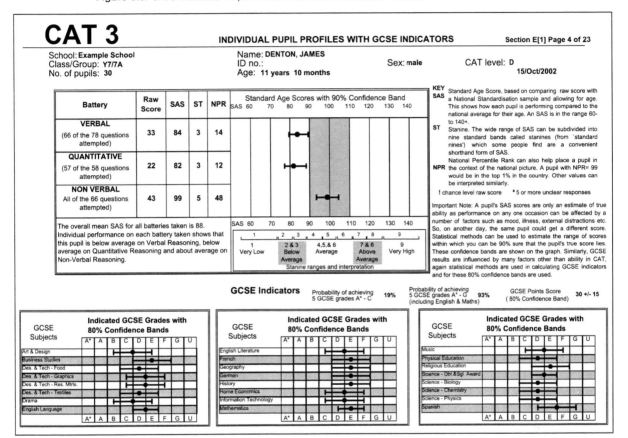

It is likely that James does not have the fundamental store of verbal and numerical concepts necessary to demonstrate his relatively well-developed non-verbal reasoning ability. However, if given some targeted intervention in basic literacy and numeracy skills, he could be expected to make very rapid progress in English and mathematics – and more widely across the curriculum. If the school were considering a group of pupils with profiles like this for targeted intervention, such a group could be expected to make rapid progress. In contrast, where *all three* reasoning scores are low, such as for pupils with even profiles like that of **Liam Hepworth** (see Figure 3.3), it is likely that progress to Level 5 by the end of Key Stage 3 will be much more gradual.

The profile may also say something about the pupil's preferred learning style. James has a strength in, and probably a preference for, *visual or spatial* rather than *verbal* modes of thinking. For example, he may prefer texts that contain pictures and graphics, and he may favour maps rather than verbal directions. He is unlikely to learn effectively from verbal methods alone; therefore you should focus on:

■ teacher or peer modelling;

■ concrete (visual) representation of abstract concepts;

■ demonstrations;

■ pictures, flowcharts, Venn diagrams or other types of illustrations;

■ films and videotapes;

■ hands-on activities.

N+ pupils often prefer to 'do' rather than to reflect about 'what to do', and this can create problems. They usually prefer practical experiments that provide a concrete learning opportunity, or require them to work with physical representations of ideas – such as cards with key words or images, which may be sorted or ranked. Transfer from spatial to verbal areas may be facilitated by practising a skill in varied contexts: for example, understanding coordinates as a general number system might be practised as practical map work, also linking into geometry and algebra.

The profile shown in Figure 3.7 is for **Emma Hartley**. As in James' profile, the relative strength of the non-verbal score in relation to the verbal and quantitative scores is apparent. However, Emma's profile differs from James' in terms of the absolute levels of performance. For Emma, *all three* standard scores are *above the national* average. Indeed her non-verbal score is in the top 10 per cent of pupils of her age.

Emma's learning needs will therefore be different from James'. For example, her levels of attainment are probably high and there will be little need to focus on core literacy and

Figure 3.7: *CAT3* Individual Pupil Profile with GCSE indicators – Emma

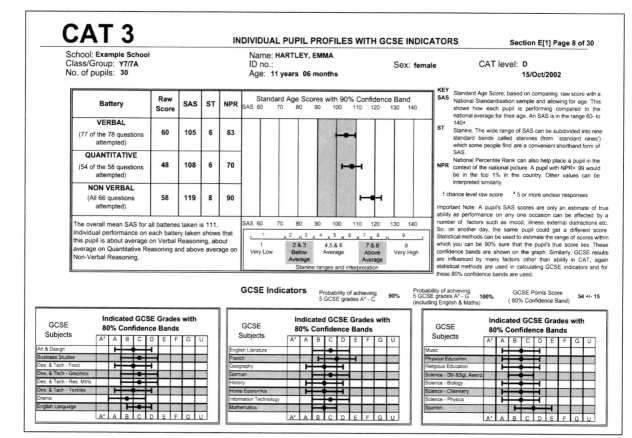

numeracy skills. Such skills are likely to be very well developed, with a wide knowledge base on which to build new learning.

However, pupils such as Emma are often overlooked because their attainment in curriculum subjects is at least average or above. While her attainment might be average, or even above average, this does not mean that it is as high as it might be. Pupils with strong non-verbal reasoning abilities are often found to excel in areas such as mathematics, science, engineering, architecture and the visual arts. However their attainment in language-based subjects such as English, modern foreign languages and humanities may represent a degree of underachievement against their non-verbal scores. It is notable when looking at Emma's GCSE indicators that the indicators for the language-based subjects – that is, English language, English literature, French, German and Spanish – are all Grade C or C/D. However, the indicators for the vast majority of the other GCSE subjects are Grade B or B/C.

The major focus for teaching and learning with Emma is to try to transfer her strengths in working with visual symbols and systems to her written work. Encourage such pupils to employ their visualising skills in considering the content, layout, length and process of writing. Topic webs or memory maps may be useful at the exploratory stage of planning a future piece of writing, when taking notes in class or when revising. Storyboards may be helpful in sequencing texts or to plot developments over time. Encouraging the use of visual plans and diagrams may be a helpful way of organising ideas: for example, using 'comparison grids' or concept explorer sheets for categorising words, sentences, themes or processes (Williams and Sutcliffe, 2000). Prompting pupils to form mental models of a scene when reading a text may help them to understand and recall the subject matter more vividly. Enacting scenes from Shakespeare's plays can provide pupils with strong visual images that later help them in written composition.

It is clear that there are differences between James and Emma because of the absolute level of their scores. However it is also clear that there are factors they have in common because of their shared N+ strength. Because of this, many of the strategies focusing on visual strengths identified for James apply equally to Emma and other N+ pupils.

Relative weakness in verbal reasoning (V–)

An example of a V– profile is shown in Figure 3.8: **Nora Williamson**. Nora's verbal score of 84 is significantly below both her quantitative and non-verbal scores. In contrast to the profile shown in Figure 3.6, where James' verbal and quantitative scores were *both* low in relation to his non-verbal score, for Nora it is *only* the verbal score that is low, while both the quantitative and the non-verbal scores are in the average range.

Figure 3.8: *CAT3* Individual Pupil Profile with GCSE indicators – Nora

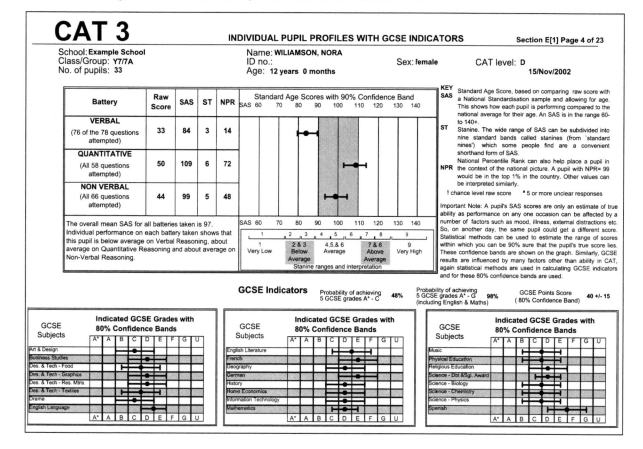

SPECIFIC READING DIFFICULTY?

It is important to determine first whether the profile results from some specific difficulty with reading. Only the Verbal Battery requires any reading ability: no reading is required for the Quantitative and Non-verbal batteries.

It may be that the pupil speaks English as an Additional Language (EAL) and is not yet fluent in reading English. In such cases, the cause of the low verbal score will be clear (but see 'low verbal scores', page 60, for further clarification). For these pupils, a more accurate estimate of their reasoning ability may be gained by considering the mean score *excluding* the verbal score. Assuming that the support and resources needed to address the pupil's language learning needs are made available, this 'adjusted' mean score may provide a sounder basis for considering targets for future attainment.

Where the pupil is a native English speaker, it is important to assess the extent of their reading skills. Low-scoring pupils may have been held back by a specific reading difficulty. As a quick check, try reading some of the questions aloud to the pupil. Does the pupil's performance improve markedly? If so, it is likely that reading skills are the problem. Detailed consideration of all the records sent by the primary school is called for. If best practice in primary–secondary liaison has occurred, then records from the primary school SENCO should indicate any specific reading difficulty. In some cases, it may be that further individual assessment is warranted. For example, if the pupil has persistent and ongoing problems at word level (as distinct from sentence or text level), he or she may have a specific reading difficulty. You may want to consider one-to-one diagnostic assessment such as the *Neale Analysis of Reading Ability* (Neale *et al.*, 1997) or the *Phonological Assessment Battery* (Frederickson, Reason and Frith, 1997). Above all, observe the pupil carefully in different contexts and when undertaking different types of activities.

LITERACY PROGRESS UNITS?

It is also possible that the low verbal score might be associated with social and economic disadvantage, reflecting little exposure to rich and varied language in the home or wider environment, or to frequent changes of school or missed or interrupted schooling, particularly for travellers, refugees, those in care or with specific medical conditions. It is important to use the pupil's strengths in the quantitative and non-verbal areas to scaffold their verbal weakness. However, verbal ability is so crucial to academic success that interventions to directly address the verbal weaknesses may be necessary, especially where verbal scores are low. If the verbal reasoning score is in the lower three stanines, you should consider whether the Progress Units of the National Literacy Strategy (England) might provide appropriate 'catch up' materials. These focus on writing organisation, information retrieval, spelling rules and strategies, using inference and deduction, using phonics to improve accuracy and developing a wider repertoire of sentence structures. The objective in employing these or other materials is to develop pupils as independent readers and writers, so they are better able to use their working memory and other resources for reasoning and thinking, rather than for decoding and processing operations.

BUILD WORD KNOWLEDGE

V– pupils may have a restricted vocabulary and may not have been exposed to rich language outside school. Activities to build word knowledge, such as word walls of key concepts in the relevant subject classroom, will support these pupils. Games such as word jigsaws, word dominoes and 'find the odd one out' can build an awareness of word families, common roots and suffixes, lexical patterns and other regularities in language. For example, how many words beginning with 'bi' can you name (*bikini, bicycle, bitter, biennial, bilateral* and so on)? Is there a common meaning to the words? Are there any exceptions? Specific work on reading, speaking and listening is needed. Reading is an excellent way to build verbal comprehension ability, particularly if combined with active techniques like asking questions, predicting, empathising and retelling.

GROUP WORK

Group work is a good way of building language use and V– pupils in particular need to build the capacity to express and communicate their ideas through words. This could build on strengths by asking pupils to describe a successful mathematics or science project. When forming groups, include pupils with verbal strengths (V+) in the group, as they can serve to model appropriate language. Groups can actively solve problems and discuss the strategies and results. Suitable problems to set might include working out the meaning of unknown words through context, morphology, prepositions etc., or inferring and deducing meanings from the evidence of target texts (by articulating problems and asking pertinent questions, by brainstorming etc.). The V– pupil might initially take a more passive role, for example as scribe, but with growing confidence may increase their active contribution. The *Framework for Teaching English* (DfEE, 2001) has many examples of good practice in the above areas.

BUILD ON VISUAL AND QUANTITATIVE STRENGTHS

Visual and quantitative strengths can be maximised, including some of the strategies reported in the N+ and Q+ profiles. For example, you could encourage the use of:

- bullet points, paragraphing and sub-headings to help structure text;
- different coloured highlighter pens to pick out key ideas, themes and linking structures in text;
- flowcharts, comparison grids and lists when pupils are planning writing;
- card- or picture-sorting activities;
- writing frames to structure writing: these can be very specific or quite general (for example, 'introduction, method, results, conclusion' for a scientific report, or 'arresting opening, developing plot, a complication, a crisis and a satisfying resolution' for a story);
- concept explorer sheets that help pupils compare and distinguish verbal concepts through generating best examples, contrary examples and borderline examples of a particular concept (see Williams and Sutcliffe, 2000);
- concept mapping or memory maps, which can provide a powerful way of interpreting texts or organising ideas and recording links between them.

Concept cartoons can be an effective way of stimulating thinking in science lessons, particularly for pupils with a V– profile (Naylor and Keogh, 2002, www.conceptcartoons.com): an example is shown in Figure 3.9. These cartoons are designed to offer new ways of looking at a situation in order to make it problematic and provide a stimulus for thinking, discussion and developing ideas. Some of the key features of concept cartoons are:

- visual representation of ideas;
- minimal text, in dialogue form;
- alternative viewpoints offered on the situation;
- alternatives are informed by common misunderstandings, so are plausible;
- the cartoon-style format and everyday setting are familiar, making the situations credible and accessible.

Figure 3.9: Concept cartoon – people with a snowman (after Naylor and Keogh, 2002)

ACTIVE LEARNING

Lecture methods, involving extended speaking to the whole class, are unlikely to benefit V– pupils. All pupils, but particularly V– pupils, will enjoy active hands-on learning, 'A lesson where you do something really sticks in your mind'. If looking at acids and alkalines in science, experiment with bread, cakes and potatoes. What do pupils expect the outcomes of the experiments to be and why? Active production is at the heart of most subjects, thus we have: art (painting), music (composing), drama (acting), media (making videos), PE (playing games), mathematics and science (solving problems) and English (writing stories, poems, scripts). Rather than lectures, other media such as film, video, whiteboard and computers, can be powerful means of presenting information to pupils. Note-taking from video can be effective because key points arise from visual input, not just words. The V– pupil may have a wider facility in using ICT, spreadsheets and databases, which can support their verbal work.

Some suggestions for activities that parents can be involved in to support the development of verbal reasoning abilities are given in Chapter 8 (page 160). When working with pupils with a V– profile, you might also want to consider such activities. These include:

■ word games, such as making up words from the letter components of car number plates;

■ '20 questions' type games, where the players guess a chosen character, object, concept or word;

- completing word searches and crossword puzzles, but especially designing your own searches or crosswords (a much more complex activity);
- writing instruction sheets on a favourite activity (for example, how to construct a model or play a favourite computer game) so as to build sequencing skills and the ability to analyse and explain a process.

Relative weakness in Quantitative reasoning (Q–)

Q– pupils are relatively weak in understanding relationships between numbers, in seeing patterns and order in numbers, and in their flexibility in combining and recombining quantitative elements in meaningful ways. An example of a Q– profile is shown in Figure 3.10. **Sally Hawkswell** has verbal and non-verbal scores that are at or above the national average, but her quantitative score is 85, placing her in stanine 3 and below average.

DYSCALCULIA?

If the absolute quantitative score is very low (stanines 1 to 3), and if in wider class work the pupil's difficulties appear to be confined to numerals, then it is possible that some

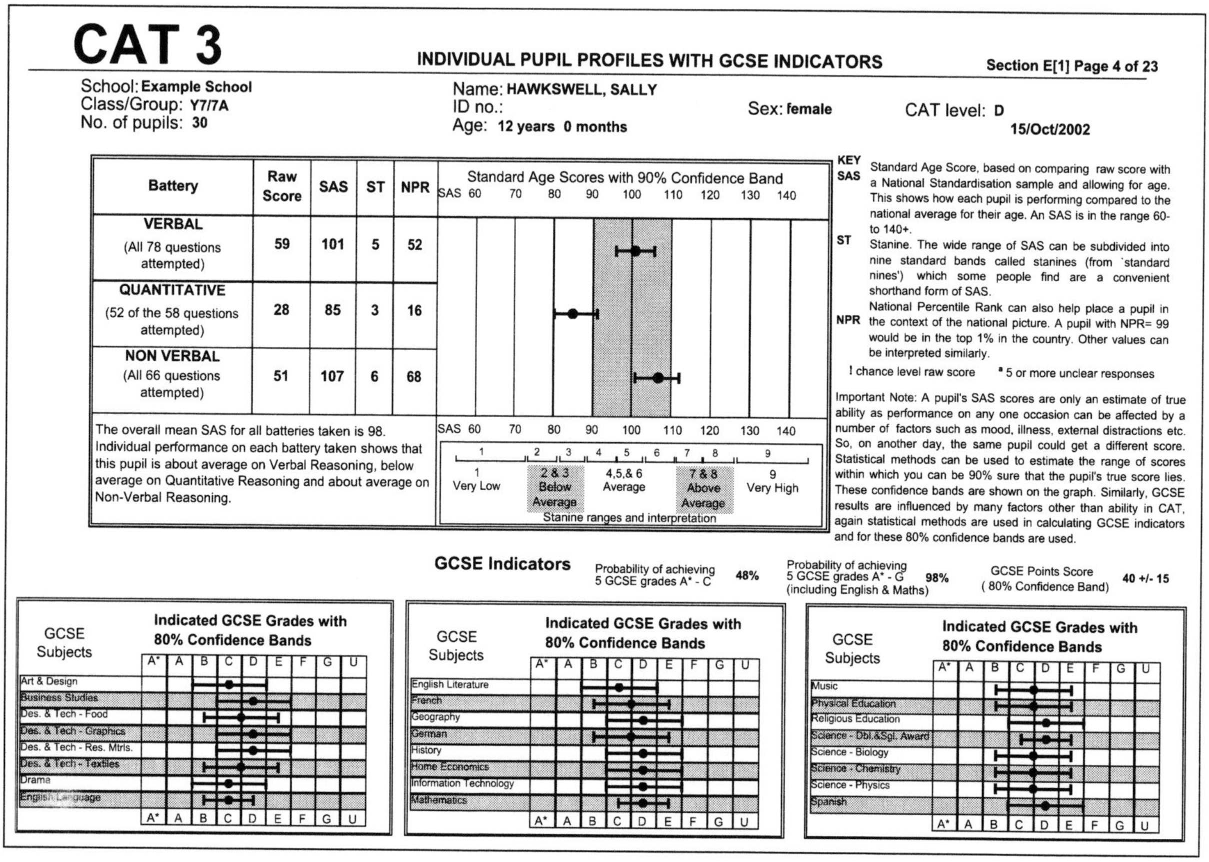

Figure 3.10: *CAT3* Individual Pupil Profile with GCSE indicators – Sally

kind of specific arithmetic difficulty (sometimes termed dyscalculia) is involved. The concept of dyscalculia, like that of dyslexia, is by no means uncontested. However, research has suggested that dyscalculic pupils may have problems understanding that number words and numerals refer to the size (or numerosity) of the sets they denote. Such pupils:

■ do not understand that collections of things have a numerosity and that manipulations – for example, combining collections or taking sub-collections away – affect the numerosity;

■ do not understand that collections need not be of visible things – they can equally be audible things, tactile things or abstract things (like wishes);

■ do not automatically recognise small numerosities – that is, collections of up to about four objects.

If you are interested in exploring this further, nferNelson has published a computerised *Dyscalculia Screener* (Butterworth, 2003).

APPEAL TO VERBAL AND VISUAL STRENGTHS
You can assist these pupils by appealing to their relative strength in verbal and visual reasoning.

In terms of verbal strengths, use verbalisation to help in counting over transitions (for example, 999, 1000, 1001), and in supporting estimation strategies. For example, when teaching the strategy 'adding nine' as the process 'add 10 then subtract one', explicitly label the steps as 'add' and 'adjust'. You can also reformulate mathematical sentences into word problems using concrete objects. For example, 'In a class of 33 pupils, 18 pupils have no pets, the others have two pets each. How many pets is that?' Also work on 'overlearning' verbal associations. Facts stored as verbal associations in exact sequences of words, such as '7 plus 8 equals 15' or '6 times 8 is 48', can be accessed through rapid mental recall. Overlearning such facts can free the pupil to spend greater working memory on the mathematical aspects of the task.

Where quantitative scores are low, pupils may benefit through emphasising the strong visual element of mathematics. Use visual aids whenever you can to illuminate meaning, making all illustrations directly relevant to text and mathematics problems. For example, you might use:

■ squared paper, as a model to understand multiplication;

■ number lines, to understand the way quantities change with addition or subtraction;

■ place value charts, to understand the significance of decimal points;

■ 'magic square' problems, to provide intense and valuable number practice (for example, 'Write the numbers from one through to nine into the cells of a three-by-three square so that every row, every column and both diagonals add up to the same number', see Figure 3.11 for solution. Parr, 2002 describes several useful variations on the magic squares theme);

■ tree diagrams, as a method of decomposing numbers or recording factors;

■ visual representations of fractions (as shown in Figure 3.12 on page 54).

Figure 3.11: Using 'magic square' problems to explore actively patterns in numbers

8	1	6
3	5	7
4	9	2

The numbers in every row, column and diagonal add up to 15

Figure 3.12: A visual representation of fractions for pupils with a weakness in quantitative reasoning

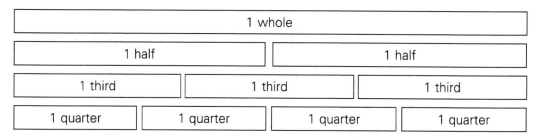

DEALING WITH ABSTRACT ELEMENTS

However, a Q– profile may stem from a more fundamental problem in dealing with abstract (as opposed to concrete) elements. Even the most elementary concepts in mathematics are abstractions: for example, relating the word 'twelve' to two numerals (1 and 2), or understanding that the number 9 in 'nine trees' means the same thing as the number 9 in 'nine coins'. Spreadsheet work – in which the pupil identifies trends in numbers, predicts the next value and then uses formulae to test their hypotheses – help build confidence and facility in reasoning with numbers. 'Number detective' games and code-and-cipher problems can also help build computational strategies. Try to use tasks that build on the pupils' interests. For example, in analysing football league tables you might ask:

- What is the average number of goals scored in a premiership match?
- What is the goal difference for each team? (involves working with negative numbers);
- For your favourite team, what fraction (or percentage) of games were home wins? What fraction were away wins?
- If your favourite team is to win the league, how many matches must it win?

… and so on.

REDUCE ANXIETY

Pupils of above average ability who do poorly in mathematics can become anxious about their poor performance, and this can lead them to avoid mathematical tasks. Strategies to reduce anxiety may be appropriate: for example, encouraging group work and cooperation, allowing more time to complete problems, giving pupils greater choice in the problems they solve, etc.

Some suggestions for activities that parents can be involved in to support the development of quantitative abilities are given in Chapter 8 (page 161). When working with pupils with a Q– profile, you might also want to consider:

■ using practical problems to practise estimation and mental maths (for example, the quantities needed to construct a model in design and technology, or the quantities needed to feed seven people if working from a recipe for two in home economics etc);

■ using timetables to plan a rail or bus journey, working out connections between services and estimating journey times;

■ working with computer games that require logical or mathematical reasoning (for example, Microsoft Minesweeper);

■ using spreadsheets for practical purposes (for example, managing money, analysing football league tables).

Relative weakness in non-verbal reasoning (N–)

An example of an N– profile is shown in Figure 3.13. **Nicola Denton** has verbal and quantitative scores in the average range, but a below average score on the Non-verbal Battery.

Figure 3.13: *CAT3* Individual Pupil Profile with GCSE indicators – Nicola

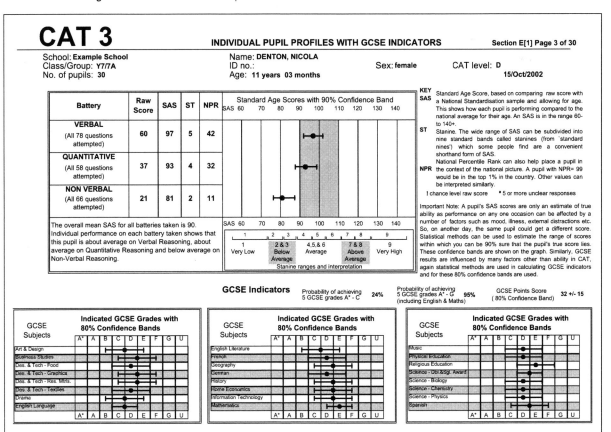

PROVIDE SUPPORT FOR HIGHER-ORDER SKILLS

Nicola achieved Level 4, the expected level for 11 year olds, in the English and mathematics tests taken in England at the end of primary school. However, this covers a very broad range of performance, with nearly half (46 per cent) of all pupils achieving Level 4 in the 2002 English and mathematics tests. Compared to other pupils achieving Level 4, Nicola's CAT profile suggests that she may need further support when it comes to higher-order problem-solving skills. For example, she may have no problem with reading accuracy, but may need more support than other Level 4 pupils in skills such as summarising, inferring and predicting. Similarly, in mathematics, she may have no difficulties with calculation and computation, but may need more support with visual problems and notational systems such as algebra, geometry and so on. She may also need specific support in other areas of the curriculum involving shape and space, such as working with charts and graphical data in science, or map reading in geography.

CHECK NUMBER OF ATTEMPTS AND PERCENTAGE CORRECT

Other explanations for N– profiles are possible. The pupil may have little experience of non-verbal assessments and his or her low non-verbal score could indicate either slow work or a lack of confidence in working with novel materials. It is important to check the number of attempts and, where this is low, the percentage of attempts that were answered correctly. If the number of attempts is low, but the percentage of attempts answered correctly is high (see Chapter 2, page 19), the student may have worked slowly on the Non-verbal Battery because he or she lacks confidence rather than ability. This is not the case for Nicola, since she has attempted all the questions on the Non-verbal Battery. However, where it *is* the case, the pupil may need support in learning to think independently when confronted with novel or unfamiliar tasks.

EXAMINE ALL RELEVANT EVIDENCE

The alternative explanations given above illustrate the general need to interpret CAT scores in the context of *all* the information you have about the pupil in order to arrive at the most appropriate interpretation of the results. For example, how does Nicola cope with classroom activities involving shape and space in mathematics? How does she perform in science or areas requiring visual modelling? How does she cope with new tasks, situations or environments? Do any of these observations support the interpretation of a weakness in reasoning with visual materials? Such observation may provide important corroboration for the CAT profile, or may suggest a need to look at your interpretation again.

SUPPORT THE USE OF VISUAL REPRESENTATIONS

Assuming that the number of attempts is high, an N– profile may indicate a general weakness in creating visual mental models, or coordinating visual models and verbal or quantitative concepts. A certain level of visual-spatial ability is important for success in many areas of the curriculum, especially in science and mathematics. For pupils whose non-verbal reasoning score is low, some direct training in visualisation and spatial thinking may be appropriate. For example, practise detecting inconsistencies between a story and a picture, or a statement and an imagined familiar scene or object. Encourage pupils to practise reproducing drawings from memory. For example, practising drawing a map of Europe from memory will result in far greater retention of the image than repeated instances of simply inspecting the map. Encourage transfer between visual and verbal areas by using drawings to summarise stories, passages of text or problem statements. When possible, do not require pupils to shift attention between two different locations, such as an illustration on an OHP or whiteboard and text in a book. Keep both in view simultaneously, or allow them to study the drawing while you read the text.

Avoid problems that require the pupil to *imagine* transformations of images. Instead, use computer graphics or physical models to *show* the pupil such transformations. For example, if you are asking pupils to conceptualise the transformation of sugar and starch to alcohol and carbon dioxide in brewing, show them a graphical form of the relationship. Show them how the graphs vary depending on a third variable, like yeast strain. Then practise mapping other verbal or quantitative concepts with similar relationships onto the figure: for example, power-to-weight ratios, how do these vary for different types of vehicles? Improving pupils' ability to work with visual models will also help them in history or geography when working with maps, including the use of coordinates and ideas of angle, direction, position, scale and ratio.

In mathematics, there may be particular problems with shape and space, for example in plotting, interpreting and predicting from graphs. Graphical calculators can be very useful in scaffolding the pupil's relative visual weakness by allowing him or her to readily view the visual form of different equations. Using data loggers to collect data, and then spreadsheets to practise modelling and simulations, also supports visualisation while building on quantitative strengths. When using visual aids such as number lines, place value charts, diagrams, mathematical shapes, measuring equipment, graphs, software etc, pay special attention to the needs of N– pupils.

Again, suggestions for activities that parents can be involved in to support the development of non-verbal abilities are given in Chapter 8 (page 161). You might also want to consider these when working with pupils with an N– profile. For example:

- encourage model-making in art and design to develop visual analysis, spatial judgement and manual dexterity;
- encourage sketching and drawing to develop the ability to estimate lengths, heights, angles and relative proportions;
- introduce computer games that require players to navigate from one area to another using grid references, distances or directions, etc.

High verbal and quantitative scores are particularly strongly related to academic success in school-related learning. Consequently the curricular attainment of N– pupils is likely to be higher than that of pupils with a similar mean *CAT* score, but with a V– or a Q– profile.

Contrast profiles

We have seen that around one third of pupils have an *even* profile of scores across the three batteries, and around 40 per cent of pupils show a *distinct* strength or weakness profile, where one of the scores is either significantly above, or significantly below, the other two scores.

The remaining profiles are *contrast* profiles (accounting for about 20 per cent of pupils) and *complete contrast* profiles (accounting for a further 5 per cent). The general form of contrast profiles is for one high score (relative strength), one middle score, and one low score (relative weakness). In the contrast profiles, only two scores differ significantly (the high and the low scores); in the complete contrast profiles, all three scores differ significantly from each other.

A contrast between two scores

Laura Wooley, whose scores are shown in Figure 3.14, has a profile that would be described as a contrast (V+,Q–) profile. This is because her verbal score (102) is the

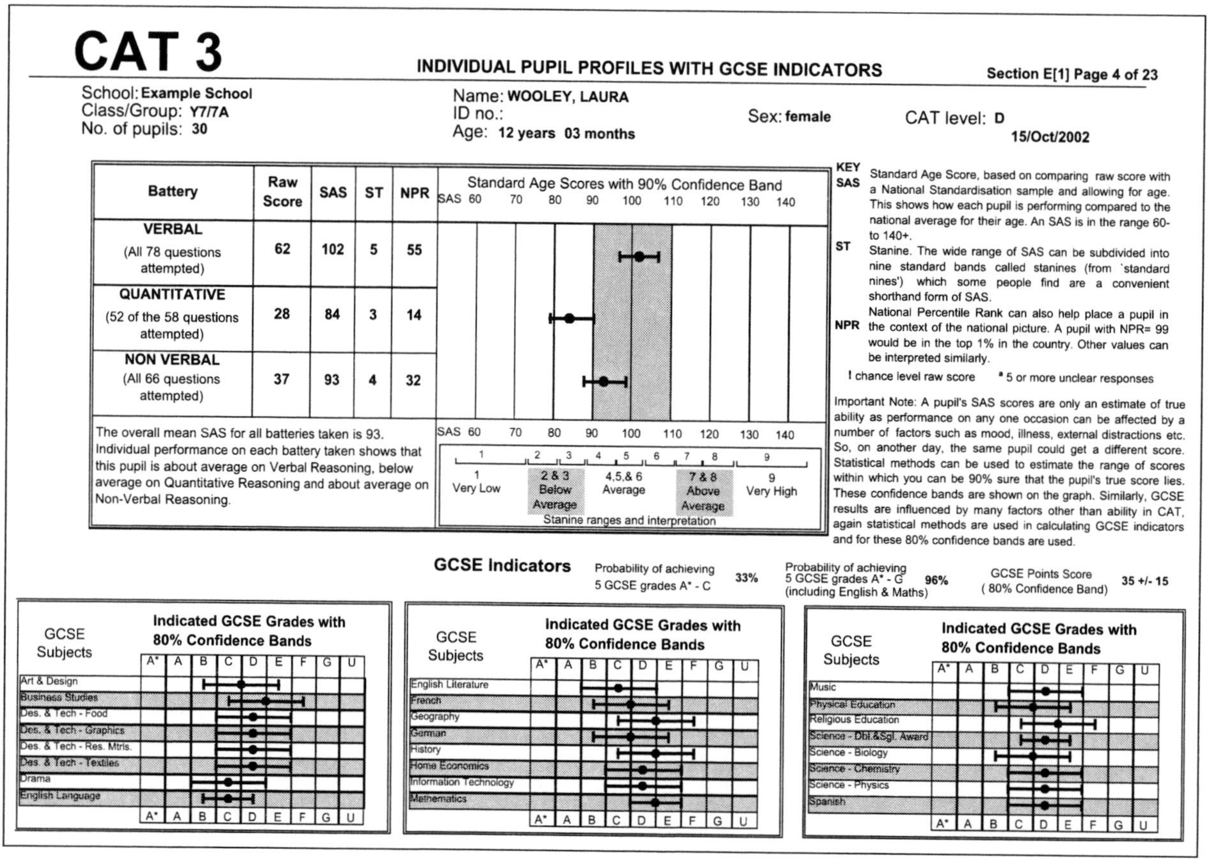

Figure 3.14: *CAT3* Individual Pupil Profile with GCSE indicators – Laura

highest of the three, and differs significantly from her quantitative score (84), which is the lowest of the three. The non-verbal score (93) is between these two extremes and does not differ significantly from either.

In general, a pupil with a contrast profile will have elements of *both* of the relevant distinct profiles. Laura may have elements of the *strengths* described in the V+ profile (see Figure 3.4, Bruce, page 41) and the *weaknesses* described in the Q– profile (see Figure 3.10, Sally, page 52). Use your detailed knowledge of the pupil to decide whether the adaptations suggested by the relative strength, or the relative weakness, are generally the most effective. Of course, as with all learning, this may vary across different learning tasks or in different situations. Similar guidance applies to each of the six variations of the contrast profile, as listed in Table 3.1 on page 34.

Complete contrast profiles

A contrast between all three scores

A small proportion of pupils have an extreme form of the contrast profile. A *complete contrast* profile is defined as a difference of 10 or more standard age score points

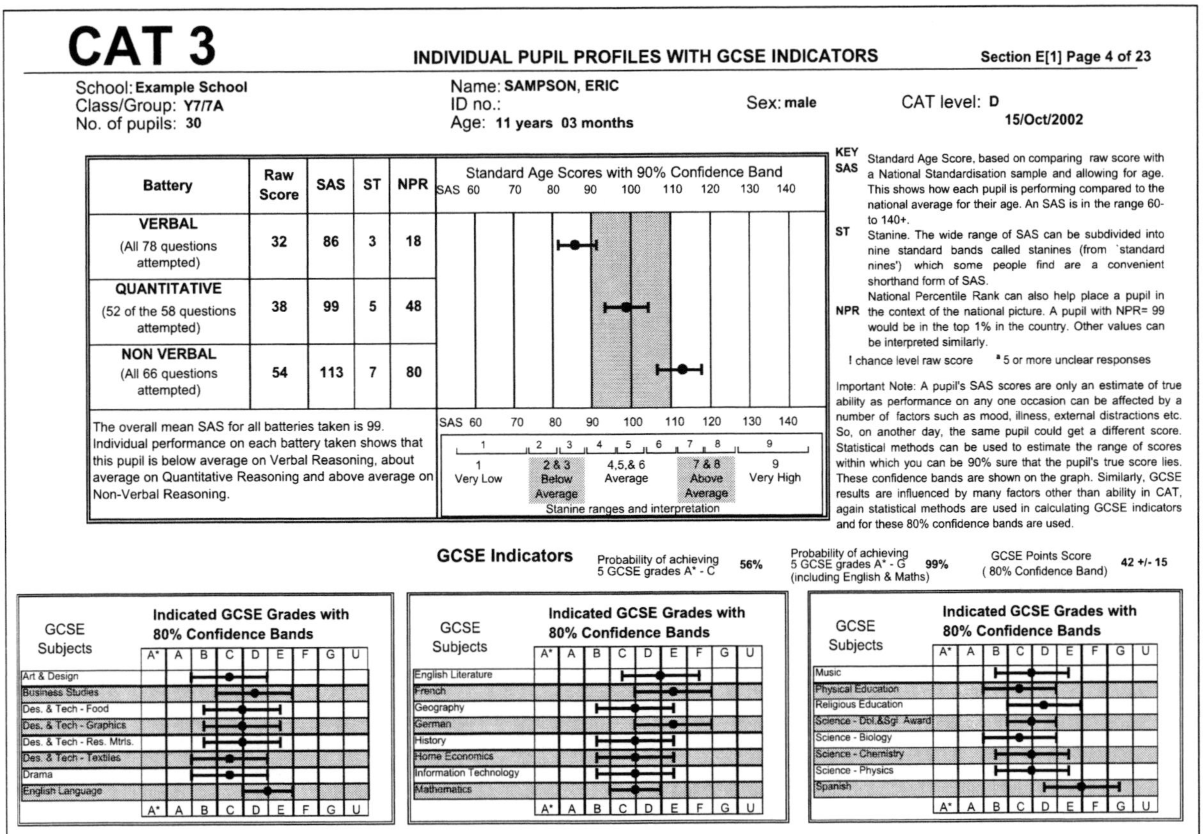

Figure 3.15: *CAT3* Individual Pupil Profile with GCSE indicators – Eric

between every battery, such that the pupil's scores on *all three batteries* are *significantly different*. Approximately 5 per cent of pupils have profiles like this: **Eric Sampson** (see Figure 3.15) is one of them. Eric's verbal reasoning score of 86 is significantly lower than his quantitative score of 99, which in turn is significantly below his non-verbal score of 113.

DISREGARD THE MEAN *CAT* SCORE

For all pupils with a complete contrast profile, little importance should be attached to the mean *CAT* score. With such a wide range of scores, the mean or average score will tend to be misleading since it will not describe accurately the pupil's strengths or weaknesses. The interpretation of the results will depend very much on the particular batteries on which the highest and lowest scores were achieved.

HIGH INCIDENCE OF LOW VERBAL SCORES

It is notable that nearly half of the pupils with complete contrast profiles have their lowest score on the Verbal Battery. Members of the single largest group (1.4 per cent of all 500,000 pupils assessed) show a complete contrast profile combining a verbal weakness with a non-verbal strength (V– N+), as shown for Eric in Figure 3.15. For these pupils, it is important to check the number of attempts and the percentage of attempts answered correctly for the Verbal Battery (see Chapter 2, pages 17 to 27) to ensure that a low number of attempts is not contributing to the outcome.

For pupils with English as an Additional Language (EAL), the low score on the Verbal Battery may indicate a lack of fluency with English language. The important factor here is not whether the pupil speaks English as an additional language, but the pupil's level of fluency in reading English. Many pupils with EAL are fully fluent both in their home language and in English; these fluent bilingual pupils can have a level of performance in the verbal domain that exceeds the average for monolingual English speakers (Strand, 1995). Where pupils have EAL *and* are not fluent in reading English, it is advisable to consider the mean score *excluding* the verbal score. This may be more informative about the pupil's true cognitive abilities. Expectations for such pupils' subsequent learning and achievement in national tests or in public examinations need to be appropriately high. This assumes that the pupil's English language learning needs are recognised and effectively resourced and addressed.

Where the pupil is a native English speaker, it is important to assess the extent of their reading skills. As a quick check, try reading some of the questions aloud to the pupil. Does the pupil's performance improve markedly? If so, and if the pupil has persistent and ongoing problems at word level (as distinct from sentence or text level), he or she may have a specific reading difficulty. You may want to consider one-to-one diagnostic assessment to more fully determine the pupil's needs (see page 49). Above all, observe the pupil carefully in different contexts and when undertaking a range of activities.

It is also possible that the low verbal score might reflect social and economic disadvantages, such as little exposure to rich and varied language in the home or wider environment. Whatever the cause of the poor verbal performance, it is vitally important that it is addressed. This is because verbal skills are so central to success in learning at school. The Progress Units of the National Literacy Strategy (DfEE, 2001a) can prove useful support for these pupils. Further strategies were discussed in relation to the V– profile (see pages 47 to 52).

VERBAL STRENGTH, QUANTITATIVE WEAKNESS

The dataset analysed for this guide (see Chapter 1, page 9) found one other complete contrast between scores that was notable in terms of a greater-than-expected frequency. This was a profile combining a *verbal strength* and *quantitative weakness* (V+ Q–). These profiles were not very common, accounting for only 0.9 per cent of all pupils. Girls were slightly over-represented in this group, reflecting a 'traditional' gender pattern of female relative strength in language and weakness in mathematics. In terms of strategies to support individual pupils, the relevant V+ and Q– profiles provide a source of ideas for teaching and learning: see the section on distinct profiles, pages 39 to 57. At a group or whole-school level, consider the total proportion of pupils with the (V+ Q–) profile, both in the 'contrast' and the 'complete contrast' form. Where this is in excess of 5 per cent of the girls, this might suggest a need to address gender issues in mathematics and other quantitative subjects at a group level. Are there particular structural or organisational factors that may have a negative impact on the performance of girls? How can the learning experiences for the group as a whole be altered to better build on the verbal strengths of the girls?

Review

This chapter should have provided you with some insights into the importance of reasoning skills for teaching and learning, and the differences in reasoning with verbal, quantitative and non-verbal concepts. The *CAT3* Individual Pupil Profiles provide a rich source of information to allow you to identify pupils' strengths and weaknesses. The different types of profile have been classified so that they can be grouped and analysed in a meaningful and structured way, and the implications for teaching and learning have been described. Given the limitations of a short text, some generalisations have been provided as a guide to further action. You will need to turn these generalisations into detailed teaching programmes for individual pupils, linking to the relevant content for your subject.

Busy professionals sometimes look for a 'cookbook' that will provide ready-made solutions. Such a desire will be frustrated. *CAT* scores often raise as many questions as they provide answers. *CAT* scores provide unique information that is not readily accessible through other methods (see Chapter 8 for a contrast between *CAT* and Key Stage 2 tests). Nevertheless, they are only one part of the 'jigsaw' that is the complete picture of the whole pupil, and must always be interpreted in this broader context. It is not possible to say that *CAT* profile *x* means that applying teaching strategy *y* will achieve a successful learning outcome. However, knowledge of a pupil's cognitive strengths and weaknesses is an excellent starting point from which to consider effective differentiation.

After reading this chapter you should be able to:

■ *understand and interpret* the *CAT3* Individual Pupil Profile;

■ use it to *identify strengths and weaknesses* in pupils' cognitive skills;

■ consider the *implications* of individual profiles for *teaching and learning*.

4 Analysing results for groups of pupils

AIMS

In this chapter we will:

- describe the scoring service reports that present the results for *groups* of pupils, including the gender difference report, and explain how these reports should be interpreted;
- learn how to compare the results for different groups of pupils and judge whether differences are significant;
- present a simple tool, used in Microsoft Excel, to evaluate a range of possible score differences in relation to gender, ethnicity, class or teaching groups;
- analyse the *CAT* results for classes or teaching groups to consider the spread of visual and verbal abilities within and between groups;
- judge the significance of the change in a pupil's scores over time, changes in mean scores for groups of pupils over time, and the implications for retesting;
- automatically convert *CAT2E* to *CAT3* scores using an Excel spreadsheet.

There are two Computer Scoring and Analysis Service reports that analyse the *CAT* results for groups of pupils:

- The *Group Distribution of Standardised Scores* report (also referred to as the group profile) presents a summary of the standardised scores for a group of pupils. When schools return their pupils' answer sheets for scoring, they sort their pupils into groups and place a 'group header sheet' on top of the answer sheets for each group. The school then receives a group report for each group it has identified, plus an additional group report based on all the pupils together. Typically, schools group pupils by their form groups. Thus a six-form entry school will receive seven group reports: one for each form group and a seventh report summarising the results for the year group as a whole.
- The *Group Summary of Results by Gender* directly contrasts the results for boys and girls within a group. You will receive this report only if you select it as an additional option.

Each of these reports is described in detail below.

The Group Distribution of Standardised Scores (group profile)

The Individual Pupil Profile presents one *individual* pupil's results against national averages and contrasts his or her performance across the three test batteries. The Group Distribution of Standardised Scores provides the same analysis, but for a *group* of pupils. An example of the two-page group profile is shown in Figure 4.1 on page 64.

Figure 4.1: Example of a Group Distribution of Standardised Scores (group profile) report

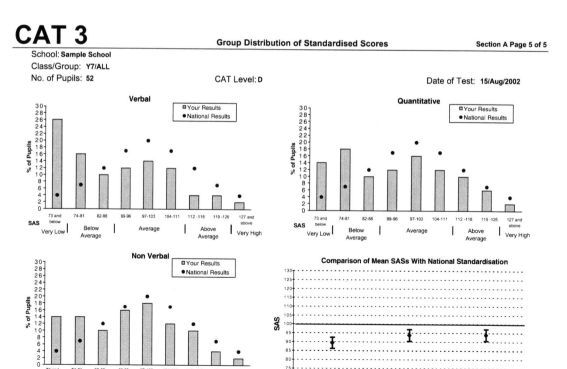

Group Distribution of Standardised Scores

School: **Sample School**
Class/Group: **Y7/ALL**
No. of pupils: **52**

Section A[1] Page 3 of 4

CAT level: **D**

Date of Test: **15/Aug/2002**

The bar charts on the following page show the percentage of your pupils' Standard Age Scores (SAS) that fall within certain ranges of scores for the Verbal, Quantitative and Non-Verbal batteries.

There is also a chart showing the average SAS of your pupils for each battery with 90% confidence bands indicated by the vertical line. If the vertical line overlaps the national '100' line the results for the group do not differ significantly from the national average.

Each battery bar chart shows the distribution of scores of your pupils as bars and also those of the National Standardisation group shown as filled circles behind the bars. The charts allow you to compare the results of your sample with the national picture as represented by the standardisation sample.

The distribution of the National Standardisation scores is a "normal" distribution. The table below summarizes your results in comparison to this normal distribution.

Cognitive AbilitiesTest
Third Edition

Your Results

	No. of Pupils [1]	Mean SAS [2]	Standard Deviation (SD) [3]	In comparison to the national average ....
Verbal	52	89.4	13.6	Your mean SAS is significantly lower than 100 Your SD is not significantly less than 15
Quantitative	52	93.8	14.6	Your mean SAS is significantly lower than 100 Your SD is not significantly less than 15
Non-Verbal	52	93.6	14.9	Your mean SAS is significantly lower than 100 Your SD is not significantly less than 15

Further information about CAT scores is provided in the Cognitive Abilities Test Administration Manual.
In case of enquiries please contact the nferNelson Customer Support and Advisory Service on 0845 602 1937.
© NFER-NELSON 2002.
nferNelson is a division of Granada Learning Limited, part of Granada plc.

Notes

1. Only pupils who have a valid SAS for a given battery are included in this analysis.
2. The mean SAS of the National Standardisation sample is 100 for each battery.
3. Standard Deviation (SD) is a statistical measure of how widely a set of scores fluctuate around the mean score. The National Standardisation sample Standard Deviation is 15 SAS points for each battery.

CAT 3

Group Distribution of Standardised Scores

Section A Page 5 of 5

School: **Sample School**
Class/Group: **Y7/ALL**
No. of Pupils: **52**

CAT Level: **D**

Date of Test: **15/Aug/2002**

Page 1

The first page of the group profile gives some general notes on interpreting the layout of the report. It also provides the following information for each *CAT* battery:

■ the number of pupils tested;

■ the mean standard age score;

■ the standard deviation (SD) of the scores.

For example, for the group shown in Figure 4.1:

■ 52 pupils were tested:

■ the mean *verbal reasoning* score was 89.4, with a standard deviation of 13.6;

■ the mean *quantitative reasoning* score was 93.8 with a standard deviation of 14.6;

■ the mean *non-verbal reasoning* score was 93.6 with a standard deviation of 14.9.

Page 2

The second page of the report consists of four graphs. The graph in the bottom right-hand corner summarises the mean scores for the group against national averages. The term 'national average' is used here, and throughout this guide, to indicate the United Kingdom (UK) average. *CAT3* was standardised on a stratified sample of pupils from England, Wales, Northern Ireland and Scotland, representative of the UK population (see Chapter 1, page 7).

Just as for the individual pupils, there are confidence bands placed around the mean scores for the group. The size of the confidence band will vary depending upon the number of pupils in the group and the range or spread of their scores, as measured by the standard deviation. Where this confidence band does not overlap with the national 100 line, the mean score is significantly different from the national average. In the example shown in Figure 4.1, the mean score for this group of pupils is significantly lower than the national average on all three *CAT* batteries.

Mean scores are a useful summary of the performance of the group as a whole, but they can obscure important information about the spread or distribution of scores within the group. The three bar graphs illustrate the distribution of scores across the nine stanines for each *CAT* battery. The percentage of pupils in each stanine is indicated by the height of the relevant bar. The percentage that would be expected if the group's results conformed to the national average is indicated by the dots. These dots form the familiar normal distribution. You can use these graphs to examine the spread or distribution of the scores for your group against the national average, and to make comparisons between the batteries.

The example group profile in Figure 4.1, suggests that:

■ The mean scores for the group are significantly below national averages on all three batteries. The mean verbal reasoning score (89.4) is particularly low.

■ Nevertheless the group includes pupils from across the entire ability range, including some pupils in the top 4 per cent nationally. For quantitative reasoning in particular, around 10 per cent of the group are in the top two score bands, not far short of the proportion that would be expected from national averages.

■ The scores are skewed to the lower end on all three batteries, with at least one third of pupils scoring in the lowest two stanines against a national average of around 11 per cent. This is particularly pronounced for the Verbal Battery, with one quarter of pupils in the bottom stanine, compared to an expectation of only 4 per cent as a national average.

■ The distribution of scores on the Verbal Battery appears skewed in relation to the Quantitative and Non-verbal battery distributions. The proportion of pupils in the 'below average' stanines is greater for the Verbal Battery than for the other two batteries. Equally, the proportion of pupils in the 'above average' stanines is lower for the Verbal Battery compared to the other two.

Some implications of these results are:

■ Core literacy and numeracy skills will be a target for a significant proportion of pupils in the group.

■ Given the large proportion of students with below average scores, there may be a need for additional classroom support.

■ It would be misleading to plan teaching solely around the low mean scores. There is a need for effective differentiation within the group to also meet the needs of some more able pupils.

■ It will be valuable to inspect the Individual Pupil Profiles to consider the possibility of a high number of pupils with V– profiles (see Chapter 3, page 47). This possibility is suggested by the particularly low mean score on the Verbal Battery as compared to the other two batteries. The relative strengths in quantitative and non-verbal reasoning of some pupils may be used to scaffold their weakness in the verbal domain (see Chapter 3 for further details).

A second example of a group profile is presented in Figure 4.2. This is the report for the pupils included in the example data file on the CD that we looked at in Chapter 2 (see pages 21 to 27). The results are for 46 pupils from P6 in Scotland (equivalent to Year 5 in England and Wales) who completed Level B of *CAT*. This group shows a very different, but equally interesting, profile compared to the group shown in Figure 4.1. The results suggest the following:

■ The mean scores for the group are not significantly different from national averages on all three batteries.

■ The group includes pupils from across the entire ability range. The scores for the Non-verbal Battery are particularly widely spread, with a standard deviation (SD) of 16.7 standard age score (SAS) points, compared with the Verbal Battery, where the standard deviation is 13.6 points.

■ Reflecting this broader distribution, the scores are slightly skewed to the top end on the Non-verbal Battery. Looking at the proportion in the 'above average' and 'very high' groups (stanines 7 to 9) we have around the expected percentage of 23 per cent for verbal reasoning, but 28 per cent for quantitative reasoning and 33 per cent for non-verbal reasoning.

Figure 4.2: Second example of a Group Distribution of Standardised Scores (group profile) report

Group Distribution of Standardised Scores

School: **Sample School**   Section A[1] Page 3 of 4
Class/Group: **P6/6**
No. of pupils: **46**   CAT level: **B**   Date of Test: **19/Sep/2001**

Cognitive AbilitiesTest
Third Edition

The bar charts on the following page show the percentage of your pupils' Standard Age Scores (SAS) that fall within certain ranges of scores for the Verbal, Quantitative and Non-Verbal batteries.

There is also a chart showing the average SAS of your pupils for each battery with 90% confidence bands indicated by the vertical line. If the vertical line overlaps the national '100' line the results for the group do not differ significantly from the national average.

Each battery bar chart shows the distribution of scores of your pupils as bars and also those of the National Standardisation group shown as filled circles behind the bars. The charts allow you to compare the results of your sample with the national picture as represented by the standardisation sample.

The distribution of the National Standardisation scores is a "normal" distribution. The table below summarizes your results in comparison to this normal distribution.

Your Results

	No. of Pupils [1]	Mean SAS [2]	Standard Deviation (SD) [3]	In comparison to the national average ....
Verbal	46	100.2	13.6	Your mean SAS is not significantly different to 100 / Your SD is not significantly less than 15
Quantitative	46	100.6	14.8	Your mean SAS is not significantly different to 100 / Your SD is not significantly less than 15
Non-Verbal	46	100.8	16.7	Your mean SAS is not significantly different to 100 / Your SD is not significantly greater than 15

Further information about CAT scores is provided in the Cognitive Abilities Test Administration Manual.
In case of enquiries please contact the nferNelson Customer Support and Advisory Service on 0845 602 1937.
© nferNelson 2002.
nferNelson is a division of Granada Learning Limited, part of Granada plc.

Notes
1. Only pupils who have a valid SAS for a given battery are included in this analysis.
2. The mean SAS of the National Standardisation sample is 100 for each battery.
3. Standard Deviation (SD) is a statistical measure of how widely a set of scores fluctuate around the mean score. The National Standardisation sample Standard Deviation is 15 SAS points for each battery.

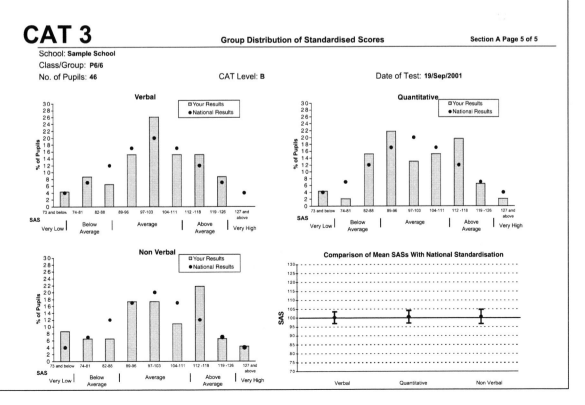

CAT 3
Group Distribution of Standardised Scores   Section A Page 5 of 5

School: **Sample School**
Class/Group: **P6/6**
No. of Pupils: **46**   CAT Level: **B**   Date of Test: **19/Sep/2001**

■ There are two peaks of scores on the Quantitative Battery, at stanine 4 and stanine 7 respectively. Relatively few pupils, and fewer than would be expected from the national distribution, fall within stanines 5 and 6 between the two peaks. Technically this is termed a 'bi-modal' distribution.

Some implications of these results are:

■ The overall pitch of teaching should be to the average and above average range.

■ There is a need for effective differentiation within the group to meet the needs of less able pupils.

■ There may be a high proportion of pupils with N+ and N− profiles, reflecting the wider spread for non-verbal scores. These pupils should be identified and the implications for teaching and learning assessed (see Chapter 3, pages 44 to 47 and 55 to 57 respectively).

■ There is a particular need for differentiation in mathematics, where teaching pitched at the average for the group might fail to match the needs of many of the pupils.

Group size

The three score distribution graphs will be sensitive to the number of pupils in the group. For the groups of around 50 pupils shown in Figures 4.1 and 4.2, any one pupil represents approximately 2 per cent of the group. However, for a group of 25 pupils one pupil will represent 4 per cent of the entire group. We must therefore be cautious in interpreting the stanine distributions for small groups, since a change in the results of a few pupils could have a disproportionate effect on the distribution. The larger the group, the greater the reliability of the score distributions. For example, the results for the whole year group are likely to be more robust than the results for individual form or tutor groups. These concerns are less marked for the comparison of mean standard age scores with the national average, since the width of the confidence bands around the mean score will reflect the size of the group under consideration.

The Group Summary of Results by Gender

Gender differences in performance have been of long-standing interest in education, but the last 10 years has seen a particular focus on the comparatively low performance of boys relative to girls in national assessments across the age range four to 16 years. At the time of writing, ministers in England have announced a further working group to look at gender differences, pulling together action across the primary strategy, the Key Stage 3 strategy and the DfES Standards and Effectiveness Unit ('Ministers launch new assault on gender gap', *Times Educational Supplement*, 2003a).

The *CAT* Computer Scoring and Analysis Service provides an optional report designed to look specifically at gender differences. The Group Summary of Results by Gender report can be selected by ticking the option box on the group header sheet (see Appendix 3 for a sample). The report provides a comparison of the *CAT* scores separately for boys and girls. The first page of the gender report gives the mean scores, standard deviation and sample size for boys and girls on each battery. The second page presents the results in the same format as the group profile we have already seen, but with boys' and girls' results presented alongside each other.

Figure 4.3 shows the gender differences report for the pupils included in the example data file on the CD, whose group profile was shown in Figure 4.2.

Some key points suggested by the report are:

▮ The mean scores for girls are generally higher than those for boys. Given the small size of the groups, none of these differences achieve statistical significance. However, this does not mean that the differences have no educational significance for the group.

▮ On the Verbal and Quantitative Batteries, the proportion of boys in the lower three score bands (28 per cent) is slightly above the national average. However, very few girls, only around 9 per cent for verbal reasoning and 14 per cent for quantitative reasoning, fall in the 'below average' or 'very low' score bands. Additional support should therefore be targeted to boys in particular.

▮ While there tend to be more boys than girls in the *lowest* two score bands for the verbal and quantitative tests, there also tend to be more boys than girls in the *highest* two score bands for these tests. This provides an important illustration of the dangers of stereotyping the performance of all boys as low achievers. It is important for the teacher to identify and meet the needs of the high-scoring boys. An analysis of the national *CAT3* dataset suggests that boys tend to be over-represented relative to girls in both the lowest *and* the highest score bands, particularly on the quantitative reasoning and non-verbal reasoning tests. For further details see Strand (2003b).

▮ The bi-modal distribution of quantitative reasoning scores seen in the group profile in Figure 4.2 arises from the distribution of girls' scores. The profile for boys is essentially flat across stanines 3 to 7; it is the girls that show the two peaks at stanine 4 and at stanine 7, with the relative 'dip' at stanine 5. Differentiation will be particularly important in mathematics and in quantitative tasks in other subjects to ensure that the diverse needs of the girls are adequately met.

Figure 4.3: Group Summary of Results by Gender for the same group as displayed in Figure 4.2

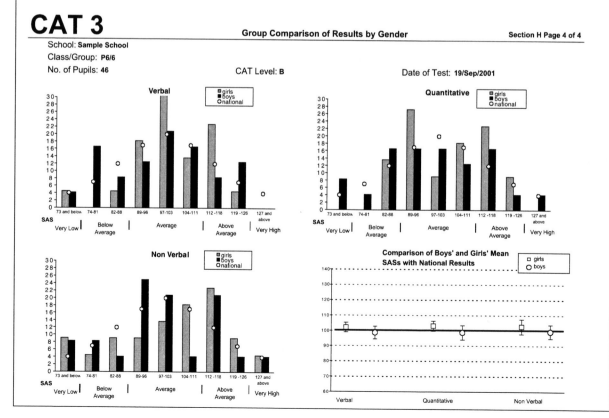

Group Summary of Results by Gender

School: **Sample School**
Class/Group: **P6/6**

Section H[1] Page 1 of 4

No. of pupils: **46**   CAT level: **B**   Date of Test: **19/Sep/2001**

Cognitive Abilities Test

Third Edition

Like previous listings, the following pages give a summary of the results achieved by your class/group on the Verbal, Quantitative and Non-Verbal batteries of CAT. The table below and the charts overleaf summarise the results separately for boys and girls. For ease of comparison, boys and girls are placed side by side.

The results of boys and girls are also listed seperately, with the female listing appearing first followed by the male listing.

Within the listings pupils are shown in alphabetical order, and the scores provided are a Raw Score (RS), a Standard Age Score (SAS), a Stanine (ST), a National Percentile Rank (NPR), and a Group Rank (GR) showing each pupil's position relative to others of the same sex in the group (unless you have requested that the latter score be omitted). A full explanation of each of these scores is provided in section A.

Further information about CAT scores is provided in the Cognitive Abilities Test Administration Manual.
In case of enquiries please contact the nferNelson Customer Support and Advisory Service on 0845 602 1937.
© nferNelson 2002.
nferNelson is a division of Granada Learning Limited, part of Granada plc.

Your Results

	Girls	Mean Age* 10:01		Boys	Mean Age* 10:5	
	Verbal	Quantitative	Non-Verbal	Verbal	Quantitative	Non-Verbal
Mean SAS	102.0	102.7	102.5	98.6	98.7	99.3
Standard Dev.	11.6	11.8	17.3	15.3	17.2	16.4
No. of pupils with valid SAS	22	22	22	24	24	24

* At the top of the page, *No. of pupils* in the class/group is the number of completed answer sheets. The *Mean Age* calculation uses estimated ages for pupils with unreadable or out of range dates of birth. *Mean SAS* includes only those pupils who attempted to answer questions in each subtest of a battery.

CAT 3

School: **Sample School**
Class/Group: **P6/6**
No. of Pupils: **46**

Group Comparison of Results by Gender

Section H Page 4 of 4

CAT Level: **B**   Date of Test: **19/Sep/2001**

Case study: Alderman Smith Secondary School

An analysis of results by gender can be revealing for a school, and the gender difference report can be a useful starting point for further analysis. As with all data, the analysis is likely to *initiate debate* rather than *provide curricular solutions*. One example of the kind of debate that can ensue is described in the case study from Alderman Smith Secondary School (see Figure 4.4). The school noted significant and substantial gender differences in pupils' end of Key Stage 3 English results at age 14. However, an analysis of pupils' *CAT* results did not show the same gender difference in verbal reasoning scores. This promoted a debate on the reasons for the relative 'under-performance' of boys at Key Stage 3, and the possible interventions the school could undertake to address the issue.

Figure 4.4: Alderman Smith Secondary School – case study

Alderman Smith Secondary School

School context

Alderman Smith is an 11 to 16 mixed comprehensive school located in Warwickshire. The total pupil roll in 2002 was around 1200 pupils, 3 per cent of whom had statements and 23 per cent of whom had non-statemented special educational needs. The school is a designated Sports College under the specialist schools programme.

CAT verbal reasoning scores and gender differences at Key Stage 3

Like many schools around the country, our school has been using *CAT* for several years. The data provides useful information from which teachers can develop academic expectations of pupils and set realistic targets for improvement. We also use the data to inform our whole-school target-setting process and our 'in-house' self-evaluation and review.

Analysing our results in detail for the entire Key Stage 3 cohort (some 720+ pupils), we identified some fundamental issues for the school in relation to gender and performance. On the basis of the *CAT* data, our boys are performing almost as well as the girls. Since the national curriculum largely tests the ability to communicate through written language, we expected that our boys would be performing as well as girls in the national tests at Key Stage 3. However, our Key Stage results, particularly in English, reveal markedly higher performance by girls. For example, 74 per cent of girls achieve Level 5 and above at the end of Key Stage 3 compared to only 52 per cent of boys.

Table 4.1: Alderman Smith Secondary School – *CAT* Verbal Battery and Key Stage 3 English results, by gender

Gender	CAT Verbal Reasoning standard age scores	KS3 English results Level 5 and above
Boys	94.0	52%
Girls	95.0	74%

Could this reflect national curriculum content being more 'girl friendly', giving girls greater opportunities to apply skills, knowledge and understanding? Either way, our girls significantly outperform boys at Key Stage 3 and the challenge is to get underneath this to find out why. We have a lot of evidence suggesting that boys need a great deal of support when it comes to extended writing activities. The *CAT* data clearly show that our boys have comparable verbal ability to the girls. The challenge is how to exploit that verbal ability in order to develop their extended writing and to foster the creativity, inspiration and motivation to connect this cognitive ability with the more creative, extended aspects of national curriculum English.

As is clear from the case study, Alderman Smith Secondary School has used its *CAT* data at a whole-school level to identify an issue and is actively engaged in responding to the challenge it identified.

Further analysis of the *CAT* results for groups of pupils

Why is it useful to carry out further analyses of the *CAT* data?

The *CAT* Computer Scoring and Analysis Service reports provide powerful analyses to support comparisons across groups of pupils. For example, you can evaluate whether there are any significant differences between the results for different teaching groups by comparing their group profiles. In this way you can determine whether the scores for any groups are above or below the national average, and whether there are any large score differences between groups.

However there are at least three reasons why it is useful to be able to complete some further analysis of your own data.

■ First, scoring service group reports will only be valid as long as the membership of the groups is stable. Over time, some pupils may change teaching groups, others may leave the school and still other pupils may join. If these changes are extensive, the analysis of group scores provided by your scoring reports may no longer be valid.

■ Second, you may wish to analyse combined data from more than one year group: for example, you may decide to analyse the *CAT* results for all pupils within a *key stage* rather than those within *one year group* alone. This is often the case in primary schools, where there may be insufficient pupils in any one year group to support an analysis.

■ Third, you may want to complete further analyses in relation to additional pupil background data that you hold on pupils. Examples might include ethnic groups, special educational needs (SEN), pupils' fluency in English, etc.

For these reasons, it is useful to be able to complete some simple group comparisons yourself. Thanks to the power of spreadsheets, this is a relatively simple task. The sorts of questions you can consider include:

■ Are there significant differences in the scores for boys and girls?

■ Are there any significant differences in *CAT* scores between classes or teaching groups?

■ Are any groups above or below the national average?

■ Are there significant differences in the results for different ethnic groups?

■ Are there significant differences between year groups?

■ Are the scores for this year's intake significantly higher or lower than last year's?

In the pages that follow, we will look at how you can complete such analyses yourself, using the data provided on your *CAT* data disk.

A general method for evaluating the results of two or more groups

The Group Summary of Results by Gender report is sufficient if you are only interested in contrasting two particular groups, and the group criterion is gender. What if you wish to compare two groups using a different criterion, such as pupils with or without an identified SEN, pupils entitled or not entitled to Free School Meals (FSM), or pupils from farming families versus those from other groups? Even more generally, what if you wish to compare *more than two* groups: for example, multiple classes or teaching groups, or multiple ethnic groups?

A more general process for evaluating and comparing the results for groups would be useful here. As well as calculating mean scores, a method for determining the significance of any score differences is required. In Chapter 3, we showed how a confidence band is placed around each pupil's standard age score. These confidence bands prevent us over-interpreting small differences between a pupil's scores on different batteries, and allow us to test whether the difference is large enough to warrant further attention.

A similar screening process is necessary for group mean scores. It is likely that the mean or average scores for groups will vary by chance alone. The smaller the number of pupils in a group, and the wider the variation in scores within the group (the standard deviation), the more likely it is that any variation is due to chance factors alone. The question is, to what extent is the variation indicative of some genuine difference in the reasoning skills of a group, rather than just random variation?

Figure 4.5 shows a method for placing a confidence band around the mean score for a group.

Figure 4.5: Calculating whether the mean score for a group is significantly different from the national average

Where SD = standard deviation of the scores for the group, and n = the number of pupils in the group with a valid score, the standard error of measurement (SEM) for a group can be approximated using the following calculation:

$$SEM = \frac{SD}{\sqrt{(n-1)}}$$

Note that:

- the *upper* limit of the 90 per cent confidence band is formed by *adding* 1.645 * SEM to the group mean;
- the *lower* limit of the 90 per cent confidence band is formed by *subtracting* 1.645 * SEM from the group mean;
- if this band *includes the score 100*, then the group mean score is *not* significantly different from the national average.

In Microsoft Excel, the term 'workbook' refers to the entire Excel file. The workbook consists of multiple 'worksheets', each identified by name at the bottom of the screen. An Excel workbook called **compare.xls** is included on the CD. In this case, the purpose of the workbook is to support you in evaluating whether the *CAT* scores achieved by different groups differ significantly both from the national average and from each other. The workbook assists by presenting the results and comparing the performance of multiple groups, and is set up to compare results of up to six concurrent groups. The use of the workbook in two different scenarios is described in detail below.

Scenario 1: Where the mean, standard deviation and sample size for each group are already known

Scenario 1 represents the 'typical' secondary school in terms of pupil roll, with six forms of entry: that is, around 180 pupils entering the school each academic year, organised into six mixed ability form/tutor groups of 30 pupils each. Let us ask two specific questions:

- Are the *CAT* battery scores of any form/tutor groups significantly different *from the national average*?

■ Are there any significant differences *between different form/tutor groups* in their average scores on the *CAT* batteries?

The example school, like most schools, has collated its pupil answer sheets by form/tutor group. In this case, the comparison process is fairly straightforward: the mean score, standard deviation and sample size for each group will already have been calculated and given on the first page of the group profile for each form/tutor group (see Figures 4.1 and 4.2 for examples). These figures can therefore be directly entered into the blue cells in the Compare workbook, together with:

■ **The name of each group:** Enter these as a short label (for example, 7E, 7F, etc.).

■ **The identity of the *CAT* battery scores being analysed (VR, QR or NVR):** The analysis can also be completed for the mean *CAT* score. However, since the mean, SD and sample size for mean *CAT* score are not included in the Group Profile, you will have to first calculate these, as demonstrated in Scenario 2 below.

■ **The desired confidence band (85 per cent, 90 per cent or 95 per cent):** If your primary purpose is comparing group mean scores against national averages, a *95 per cent confidence band* is suggested. However if your primary purpose is comparing different group mean scores with each other, then an *85 per cent confidence band* will give a more accurate indication of the results that would be obtained through a direct evaluation of the difference in mean scores between the groups. The *90 per cent confidence band* option is included to provide a generic balance between these two purposes. As previously indicated, where the confidence bands for two groups do not overlap, then we conclude that there is a significant difference in the mean score for the two groups.

The output from the Compare workbook for our example school, entering the results from the Non-verbal Battery and using a 90 per cent confidence band, is shown in Figure 4.6. It is apparent from the graph that:

■ the confidence bands around the *mean non-verbal reasoning scores* for four of the tutor groups overlap the national '100' line, indicating that the group mean scores *do not differ significantly from the national average*;

■ the *mean scores for groups 7F and 7I* are *significantly below the national average*;

■ the *confidence bands* for most of the groups *overlap*, indicating that we cannot reliably distinguish between the groups;

■ the *confidence bands* for the *lowest* (7F) and the *highest* (7S) scoring groups *do not overlap*, indicating that the two tutor groups *differ significantly in their non-verbal reasoning scores*.

Figure 4.6: Example output from the Compare workbook for six tutor groups

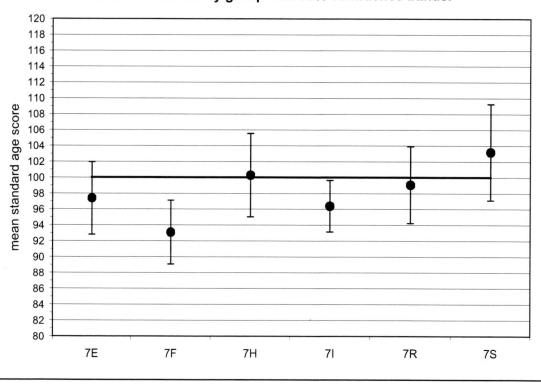

Using CAT to compare the mean scores for multiple groups of pupils

Enter your data in the cells highlighted in blue. The red cells are automatically calculated from your data.

Which CAT battery is being analysed (VR, QR or NVR)?   **NVR**

Choose the confidence band (85%, 90% or 95%)?:   **90%   1.65**

Group name	Mean score	SD	Number of pupils	SEM	SEM * Sig. Level	Lower CI	Upper CI	Nat average
7E	97.4	15.0	30	2.79	4.58	92.8	102.0	100
7F	93.1	12.5	27	2.45	4.03	89.1	97.1	100
7H	100.3	17.8	32	3.20	5.26	95.0	105.6	100
7I	96.4	11.2	33	1.98	3.26	93.1	99.7	100
7R	99.1	13.5	22	2.95	4.85	94.3	103.9	100
7S	103.2	19.5	29	3.69	6.06	97.1	109.3	100
Total	98.3	11.2	173	0.85	1.40	96.8	99.7	100

Mean NVR scores by group with 90% confidence bands.

Analysis of the verbal reasoning and quantitative reasoning scores for the school revealed a similar pattern as shown for the non-verbal scores. The analysis suggests a number of messages for the school:

■ The head of Year 7, who believed that he had six mixed-ability groups, will need in future to monitor carefully the allocation of pupils to tutor groups. Given the large number of factors to consider, including friendship groups, gender balance, curricular attainments etc., it may not always prove possible to create totally equivalent groups. The key is to be *aware* of any differences, should they exist.

■ Subject teachers should be aware of the implications for differentiation, particularly when planning lessons for classes 7F and 7S.

■ Senior management, when considering issues such as performance management, should be wary of making judgements concerning teaching quality based solely on levels of pupil attainment, such as may be indicated by English, mathematics or science tests. Attainment may vary quite substantially between these tutor groups for reasons unrelated to the quality of teaching.

Scenario 2: Where the mean, standard deviation and sample size of the groups are not already known

What if the groups you wish to compare are not class or tutor groups, for which you already have Group Profiles? In such cases, you will need to calculate the mean score, the standard deviation and the sample size for each of the groups you wish to consider. This can be completed readily in Microsoft Excel. The relevant Excel functions are listed in Table 4.2.

Table 4.2: Values needed for each group and corresponding Microsoft Excel functions

Values you need to calculate for each group	Microsoft Excel function
Mean score ($\bar{X}$)	=AVERAGE()
Standard deviation of the scores (SD)	=STDEV()
Number of pupils in the group with valid scores (n)	=COUNT()

As an example, we will use the data file included on the CD, called **dataset2.xls**. This file contains the *CAT* results for a group of 46 pupils, 22 of whom are entitled to free school meals (FSM) as indicated by the value '1' in column E of the spreadsheet. The remaining 24 pupils are not entitled to free school meals, indicated by '0' in column E. Let us compare the results for these two groups of pupils: do the scores of either group differ significantly from the national average or from each other?

First, we need to sort the file by the grouping variable (in this case, FSM entitlement) so that all the pupils from the same group are listed sequentially.

We looked at how to sort an Excel spreadsheet in Chapter 2:

■ select Data/Sort from the menu;

■ in the drop-down selection box that appears, select 'FSM' and press return;

■ the pupils not entitled to FSM are now listed in rows 2 to 25 and the pupils entitled to FSM are listed in rows 26 to 47.

To compare the verbal reasoning scores for these two groups, we need to locate the column that contains the verbal standard age scores and enter the appropriate cell ranges in the brackets after the function. The verbal standard age scores are contained in column W. To calculate the mean, SD and n of the verbal scores for the two groups, the formulae shown in Table 4.3 have been typed into a block of cells starting in cell U50 at the foot of the **dataset2.xls** spreadsheet.

Table 4.3: Formulae needed for the calculation of defined values within dataset2.xls

Verbal Reasoning	**Mean**	**SD**	**n**
Entitled FSM	=AVERAGE(W2:W25)	=STDEV(W2:W25)	=COUNT(W2:W25)
Not entitled FSM	=AVERAGE(W26:W47)	=STDEV(W26:W47)	=COUNT(W26:W47)

We can also calculate the same measures for quantitative reasoning, non-verbal reasoning and mean *CAT* score: these are contained in columns AI, AW and BF respectively. The values calculated by the formulae are shown in Figure 4.7.

Figure 4.7: Extract from the Excel workbook **dataset2** showing values calculated for pupils not entitled and entitled to FSM

		Mean	**SD**	**n**
Verbal	Not entitled FSM	105.2 94.8	12.3 13.1	24 22
Quantitative	Not entitled FSM	103.1 98.2	15.1 14.2	24 22
Non-verbal	Not entitled FSM	103.8 97.6	16.6 16.6	24 22
Mean CAT	Not entitled FSM	104.0 97.0	13.7 12.9	24 22

We can enter these figures directly into the Compare workbook to calculate and display the mean scores and confidence bands for each group on each of the three *CAT* batteries. This has been done in the workbook **compare_dataset2.xls**. The results, using 85 per cent confidence bands, are shown in Figure 4.8.

Figure 4.8: Chart output from the Compare workbook for the example file **Dataset2** (see compare_dataset2.xls)

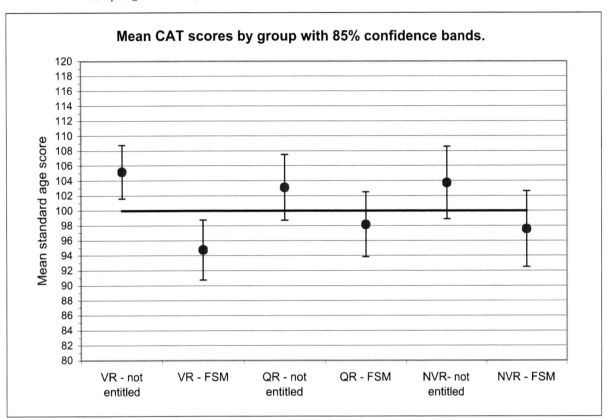

We conclude that there is a significant difference in the mean verbal scores for the two groups. The verbal scores for those pupils not entitled to FSM are significantly above the national average, while the verbal scores of those entitled to FSM are significantly below the national average. However, there are no significant differences between the groups or against national averages for quantitative or non-verbal scores. The results suggest the school should focus particularly on developing the verbal skills of pupils from disadvantaged circumstances. Some strategies were considered in Chapter 3 in relation to the V-profile, among others (see pages 47 to 52).

Case study: Burntwood Girls Secondary School

Analyses involving groups of pupils are not restricted to the direct comparison of mean scores as illustrated in the examples given above. We may also be interested in the *distribution* of scores for a particular group and how this distribution can change *over time.* Figure 4.9 shows a case study from Burntwood Girls Secondary School. Of particular interest here is the way the school utilises *CAT* to monitor change over time in scores for particular ethnic groups; this information is related to the curriculum and special provision of the school.

Figure 4.9: Burntwood Girls Secondary School – case study

Burntwood Girls Secondary School

School context

Burntwood is an all-girls 11 to 18 mixed-ability foundation school, located in an inner London LEA with high levels of social disadvantage. Nearly half (47 per cent) of pupils are entitled to free school meals, compared to an England average of 18 per cent. The school serves a multi-ethnic population with over two-thirds of girls drawn from ethnic minority groups, particularly from the Caribbean, Indian and Pakistani communities. In contrast to many schools in such circumstances, the school achieves high levels of success in GCSE examinations. In 2002, for example, 62 per cent of pupils achieved five or more A* to C grades (LEA average 49 per cent, England average 52 per cent). The school figured prominently in the report *Success against the odds: effective schools in disadvantaged areas* (National Commission on Education, 1996). The school was named as an outstanding school in the Her Majesty's Chief Inspector (HMCI) 1997/98 Annual Report.

Using *CAT* to monitor the ability of the intake

The school felt that the ability of the intake was changing, but had no hard information to support these perceptions. Key Stage 2 results varied widely across feeder primary schools, raising some concerns about the consistency and validity of the results. Key Stage 2 results were also not available for 17 per cent of the Year 7 intake. The school started using *CAT* to gain a consistent picture of the ability of the intake, and to monitor changes in the intake over time. *CAT* was first used in September 1996 with both Year 7 and Year 9, and administered annually thereafter. *CAT* results confirmed the perception that the ability of the intake was increasing. The school is considering what implications, if any, this may have for the curriculum.

Using *CAT* to monitor for equal opportunities

The school has a strong commitment to monitoring for equal opportunities and therefore undertook an analysis of *CAT* scores in relation to pupils' ethnic background. It was apparent from the school's analysis that an increasing proportion of the Caribbean girls were scoring in the higher stanines (see Figure 4.10). Thus the proportion of the girls in stanines 2, 3 and 4 was dropping, while the proportion in stanines 5, 6 and 7 was increasing.

However, this increase in the ability profile of Caribbean girls was not being reflected in increased representation within the school's programme for Students of Marked Aptitude (SOMA). The school is reviewing issues around the identification and support of pupils in the SOMA programme. For example, following two professional days on target setting, *CAT* results are distributed to all class teachers to assist in a full appraisal of all pupils.

Figure 4.10: Burntwood Girls Secondary School – *CAT* scores for Caribbean girls over three successive intakes

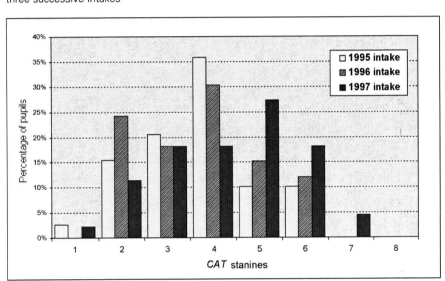

Realistic and honest pupil targets

In common with many schools, teachers' reports to parents tend to focus on effort: for example, 'Mary is trying very hard and has improved significantly this term'. Such feedback is a valuable and important part of any pupil report. However, from the perspective of the Senior Management Team (SMT), it was sometimes difficult to determine a pupil's levels of attainment from the reports. One member of the SMT commented that 'from reading the reports it was difficult to tell the difference between a pupil with SEN and a high-achieving pupil'.

The *CAT* results are given to all class teachers. Teachers are asked to consider, together with the pupil, targets for the pupil's attainment at the end of each key stage. The school believes that the *CAT* scores, alongside other pupil assessment information, help teachers to focus on the attainment and ability of individual pupils, and to be honest and realistic in their expectations. These targets are reviewed twice a year and are shared with parents. All targets form part of the pupil's annual report.

A group profile of relative cognitive strengths and weaknesses

As we saw in Chapter 3, considerable insight into a pupil's learning style can be gained through examination of the *CAT3* Individual Pupil Profiles. We saw how some pupils might be consistent in their abilities to reason across different modalities, but that others might show distinct strengths (V+, Q+, N+) or weaknesses (V–, Q–, N–) in different areas. Still others might have a contrast profile showing a combination of strengths and weaknesses (for example, V+, N–). This information will always be the most detailed and reliable available from *CAT* on the learning style of any individual pupil.

However, in addition to looking in detail at individual pupils, you may want to get a broad feel for the composition or spread of abilities in working with different symbol systems across a group of pupils.

Visual–verbal preferences

One of the most consistent dimensions highlighted in learning styles research is the visualiser–verbaliser dimension. The roots of this research can be traced back to Francis Galton and his 'breakfast table' questionnaire (Galton, 1883). This enquired into the quality of images elicited by individuals when visualising certain scenes (for example, the breakfast they had eaten that morning). Whilst some authors have focused on the three physical sensory modalities (visual, auditory and kinesthetic), factor analytic studies have consistently emphasised the dominance of visual or verbal processes in learning (for example, see Paivio, 1971).

There are two key issues in the assessment of visual–verbal preferences:

■ First, many authors have attempted to assess visual–verbal preferences via introspective self-report measures, such as questionnaires. This approach has the weakness that pupils may not be able to accurately introspect on and report their behaviour, or may tend to give responses perceived as more socially positive or desirable. By contrast, *CAT* measures reasoning abilities, and arguably these are the most important aspects in relation to school learning. For example, it may not be the ability to *generate* visual images that matters for effective learning, but the ability to *reason with and about* those images. Similarly, it may not be the ability to *remember* words or to *speak fluently* that matters, but rather the ability to *reason about the concepts that the words signify* (Lohman and Hagen, 2001).

■ Second, should we consider verbaliser and visualiser as opposite poles on a single dimension? The best-known scales (Paivio, 1971; Richardson, 1977) are scored on a single dimension, assuming that pupils with a *strength in visual learning* will necessarily be *weaker in verbal learning*. However, it would seem reasonable to assume that some pupils may be *strong in both* areas – they may be good at learning *verbally* (in words, by reading or listening) and *visually* (in processing images, graphs, diagrams or pictures) – or they may be *weak in both* domains.

For these reasons, a specific contrast between the *CAT* Non-verbal and Verbal batteries, contrasting pupils' abilities to reason with visual images and with words, may be particularly well placed to illustrate both the range of abilities and the balance of visual–verbal preferences within a group of pupils.

The group visual–verbal learning profile

A simple way to show the spread and balance of visual–verbal abilities for a group is to plot the non-verbal scores of the pupils in the group along the x-axis and their verbal scores along the y-axis. To get a sense of the distribution against national averages, draw in the national average lines at the mean standard age score of 100 for both verbal reasoning and non-verbal reasoning. Finally, draw an ellipse to contain the central area where scores are average and broadly balanced: that is, where both verbal and non-verbal reasoning scores are in the range 90 to 110 on each battery. This creates a chart with five cells, labelled A, B, C and D for the top left, top right, bottom left and bottom right cells respectively, and E for the central area.

Figure 4.11 shows a scatterchart of the cells, taken from a Microsoft Excel workbook included on the CD. This workbook will let you enter and plot your own data on the scatterchart (see 'Completing your own group visual–verbal learning profile', page 86).

Figure 4.11: Group visual–verbal learning profile

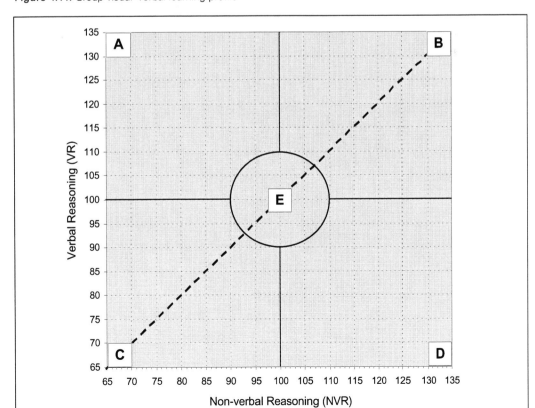

Pupils included in the central cell E represent the reference or 'average' group, against which the other cells are compared. Their reasoning abilities are typical of their age and they are broadly balanced in their visual–verbal strengths. The pupils in cells A to D may be contrasted with this average group, as follows:

■ those in cell A are above average in verbal reasoning but below average in non-verbal reasoning;

■ those in cell B are above average in both verbal and non-verbal reasoning;

■ those in cell C are below average in both verbal and non-verbal reasoning;

■ those in cell D are above average in non-verbal reasoning but below average in verbal reasoning.

This is not recommended as a system for categorising individual pupils; we do not want to label pupils as 'cell A' or 'cell B' learners (see 'Health warning', page 87). However, the graphical layout is useful to identify the broad range of abilities that might be represented within any particular group. To support this aim, Figure 4.12 gives a 'thumbnail sketch' of some of the attributes that might be typical of pupils in each of cells A through to D, in terms of their reasoning abilities and relative visual–verbal strengths.

Figure 4.12: Thumbnail sketch of 'typical' learners in the group visual–verbal learning profile

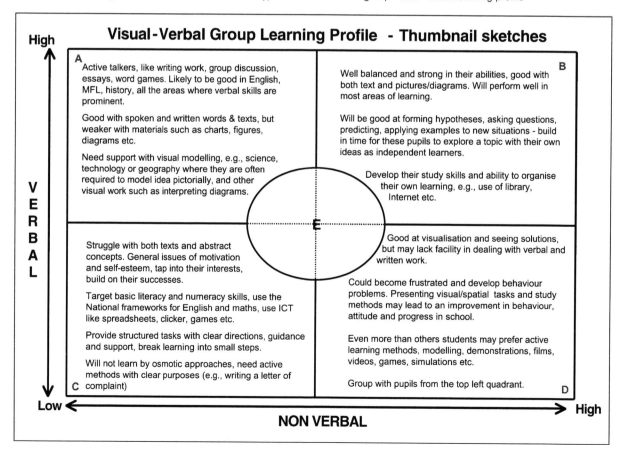

A practical example of using the group visual–verbal learning profile in a school

Let us consider some practical examples of the use of the visual–verbal profile. Figure 4.13 shows the group visual–verbal learning profiles for four tutor groups from within a single school. What might these group profiles tell us about the learning needs of each group?

Figure 4.13: Group visual–verbal learning profiles for four form/tutor groups in one school

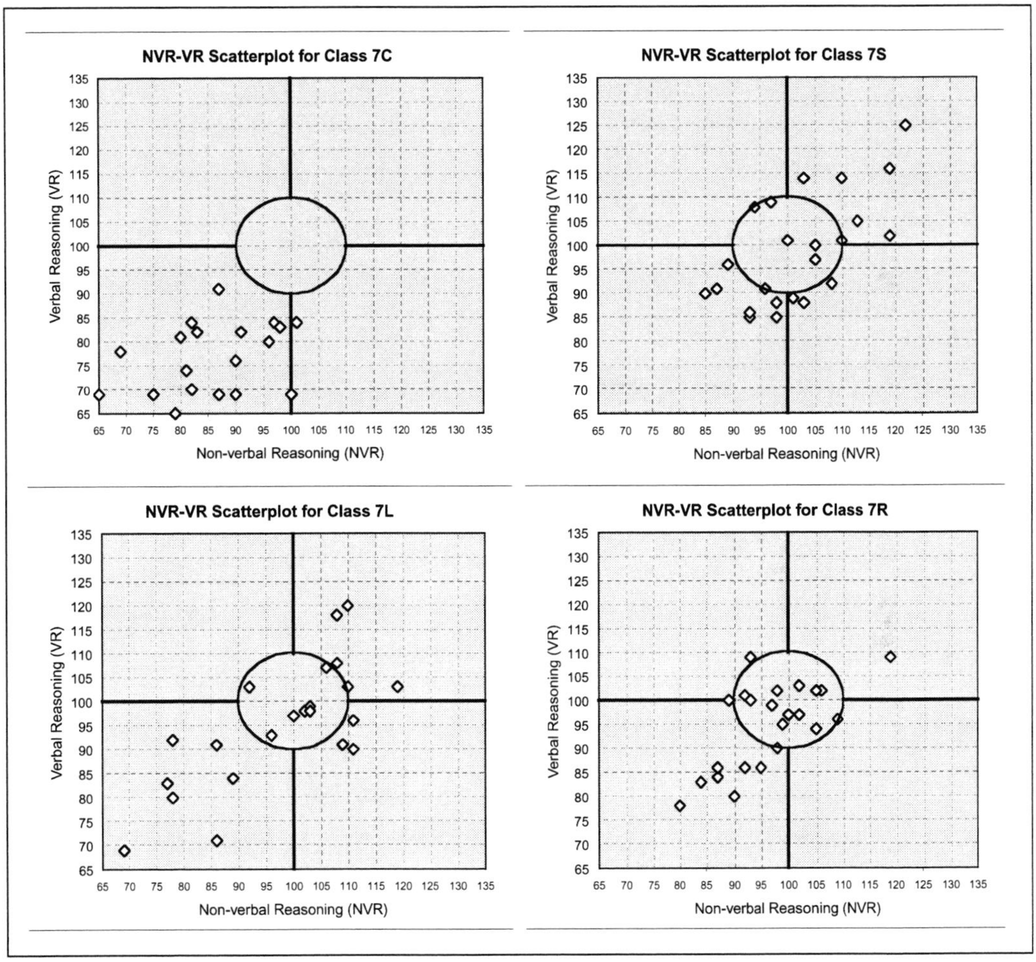

Class 7C

The majority of pupils in class 7C are likely to need a high level of additional support. This was not a particular surprise to the school, since this group had been created to support pupils likely to have additional needs. For this class, core literacy and numeracy skills are likely to be a focus throughout Year 7. However it is noticeable that almost one third of the group, those towards the right-hand side of cell C, have verbal reasoning scores 10 or more points below their non-verbal reasoning scores. The teacher should therefore consider whether some of the low verbal performance might represent underachievement, and how he or she might build on the relative strength of these pupils in working with visual symbols.

Class 7S

There is a moderate spread of ability across the group, but the majority of pupils either fall within cell E or are closely clustered around it. Early in Year 7 it may pay dividends to give particular attention to motivating and engaging the pupils just below cell E, whose verbal scores are just below the national average range. Planning will need to include extension work for the group of pupils in cell B who will require more stretching and demanding activities.

Class 7L

This is a very wide-ranging and heterogeneous group. There are several pupils within 7L who would not be out of place in class 7C in terms of their verbal and non-verbal reasoning scores. At the same time there are also some pupils with scores in cell B who are more akin to the group in class 7S. There are also three pupils in cell D, with verbal reasoning scores that are significantly lower than would be expected from their non-verbal reasoning scores. This class will require careful differentiation to address the wide range of needs.

Class 7R

This class shows a relatively restricted range of scores, dividing primarily into two distinct clusters. Most pupils are grouped in cell E, with abilities in the average range and no discernable visual–verbal preference. However, a sizeable minority are placed in cell C. When forming groups for discussion and other activities it may be beneficial to mix pupils from cells C and E, so that there are opportunities for modelling and learning by observation and association. One pupil falls in cell A and has a verbal score more than 10 points below his non-verbal score. He may cope well with text and written work, but needs more support with visual material such as graphs, figures and diagrams.

Completing your own group visual–verbal learning profile

A Microsoft Excel workbook, allowing you to plot group visual–verbal learning profiles based on your own data, is included on the CD: it is named **scatter_blank.xls**. Instructions on using the workbook are given in the first worksheet of the workbook. If you enter your pupil data into the blue columns of the second worksheet, your results will automatically be plotted in the scatterchart in the third worksheet. By copying and saving multiple copies of the workbook, you can produce a scatterchart for each teaching group in your school or department.

The workbook has two additional features to the scattercharts presented in Figure 4.13:

- The graph will identify separately each point as a girl (white diamond) or a boy (black circle). To ensure this happens you must identify boys and girls using the letters M or F (for male or female), in column B of the data sheet.

■ The graph will label each point with the name of the pupil. To do this you must install some free software which can be downloaded from the web. Full instructions are contained in the first worksheet, and are summarised in Chapter 7, page 136).

Figure 4.14 shows the results for class 7C (as displayed in Figure 4.13), but includes the additional features contained in the scatter workbook.

From the results we can see that the group of pupils whose verbal reasoning scores were low compared to their non-verbal reasoning scores are predominantly boys: six of the seven boys fall within this group. Whilst the teacher will wish to respond to each pupil as an individual, the results reveal a general issue of verbal underperformance by boys in particular.

'Health warning' on using the group visual–verbal learning profile

The group visual–verbal learning profile is a useful device for planning. The purpose is to illustrate the wide range of abilities in working with visual or verbal symbols that are likely to be represented by the pupils in your class. However, there is a substantial difference between a *planning* or *illustrative* device and a *classification* system. As

Figure 4.14: Output from the Scatter workbook for class 7C as identified in Figure 4.13

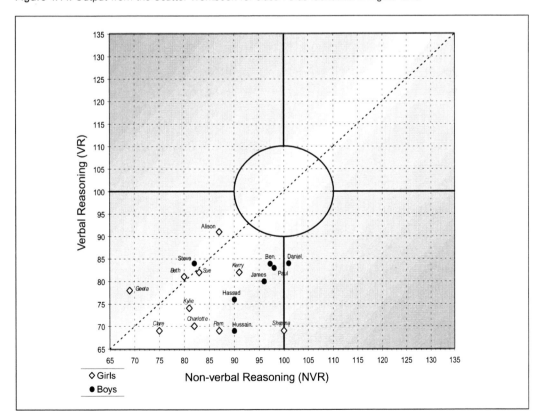

Note: in the workbook, scores are plotted in red for girls and blue for boys. The white diamonds (girls) and the black circles (boys) appear only in Figure 4.14.

mentioned earlier, you are strongly advised against using the results as a classification system: for example, you should avoid talking about 'cell A' or 'cell B' learners. A few examples will demonstrate the reasons for this.

First, most readers will probably understand intuitively that whilst cell E may be small in terms of absolute size in the scatterchart, it will contain a disproportionately large percentage of pupils. This is because cell E includes the typical or most frequent range of scores, and indeed cell E contains around 27 per cent of all pupils. However, because cells A to D are of equal physical size in the scatterchart, it may be falsely assumed that an equal proportion of pupils would be found in each of these four cells. This is not the case, because verbal and non-verbal scores are positively correlated, as is illustrated by the diagonal 'line of equity' running from the bottom left to the top right of the scattercharts. The majority of pupils will have verbal scores that lie within nine standard age score points above or nine standard age score points below this line. As a consequence of this correlation, the majority of pupils who are not in cell E are found in cells B or C (about 30 per cent in each), and only a much smaller proportion (around 7 per cent each) in cells A and D.

Second, some pupils will be misdiagnosed in terms of their verbal and non-verbal strengths or weaknesses. A pupil with a non-verbal reasoning score of 102 and a verbal reasoning score of 130 will be in cell B, which is characterised as *'both scores high'*. In reality, it would be more accurate to interpret the pupil's scores as *'non-verbal reasoning average, verbal reasoning high'*. Similarly, a pupil with a non-verbal reasoning score of 115 and a verbal reasoning score of 102 would fall within cell B, while a pupil with a non-verbal reasoning score of 115 but a verbal reasoning score of 98 would fall within cell D. While the pupils fall in different cells, both, in reality, would most accurately be described as *'non-verbal reasoning high, verbal reasoning average'*. Again, it is important to consider the line of equity here. Pupils whose scores are 10 or more points above or below the diagonal line have a significant difference between their verbal and non-verbal scores, regardless of the cell in which they fall.

Third, the interpretation offered by the visual–verbal profile is partial because it does not include all the information on pupils' reasoning abilities provided by *CAT*. Suppose that a pupil has a non-verbal reasoning score of 110 and a verbal reasoning score of 95, placing him or her in cell D. In this case, the difference is 10 or more SAS points, meaning that the cell D characterisation (*'non-verbal reasoning high, verbal reasoning low '*) is probably accurate. However, if the quantitative reasoning score is nearer 95, matching the verbal score, then we are looking predominantly at a non-verbal strength (N+). Alternatively, if the quantitative score is nearer to 110, matching more closely the non-verbal reasoning score, then we are looking predominantly at a verbal weakness (V–). These two interpretations are different: in the first we are building on a strength; in the second we are looking at support for a relative weakness.

It will be clear from the above that you must look at the scores themselves, and consider the size of the actual score difference, as evidence of the strength of any cognitive or modality preference. While the group profile is helpful, the temptation to apply cell labels to pupils should be resisted. The *CAT3* Individual Pupil Profile described in Chapter 3 is the most appropriate tool for interpreting the scores of individual pupils.

Understanding changes in *CAT* scores over time

This section considers changes in *CAT* scores in three related but distinct ways:

- for individual pupils over time;
- for evaluating the new intake each academic year, in relation to previous intakes;
- for tracking a whole cohort over time, as it progresses through the school.

Individual pupils

In areas of attainment testing – such as reading, writing, spelling, mathematics or science – it is not unusual to test pupils at regular intervals. In terms of formal standardised tests, this is often an annual occurrence, usually at the beginning or end of the academic year. Since the test content typically reflects the material that has been taught during the year, the rationale for the test is to assess what the pupil has learned during the course of study.

The situation is somewhat different with reasoning tests such as *CAT*:

- Unlike attainment tests, *CAT does not assess areas of the taught curriculum*, so there is no direct rationale for annual testing.
- Research suggests that reasoning test scores tend to be *highly correlated over time* – more so than attainment test scores, indicating greater consistency over time. For example, a large-scale study with *CAT2E,* following pupils between the ages of 10 and 13 years, revealed a correlation of 0.89 in mean *CAT* score over the three-year period (Strand, 2003a).

For both of the above reasons, it is not common to administer *CAT* annually. However, high correlation coefficients can conceal important change within individuals over time. For example, the study referred to above (Strand, 2003a) also revealed a change of 10 or more standard score points for approximately one sixth of pupils on the *CAT2E* Verbal Battery and for about one fifth of pupils on the *CAT2E* Quantitative and Non-verbal batteries. As a rough rule, a change of 10 or more standard age score points in a pupil's score on the same *CAT3* battery, with an interval of a year or more between test occasions, would be considered a statistically significant change (see the *CAT3 Technical Manual*, pages 12 and 13, for the statistical basis of this calculation). Table 4.4 on page 90 gives an indication of the proportion of pupils that might experience changes of a certain size and direction in standard age scores. For example:

- a small minority, around 15 per cent, might be expected to show an *increase* of 10 or more standard age score points;

■ a small proportion, around 15 per cent, might be expected to show a *decrease* of 10 or more standard age score points.

For these pupils, the score changes may have important educational implications.

To summarise, high test–retest correlations suggest that a programme of annual testing with *CAT* is not necessary. However, the extent of individual change also suggests that *it is important to retest pupils at times when key educational decisions are required.* For example, a school may use *CAT* in Year 7 for a range of purposes, including to generate indicators for performance in national end of Key Stage 3 tests. When the pupils have completed Key Stage 3, and if the school wishes to generate GCSE indicators for the same pupils, the pupils should be retested to ensure that GCSE indicators are based on the most up-to-date and relevant *CAT* scores available.

It is important to note that the relative stability of reasoning test scores has no direct bearing on the long-running debate over the relative influence of heredity and environment on intelligence. For example, the high correlation over time may simply reflect systematic and stable environmental influences, such as the socio-economic status of the home. The most likely explanation is that reasoning skills are prerequisites for subsequent learning in a cumulative manner:

> Not only does the individual retain prior learning, but much of their prior learning provides tools for subsequent learning. Hence the more progress they have made in the acquisition of intellectual skills and knowledge at any one point in time, the better able they are to profit from subsequent learning experiences.

Anastasi, 1976, page 328

In short, nothing succeeds like success.

Table 4.4: Differences between scores on the same *CAT3* battery on two different occasions and the percentage of pupils obtaining such changes

Difference in standard age score from first to second occasion and direction of difference	Percentage of pupils showing the size of difference
Increases by >16	5
Increases by >12	10
Increases by > 9	15
Decreases by > 9	15
Decreases by >12	10
Decreases by >16	5

Note: the figures assume an average intercorrelation of 0.80 between battery scores over time.

Evaluating the new intake each year

An important use of *CAT* scores is to monitor change over time in the abilities of each new cohort entering the school each academic year. The case study for Burntwood School (page 80) shows that *CAT* was able to provide hard information to support the school's perceptions of changes in the abilities of the intake and that this had important implications for the school's equal opportunities policy. Another case study (Ringmer Community College, see Chapter 7, page 131) further demonstrates the importance – for self-evaluation and accountability purposes – of having empirical evidence on the reasoning abilities of cohorts of pupils as they enter the school.

Converting from *CAT2E* to *CAT3*

Schools currently using *CAT2E* may be concerned about how they can maintain the integrity and consistency of their records if they move over to *CAT3*. How can the school maintain consistency in time series data across the *CAT2E* / *CAT3* changeover and not lose the benefit of its long-term records?

Anticipating this issue, the development of *CAT3* included a substantial equivalence study involving over 10,000 pupils in over 420 schools. Schools in the equivalence study administered both the *CAT2E* and *CAT3* version of one battery, with the order of administration being counterbalanced within each battery and *CAT* test level. That is, half the schools gave pupils the *CAT2E* version first, and half gave the *CAT3* version first. This has allowed the publication of detailed equivalence tables that allow users to convert any *CAT2E* verbal reasoning, quantitative reasoning, non-verbal reasoning or mean *CAT2E* score to the *CAT3* equivalent. Full details are given in the *CAT3 Technical Manual*, pages 30 to 41.

Whilst all the tables necessary to complete the conversion are given in the *CAT3 Technical Manual*, it would be a lengthy process to complete this conversion by hand. However, the attached CD contains a Microsoft Excel workbook that will allow you to automatically convert *CAT2E* to *CAT3* scores. The use of the workbook is described in the first worksheet of the workbook. The workbook will enable you to cut and paste the *CAT2E* results of up to 200 pupils and, at the touch of a button, generate the *CAT3* equivalents for their verbal reasoning, quantitative reasoning, non-verbal reasoning and mean *CAT* scores. Full instructions are included in the first worksheet.

Tracking a whole cohort

The two examples described above consider changes associated with different groups of pupils over time, showing how *CAT* may be used to identify change in the scores of the new intake each academic year. However, just as the scores of individual pupils can change over time, so can the average scores for a whole cohort. Let us consider the three-year period between entry to secondary school and the end of Year 9. There are two situations in which significant changes in scores for a whole cohort have been observed.

■ Where *CAT* scores are generally low on entry to secondary school, and the school has implemented specific targeted interventions to address core literacy and numeracy skills, then a substantial increase in *CAT* scores may be noted during the course of Key Stage 3, particularly on the Verbal and Quantitative batteries.

■ Whatever their initial level of scores, some schools seem more effective than others in raising *CAT* scores during the first three years of secondary school. Across the first three years of secondary school, we noted a 'school effect' of around five standard age score points on the Quantitative Battery. In the most effective schools, quantitative reasoning scores at the end of Key Stage 3 were around 2.5 points higher than expected from Year 7 scores, while in others they were around 2.5 points lower. While the 'school effects' for verbal reasoning and non-verbal reasoning were more modest (two and three standard age score points respectively compared to five points for quantitative reasoning), a small number of schools (around one in six, which is 16 per cent) also showed significant changes in verbal reasoning and non-verbal reasoning scores. These results are discussed in more detail in Strand, 2003a.

Other issues that may impact on *CAT* scores, such as the explicit development of thinking skills, are discussed in Chapter 8.

In conclusion, these findings suggest it is important to retest pupils during Year 9 if the purpose is to generate GCSE or Scottish standard grade indicators – for example, to assist in target setting. Not only may some individual pupils have made significant progress over the period, but the performance of the cohort as a whole may also have improved. Both these changes would need to be reflected in raised targets for public examination results relative to those based on Year 7 *CAT* scores.

Review

Having read this chapter, you should be able to:

■ check that you have completed a *group header sheet* for each group for which you wish to have a separate report;

■ for mixed sex schools, decide if you wish to order the *Group Summary of Results by Gender*;

■ analyse your *CAT* data disk to *identify separately the results for boys and girls* (What differences, if any, are there in mean scores or in the distribution of scores for boys and girls? What implications might this have?);

■ use the *Excel 'Compare' workbook* to *contrast the mean scores for different groups*: these may be form groups or classes, this year's intake compared to those of previous years, pupils from different ethnic groups and so on, *calculating the mean, SD and n for groups* as required;

■ if necessary, use the Excel 'Convert' workbook to *convert pupils' CAT2E scores to the CAT3 equivalent scores* before completing time series analyses;

■ use the Excel 'Scatter' workbook to produce the *group visual–verbal learning profile*;

■ *analyse the profile to identify strengths and weaknesses for groups of pupils*, and consider what the implications may be for teaching and learning;

■ *retest pupils during or at the end of Year 9*: this is a point where key educational decisions are made and these should be based on the most up-to-date and relevant *CAT* data available;

■ *identify* any pupils for whom there may have been *significant change in CAT scores*; evaluate the extent of *change in scores for the group as a whole*.

5 Indicators and target setting

AIMS

This chapter will:

■ *describe the key features and benefits* of the reports that indicate pupils' possible future performance in Key Stage 3 tests, GCSE or Standard Grade examinations based on their *CAT* results on entry to secondary school – these reports are referred to as *CAT indicators*;

■ explain *how the indicators are calculated*;

■ describe the *Key Stage 3, GCSE and Scottish Standard Grade indicator reports* from the *CAT* Computer Scoring and Analysis Service;

■ consider the range of *factors influencing pupils' attainment* in national tests and public examinations;

■ show how *CAT* Progress Charts can be used in *pupil target setting*.

An introduction to the *CAT* indicator reports

There has always been a significant and positive correlation between pupils' scores on reasoning tests and their school performance as measured by national tests or examinations. The link may exist because much school activity concerns the application of reasoning abilities in the initial learning of curriculum knowledge, and then building on and recombining that knowledge as learning progresses. Thus, pupils' scores on *CAT* on entry to secondary school are very strongly related to their subsequent attainment in national tests at the end of Key Stage 3 and in GCSE or Scottish Standard Grade public examinations at around age 16.

Since 1996 the *CAT* Computer Scoring and Analysis Service has provided secondary schools with indicators of pupils' GCSE outcomes based on their prior *CAT* scores. Key Stage 3 indicators were introduced in autumn 1999, and Scottish Standard Grade indicators in autumn 2002. Schools have requested the indicators for a variety of reasons:

■ to monitor pupils' progress during secondary school;

■ to help with setting realistic but challenging targets for Key Stage 3 tests or GCSE/ Standard Grade examinations with individual pupils;

■ to set 'targets for learning' through a dialogue with pupils, focused on both their potential and their attainment;

■ to gain a view of the viability of various school-level targets;

■ to support the assessment of 'value added' by comparing indicated with actual outcomes (see Chapter 7).

How the indicators are calculated

The method by which the Key Stage 3, GCSE and Standard Grade indicators are calculated is described in Part 5 of the *CAT3 Technical Manual* (pages 54 to 62) and in detailed technical reports downloadable from the *CAT* website (www.nfer-nelson.co.uk/cat): only a summary will be given here. The key points to note are as listed below.

■ The indicators are based on the actual progress of real pupils over time. This is done by tracking a sample of pupils from the time they take their *CAT* tests in Year 7 (equivalent to S1 in Scotland, Year 8 in Northern Ireland) until they take their Key Stage 3 tests or public examinations some three to five years later.

■ The samples of pupils employed to generate the indicators are extremely large and nationally representative. For example, the GCSE indicators for autumn 2003 were based on results for nearly 100,000 pupils from 974 schools across 104 local education authorities (LEAs). The Key Stage 3 indicators for autumn 2002 were based on results for over 126,000 pupils from 1120 schools in 132 LEAs.

■ The indicators are updated every year to ensure that they stay in line with national changes in performance. For example, during the period 1998 to 2002 the proportion of pupils in England achieving five or more GCSEs at Grades A* to C increased by over 5 percentage points, from 46.3 per cent in 1998 to 51.5 per cent in 2002. It is important that we regularly update the indicators so that they reflect this national upward trend.

In this chapter, the relationship between *CAT* scores and GCSE results is used to illustrate some basic features of the relationship between *CAT* and measures of pupil attainment. Similar findings apply to Key Stage 3 and to Standard Grade outcomes, but it is easiest to demonstrate these principles using just one of the relevant datasets.

CAT scores and GCSE performance

The strength of relationship

As explained earlier, the strength of relationship between two variables can be measured by a statistic called the *correlation coefficient*. A value of zero indicates no relationship, while a value of 1 indicates a perfect positive relationship between two measures.

Table 5.1: Correlations between the *CAT* standard age scores and selected GCSE outcomes

GCSE measure	Mean *CAT* score	*CAT* battery		
		Verbal	**Quantitative**	**Non-verbal**
GCSE/GNVQ total points score	**.71**	.69	.64	.58
GCSE/GNVQ Best 8 points score	**.75**	.72	.68	.62
Number of A* to C GCSE grades	**.63**	.61	.55	.48
Art and Design	**.44**	.40	.38	.40
Business Studies	**.57**	.56	.52	.43
Design and Technology – Food Technology	**.55**	.54	.50	.45
Design and Technology – Graphics Products	**.50**	.46	.43	.44
Design and Technology – Resistant Materials	**.50**	.45	.43	.44
Design and Technology – Textiles	**.56**	.55	.49	.46
Drama	**.50**	.50	.42	.41
English Language	.68	**.70**	.61	.53
English Literature	.61	**.63**	.54	.47
French	.66	**.67**	.59	.51
Geography	**.67**	.65	.59	.54
German	.64	**.64**	.57	.49
History	**.64**	.64	.57	.50
Home Economics	**.54**	.52	.47	.42
Information Technology	**.50**	.47	.45	.40
Mathematics	**.77**	.68	.73	.66
Media and Film Studies	**.60**	.56	.54	.48
Music	**.58**	.56	.52	.49
Physical Education	**.56**	.54	.51	.44
Religious Education	**.55**	.55	.49	.42
Science – double award	**.69**	.65	.61	.57
Science – singe award	**.58**	.55	.51	.49
Sociology	**.59**	.62	.51	.40
Spanish	.58	**.59**	.55	.42
Statistics	**.62**	.55	.56	.50

Note: figures in bold are the highest correlations for each GCSE outcome.

Table 5.1 shows the correlations between Year 7 *CAT* scores and a range of GCSE results five years later. Three main points may be noted, as described below.

Strong correlation

There is a very strong correlation between *CAT* scores in Year 7 and GCSE results five years later. The measure used to summarise a pupil's GCSE/GNVQ results is the 'Best 8' point score, which is obtained by adding together the points scores for his or her best eight subjects. The correlation between the mean *CAT* score and the Best 8 point score is 0.75.

In the field of social sciences, and educational measurement in particular, it is relatively rare to find such a high degree of association. In the physical sciences we can make statements with almost absolute certainty: mix chemical x with chemical y and a specified reaction will occur. Other areas, such as weather forecasting, are more likely to use expressions of probability: there is a 10 per cent chance that it will rain today, or a 20 per cent chance that it might rain within the next week. However, as far as human beings are concerned, it is often hard to make any but the vaguest generalisations about future behaviour or attainments. A correlation of 0.75 is therefore very significant.

Matching patterns and abilities

Looking at the three *CAT* batteries separately, the highest correlations are as follows:

- GCSE English with the Verbal Battery;
- GCSE mathematics with the Quantitative Battery;
- GCSE art and design with the Non-verbal Battery.

This reflects the pattern of intercorrelations that we might expect given the content of the *CAT* batteries and the abilities assessed.

Significance of the mean *CAT* score

With the exception of the GCSE language subjects, the highest correlation is always with the *mean CAT score* (that is, the pupil's average score over all three *CAT* batteries). This indicates a general principle that an overall measure of the pupil's ability to reason with words, with numbers and with shape and space, is the best basis for predicting success across the whole range of GCSE subjects, with the exception of languages. Therefore, the GCSE indicators for languages (English, French, German and Spanish) are calculated from the pupil's verbal reasoning score, while indicators for all other subjects are calculated from the pupil's mean *CAT* score. The same is true for Standard Grade indicators. Similarly, Key Stage 3 English indicators are based on the verbal reasoning score while Key Stage 3 mathematics and science indicators are based on the mean *CAT* score.

Visualising the relationship

GCSE/GNVQ points score

Chapter 3 stressed the importance of presenting ideas and concepts in a variety of media. Key ideas and concepts are more likely to be understood when received via a variety of senses to reinforce the message, and this applies equally to teachers as to their pupils. The relationship between *CAT* scores and GCSE grades is therefore presented in graphic form – as a scatterplot – as well as in tabular form. Figure 5.1, on page 98, shows the relationship between:

- the mean *CAT* score (*x*-axis);
- the GCSE/GNVQ Best 8 points score (*y*-axis) …

... for a random sample of around 1000 pupils drawn from the *CAT*-GCSE dataset described above.

Figure 5.1: Mean *CAT3* standard age score *versus* GCSE/GNVQ Best 8 points score

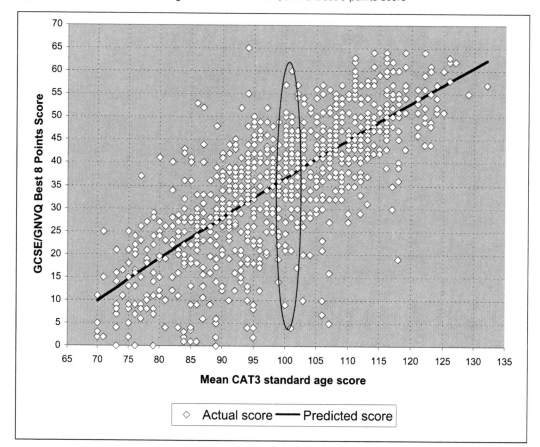

Each individual pupil's result is shown by a dot. We can summarise the data by drawing a *regression line* through it: this is the thick black diagonal line. The scatterplot shows that as the mean *CAT* score increases, so does the Best 8 points score – which is the same fact indicated by the correlation coefficient of 0.75. For example:

■ a pupil with a mean *CAT* score of *90* achieves a Best 8 points score of around *29* points, equivalent to *five subjects at Grade D* and *three at Grade E*;

■ a pupil with a mean *CAT* score of *100* typically achieves a Best 8 points score of around *38* points, equivalent to *six subjects at Grade C* and *two at Grade D*;

■ a pupil with a mean *CAT* score of *110* typically achieves a Best 8 points score of around *46*, equivalent to *five subjects at Grade B* and *three at Grade C*.

Please note that the Best 8 point scores quoted above are taken from the full dataset of 100,000 pupils – rather than the sample of 1000 pupils shown in Figure 5.1: the scores may therefore vary slightly from the points that would be read from the *y*-axis of the figure.

The scatterplot is especially helpful because it clearly shows another important aspect of the relationship between *CAT* and GCSE: the very *wide* range of GCSE/GNVQ outcomes that are achieved by pupils with very *similar* mean *CAT* scores. Thus, although the typical pupil with a mean *CAT* score of 100 achieves a Best 8 points score of 38, some pupils with the same *CAT* score achieve up to 60 or more points, while others achieve as few as 10 points as shown by the ellipse in Figure 5.1. This fact is true across the whole range of *CAT* scores. Some pupils achieve much higher points scores than expected, others achieve much lower scores than expected. Some reasons for this variety are given on pages 100 to 101.

Progress Charts

A similar range of variation is apparent for individual GCSE subjects. This can best be shown through the use of Progress Charts, which divide *CAT* scores into 12 score bands and present the GCSE grades achieved by pupils within each of these score bands. Figure 5.2 shows the Progress Chart for GCSE Geography.

The Progress Charts demonstrate for individual GCSE subjects the same two key principles demonstrated by the scatterplot shown in Figure 5.1:

■ *CAT* scores are strongly associated with subsequent GCSE attainment: thus we can see that pupils with higher *CAT* scores tend to achieve higher GCSE grades;

■ there is a wide range of GCSE outcomes achieved by pupils with similar *CAT* scores.

Consider, for example, the Progress Chart for pupils with a mean *CAT* score in the range 100 to 104, as shown in Figure 5.2 on page 100.

The most likely outcome is a Grade C, since this is the grade that was achieved by almost one third (32 per cent) of pupils with a mean *CAT* score in this range. The indicated grade for GCSE Geography for pupils with mean *CAT* scores of 100 to 104 would therefore be Grade C. However, this does not mean that pupils are guaranteed to *achieve* a Grade C, merely that it is the *most likely outcome*. Grades B, A or even A* are also possible, since these are achieved by 16 per cent, 8 per cent and 2 per cent of pupils respectively. Equally, over one fifth (22 per cent) achieve a Grade D, 11 per cent achieve a Grade E, and around 5 per cent achieve a Grade F or lower.

We consider the use of the Progress Charts in more detail later in this chapter (see pages 111 to 116).

Figure 5.2: *CAT3* to GCSE Geography Progress Chart – autumn 2003

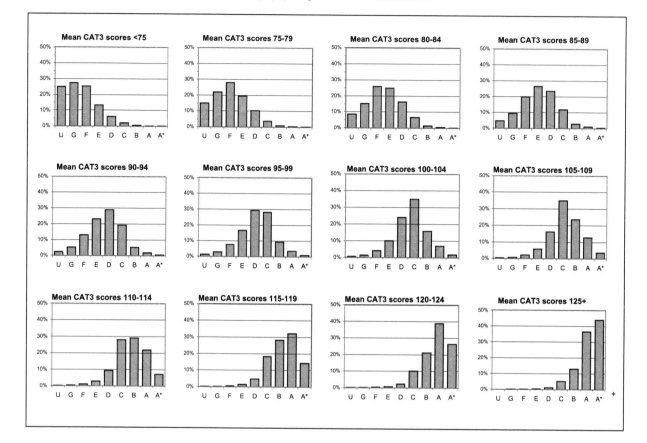

Factors influencing pupil attainment

Since *CAT* is such a good predictor of subsequent attainment, some teachers ask why the correlations between *CAT* and GCSE/GNVQ are not perfect. Why is the correlation not 1.00, rather than 0.75? A good way to address this is to ask yourself the question, 'What factors occurring between Years 7 and 11 may affect a pupil's GCSE results?' Spend a couple of minutes considering your answer. The question is often used as a 'brainstorming' activity and usually generates a large number of responses; the factors suggested include:

- pupils' health, both physical and mental;
- continued growth of cognitive ability;
- effort and motivation;

- extent of parental support and parental expectations;
- homework completion;
- quality of teaching;
- teacher expectations;
- pupils' self-confidence and self-esteem;
- whether special educational needs are identified and addressed;
- attendance/absence – from school or from particular subjects;
- English as an Additional Language – whether support is provided;
- peer influences, both positive (being placed in a high-ability set) and negative (anti-social behaviour);
- school ethos and values;
- leadership, both whole-school and within subject departments;
- community support (for example, attendance at supplementary or Saturday schools);
- pupil mentoring;
- targeted interventions (for example, summer schools).

When all these factors are considered, it is perhaps surprising that the correlation exists at all, let alone that it is as high as 0.75. We should perhaps reflect on what a perfect correlation would mean:

- pupils' GCSE/GNVQ outcomes could be perfectly predicted from their *CAT* scores alone;
- none of the factors listed above would make a difference to their results;
- whatever school they attended, whoever taught them and whether they worked hard or not, pupils would always achieve the indicated GCSE/GNVQ outcome.

This is, of course, contrary to our experience. To recap, the relationship between *CAT* scores and public examination outcomes is not perfect. Therefore, the indicators cannot be precise. The indicator can only give the typical or most frequent outcome, and there will be a broad range of performance around it.

While all the factors included in the above list are important, there are two key general factors that are likely to explain a substantial part of this variation around the indicator:

- the pupil's motivation and effort;
- school or teaching effects.

We will consider how you can use the *CAT* results to address these issues (for example, using Progress Charts to address motivation and effort, see page 110). First, let us review what the *CAT* Computer Scoring and Analysis Service indicator reports look like and what data they contain.

Some examples of the *CAT* indicator reports

When submitting *CAT* answer sheets to the *CAT* Computer Scoring and Analysis Service, secondary schools can choose from Key Stage 3, GCSE or Scottish Standard Grade indicator options. Primary schools can choose a Key Stage 2 indicator option. The Key Stage 2 indicators are not described in detail in this guide, but the basis for their annual calculation and the format of the reports is similar to those provided for Key Stage 3.

Examples of the *CAT* Computer Scoring Service reports for the Key Stage 3, GCSE and Standard Grade indicators are given below. For each indicator, the report headed 'Group Summary' comprises two components:

■ the *pupil listing page/s*, which list/s the indicators for each pupil, with 25 pupils listed per page;

■ the *group summary report*, which gives an overall summary of the results for the group.

In addition, you can choose to have the indicators included on the Individual Pupil Profiles. Finally, if you selected the *CAT* disk option, then your data disk will also contain any indicators you selected such as indicated Key Stage 3 levels in English, mathematics and science, and indicated grades in each of 30 GCSE or 24 Standard Grade subjects.

Key Stage 3 indicator reports

Pupil listing page/s

For each pupil, the indicator report shows his or her probability of achieving each level in each Key Stage 3 test, given his or her current *CAT* score. In the report shown in Figure 5.3, for example, the following indicators are given concerning the Key Stage 3 English results for **Sarah Armstrong**, who has:

■ a 9 per cent chance of achieving Level 3 or lower;

■ a 38 per cent chance of achieving Level 4;

■ a 43 per cent chance of achieving Level 5;

■ a 9 per cent chance of achieving Level 6 or above.

Figure 5.3: Example of a *CAT3* Key Stage 3 indicator report – pupil listing page

CAT 3

Group Summary of KS3 Indicators

Section L[2] Page 2 of 3

School: **Sample School**
Class/Group: **Y9/9A**　　No. of Pupils: **22**　　CAT level: **E**　　Date of Test: **15/Aug/2002**

ID Number	Name Of Pupil	Age	Sex	Mean SAS	Indicated KS3 Level (+/- 0.5 grades)			Probability of obtaining KS3 English Level						Probability of obtaining KS3 Mathematics Level						Probability of obtaining KS3 Science Level					
					English	Maths	Science	<=3	4	5	6	7	8	<=3	4	5	6	7	8	<=3	4	5	6	7	8
	ARMSTRONG, SARAH	12:2	F	93	5C	5C	5C	9%	38%	43%	8%	1%	<1%	4%	40%	48%	7%	<1%	<1%	5%	39%	49%	6%	<1%	<1%
	CLERKSON, PHIL	12:3	M	125	6A	8	7B	<1%	2%	17%	47%	31%	4%	<1%	<1%	<1%	2%	44%	54%	<1%	<1%	1%	23%	60%	16%
	CULPER, ASHLEY	13:1	M	96	5C	5B	5C	9%	38%	43%	8%	1%	<1%	2%	25%	58%	15%	1%	<1%	3%	27%	59%	11%	<1%	<1%
	DAGNALL, REBEKAH	12:10	F	118	6A	7B	6A	<1%	1%	12%	43%	38%	6%	<1%	<1%	1%	14%	71%	14%	<1%	<1%	7%	54%	35%	4%
	DAYTON, NIGEL E	12:2	M	104	5B	6C	5A	5%	26%	52%	15%	2%	<1%	<1%	4%	34%	51%	11%	<1%	<1%	7%	53%	36%	3%	<1%
	EWELL, EDWARD	12:7	M	70	3	3	3	65%	29%	5%	<1%	<1%	<1%	92%	7%	<1%	<1%	<1%	<1%	80%	19%	1%	<1%	<1%	<1%
	FERRER, ALBERT	13:8	M	107	6C	6B	6C	<1%	5%	34%	45%	14%	1%	<1%	2%	20%	57%	21%	<1%	<1%	4%	41%	50%	5%	<1%
	FLECK, ALISON	13:5	F	90	4B	4A	4A	26%	50%	22%	3%	<1%	<1%	8%	55%	33%	4%	<1%	<1%	8%	51%	37%	3%	<1%	<1%
	GILBRIDE, RACHAEL	14:0[4]	F	132	7B	8	7A	<1%	<1%	3%	19%	57%	20%	<1%	<1%	<1%	<1%	10%	90%	<1%	<1%	<1%	6%	46%	48%
	GLEWER, RICHARD	12:7	M	100	5B	5A	5B	5%	26%	52%	15%	2%	<1%	<1%	10%	53%	32%	4%	<1%	1%	15%	62%	21%	1%	<1%
	HARRISON, KATIE	12:11	F	137	7B	8	8	<1%	<1%	3%	19%	57%	20%	<1%	<1%	<1%	<1%	3%	97%	<1%	<1%	<1%	2%	23%	75%
	HAZELGROVE, EMMIE	12:0	F	112	6B	6A	6B	<1%	2%	18%	46%	29%	4%	<1%	<1%	6%	42%	49%	3%	<1%	1%	20%	64%	14%	1%
	HUNTE, LARRY	13:4	M	110	6B	6A	6C	<1%	2%	21%	46%	25%	3%	<1%	<1%	10%	51%	36%	2%	<1%	2%	28%	60%	9%	<1%
	JOHNS, LONNY	12:10	M	108[2]§	6C	6B	6C	<1%	7%	40%	41%	11%	<1%	<1%	1%	16%	56%	25%	1%	<1%	3%	36%	54%	6%	<1%
	KITCHENER, DAMIAN	12:11	M	64	3	3	3	94%	5%	<1%	<1%	<1%	<1%	98%	2%	<1%	<1%	<1%	<1%	92%	8%	<1%	<1%	<1%	<1%
	LEECHING, KIM	11:10	M	120	6C	7B	7C	<1%	7%	40%	41%	11%	<1%	<1%	<1%	<1%	9%	69%	22%	<1%	<1%	4%	45%	44%	6%
	MALCOLM, ANGUS	12:6	M	73	4C	3	3	52%	38%	8%	<1%	<1%	<1%	85%	14%	<1%	<1%	<1%	<1%	69%	28%	3%	<1%	<1%	<1%
	MCPHAIL, NICHOLAS	11:9	M	80	3	4C	4C	72%	23%	4%	<1%	<1%	<1%	51%	45%	4%	<1%	<1%	<1%	38%	53%	9%	<1%	<1%	<1%
	MILLINGTON, CARLA	13:5	F	73	4B	3	3	32%	48%	17%	2%	<1%	<1%	85%	14%	<1%	<1%	<1%	<1%	69%	28%	3%	<1%	<1%	<1%
	TABERNER, JAMIE	12:8	M	118	6C	7B	6A	<1%	5%	36%	44%	13%	1%	<1%	1%	1%	14%	71%	14%	<1%	<1%	7%	54%	35%	4%
	WILLIAMSON, NORA	13:1	F	121	7C	7A	7C	<1%	<1%	6%	31%	51%	11%	<1%	<1%	<1%	7%	66%	27%	<1%	<1%	3%	41%	49%	7%
	WINSTANLEY, COLIN	11:11	M	111	6C	6A	6B	<1%	6%	38%	42%	12%	1%	<1%	<1%	8%	47%	42%	2%	<1%	2%	24%	62%	11%	<1%

Key:
> Letter unreadable in name.

1. Unclear date of birth. Estimated age used.
2. Age unknown. Average age used.
3. Age out of range. Youngest allowed used.
4. Age out of range. Oldest allowed used.

§ WARNING Mean SAS calculated on only 1 or 2 batteries.
[2] KS3 English indicator is based on the Mean SAS **not** the Verbal SAS, see section front page.

In addition to this detailed data, a summary 'indicated level' is also given for each test. In Sarah's case the indicator is 5C for each test. The indicators for the English test are based on the pupil's verbal reasoning score, while the indicators for mathematics and science are based on the pupil's mean *CAT* score.

Group summary page

The last page of the report comprises a summary of the results for the group as a whole: an example is shown in Figure 5.4 on page 104. This report indicates what proportion of the group might be expected to achieve each level. The group summary indicators are the means of the probabilities across all pupils. For example, if we take the average of all 22 results in the English '3 or less' column, as shown in Figure 5.3, this will give a figure of 27 per cent, as shown by the first column in the Key Stage 3 English bar chart in Figure 5.4. Similarly, the average of the 22 results in the English 'Level 4' column is 16 per cent, and so on.

Figure 5.4: Example of a *CAT3* Key Stage 3 indicator report – group summary page

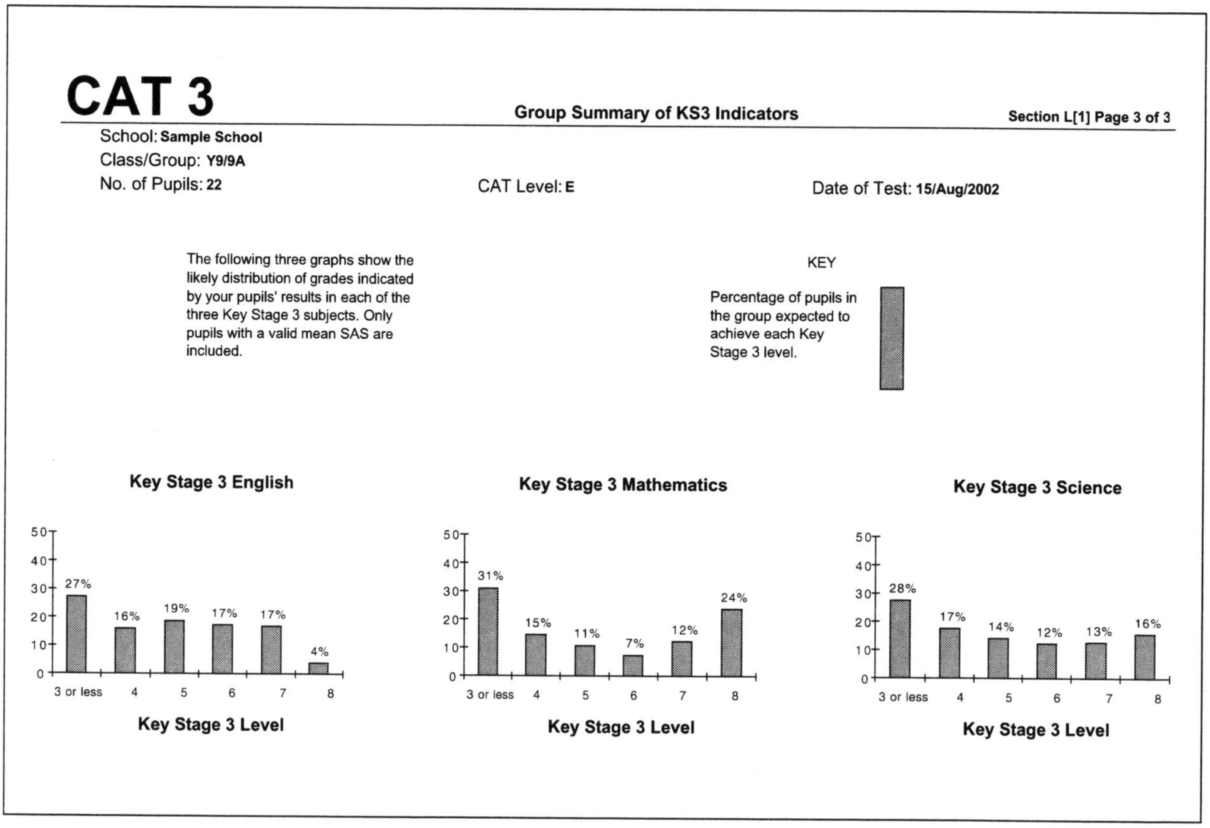

Individual Pupil Profile with Key Stage 3 indicators

The Key Stage 3 indicators for each pupil may be added to their Individual Pupil Profile, as shown in Figure 5.5. The detailed Progress Chart data is shown as three bar charts down the right-hand side of the Profile, and the summary indicated levels appear above the bar charts, with confidence bands of plus or minus one sub-level.

Figure 5.5: Example of a *CAT3* Individual Pupil Profile with Key Stage 3 indicators

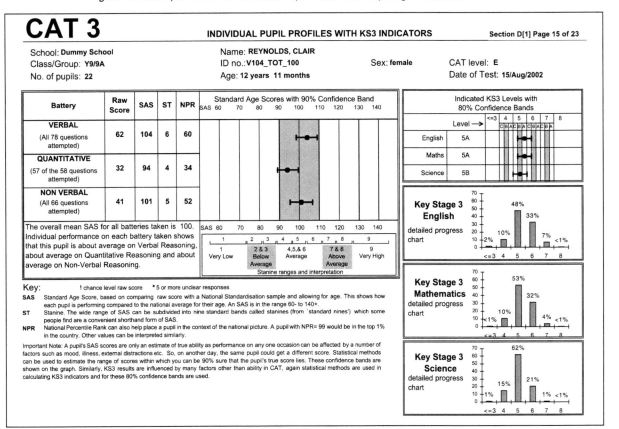

GCSE indicator reports

Pupil listing page/s

Schools often request a specific indicated grade for each subject – because, for example, they require a summary of the extensive Progress Chart data. Whilst they recognise that the Progress Charts provide the most detailed data, they still want a specific indicated grade. To meet this demand, the *CAT* Computer Scoring and Analysis Service report gives an overall indicated grade for each subject on the Group Summary pupil listing page. This indicator is a 'best fit' summary relative to the probability data contained in the Progress Charts and indicates the 'typical' outcome. The indicated grade may be a whole grade (Grade A, B, C etc.) or, where the *CAT* score indicates that the pupil may be at a boundary between grades, a split grade (Grade A/B, B/C, C/D etc.). Schools must recognise that, while it is useful for administrative purposes to have a single 'indicated outcome', it is still the Progress Charts that provide the most sophisticated and detailed information on pupils' possible outcomes (see page 111).

An example of a pupil listing page is shown in Figure 5.6 on the next page. For each pupil, this lists their indicated GCSE grade in each of 24 key GCSE subjects. Results for a further six GCSE subjects are included on the *CAT* data disk or can be downloaded from the *CAT* website. In addition, there are three summary indicators for each pupil (appearing on the far right of the sheet):

■ the percentage probability that they will achieve five or more GCSE Grades A* to C;

■ the percentage probability they will achieve five or more GCSE Grades A* to G (including English and mathematics);

■ their indicated GCSE/GNVQ Best 8 points score.

Figure 5.6: Example of a *CAT3* GCSE indicator report – pupil listing page

CAT 3

Group Summary of GCSE Indicators Section M[2] Page 2 of 3

School **Sample School**
Class/Group: **Y9/9B**
No. of Pupils: **22** CAT level: **E** Date of Test: **15/Aug/2002**

ID Number	Name Of Pupil	CAT Verbal SAS	CAT Mean SAS	Art & Design	Business Studies	Design & Tech - Food	Design & Tech - Graphics	Design & Tech - Res. Materials	Design & Tech - Textiles	Drama	English Language	English Literature	French	Geography	German	History	Home Economics	Information Technology	Mathematics	Music	Physical Education	Religious Education	Science - Double Award	Science - Biology	Science - Chemistry	Science - Physics	Spanish	%Probability of 5 A*-C	% Prob. of 5 A*-G (including English and Mathematics)	GCSE Best 8 Points Score
322	BAILEY, AMY	90	93	C/D	D/E	D	D	D	D	C	D	D	D/E	D/E	D/E	D/E	D	D	D/E	D	C/D	D/E	D	C/D	D	D	E	33%	96%	33
367	CLERKSON, PHIL	121	125	A/B	A/B	A/B	A/B	B	A	A/B	A/B	B	B	A	B	A	A	A/B	A	A	A	A	A	A	A/B	A/B	B	100%	100%	57
456	CULPER, ASHLEY	90	96	C	D	C/D	D	C/D	C	D	D	D/E	D	D/E	D	D	D	C/D	C/D	D	D	C/D	C/D	C/D	E			44%	98%	36
867	DAGNALL, REBEKAH	125	118	B	B	B	B	B/C	A/B	A/B	A/B	A/B	A/B	A/B	A/B	A/B	A/B	B	A/B	A/B	A/B	B	A/B	A/B	B	B	B	98%	100%	53
502	DAYTON, NIGEL E	95	104	B/C	C/D	C	C/D	C/D	C	B/C	C/D	C/D	D	C	D	C	C	C/D	C	C	C	C/D	C	C	C	C	D/E	75%	100%	42
507	EWELL, EDWARD	72	70	E	F/G	E/F	F	E/F	F	E	E/F	E/F	F	G	F	F/G	F	G	F	E/F	F/G	F/G	E/F	E	E/F	F/G	D/E	3%	60%	10
322	FERRER, ALBERT	111	107	B/C	C	B/C	C	C	B/C	B/C	B/C	B/C	C	C	C	C	B/C	C	C	B/C	B/C	C	C	B/C	C	C	D/E	83%	100%	45
245	FLECK, ALISON	82	90	C/D	D/E	D	D/E	D/E	D	C/D	D/E	D/E	E/F	D/E	E	D/E	D/E	D/E	E	D	D	E	D/E	D	D	D	E/F	24%	95%	30
449	GILBRIDE, RACHAEL	140+	132	A	A	A	A/B	A/B	A	A	A*/A	A	A*/A	A*/A	A*/A	A	A*/A	A	A	A*/A	A*/A	A*/A	A*/A	A*/A	A*/A	A*/A		100%	100%	62
634	GLEWER, RICHARD R	95	100	C	C/D	C	C/D	C/D	C	B/C	C/D	C/D	D	C/D	D	C/D	C/D	C/D	C/D	C	C	D	C/D	C	C/D	C/D	D/E	60%	99%	39
404	HARRISON, KATIE	140+	137	A	A*/A	A*/A	A	A	A*/A	A	A*/A	A	A*/A	A*/A	A*/A	A*/A	A*	A*/A	A*	A*/A	A*/A	A*/A	A*	A*/A	A*/A	A*/A	A*/A	100%	100%	64
412	HAZELGROVE, EMMIE	120	112	B	B/C	B/C	B/C	C	B	B	B	B	B	B	B	B/C	B	B/C	B	B	B/C	B	B/C	B	B/C	B/C	B/C	93%	100%	48
353	HUNTE, LARRY	118	110	B/C	C	B/C	C	C	B/C	B	B	B	B	B/C	B	B/C	B/C	C	B/C	B/C	B/C	C	B/C	B/C	B/C	B/C		90%	100%	47
400	JOHNS, LONNY	--²	108 §	B/C	C	B/C	C	C	B/C	B/C	B/C	B/C	C	B/C	C	B/C	B/C	C	B/C	B/C	B/C	C	B/C	B/C	B/C	B/C	C/D	86%	100%	45
410	KITCHENER, DAMIAN	60	64	E	G	F	F/G	F	E/F	G	G	G	G	F/G	F	G	F/G	F	G	F	E	E/F	G					2%	46%	4
421	LEECHING, KIM	108	120	A/B	B	A/B	B	B	A/B	A/B	B/C	B/C	C	A/B	C	A/B	A/B	B	A/B	A/B	A/B	A/B	A/B	A/B	A/B	B	C/D	98%	100%	54
498	MALCOLM, ANGUS	75	73	D/E	F	E/F	E/F	E/F	E/F	D/E	E/F	E/F	F	F/G	F	F/G	F	E/F	F/G	F	E	F	F	E	E	E	F	4%	67%	14
478	MCPHAIL, NICHOLAS	70	80	D	E/F	E	E	E	E	D	F	F	F/G	F	F	F	E/F	E	E	E	D/E	E/F	E/F	D/E	D/E	D/E	F/G	8%	82%	21
465	MILLINGTON, CARLA	80	73	D/E	E	E/F	E/F	E/F	E/F	D/E	E	E	E/F	F/G	E/F	F/G	F	E	F	E/F	F	E	E	E	E	E	E/F	4%	67%	14
462	TABERNER, JAMIE	110	118	B	B	B	B	B/C	A/B	A/B	B/C	B/C	C	A/B	C	A/B	A/B	B	A/B	A/B	A/B	B	A/B	A/B	B	B	C	98%	100%	53
463	WILLIAMSON, NORA	134	121	A/B	B	A/B	B	B	A/B	A/B	A	A	A	A/B	A	A/B	A/B	B	A/B	A/B	A/B	A/B	A/B	A/B	A/B	A/B	A	99%	100%	55
456	WINSTANLEY, COLIN	109	111	B	B/C	B/C	C	C	B	B	B/C	B/C	C	B/C	C	B/C	B/C	B/C	B/C	B/C	B/C	B/C	B/C	B/C	B/C	B/C	C	91%	100%	48

Key: > Letter unreadable in name.

§ *WARNING Mean SAS calculated on only 1 or 2 batteries.*
² *Language indicators are based on the Mean SAS **not** the Verbal SAS, see section front page.*

Group summary page

The last page of the listing gives a summary of the indicators for the group. An example is shown in Figure 5.7. From this summary you can see, for example, that:

■ 63 per cent of the group may be expected to achieve five or more Grades A* to C or equivalent;

■ 91 per cent may be expected to achieve five or more Grades A* to G or equivalent;

■ the group total points score may be 46 (plus or minus three points);

■ the proportion of the group likely to achieve Grades A* to C and A* to G in English, mathematics and science is shown;

■ the proportions of the group likely to achieve each grade in English, mathematics and science are also shown (by the three graphs running across the bottom of the page).

Figure 5.7: Example of a *CAT3* GCSE indicator report – group summary page

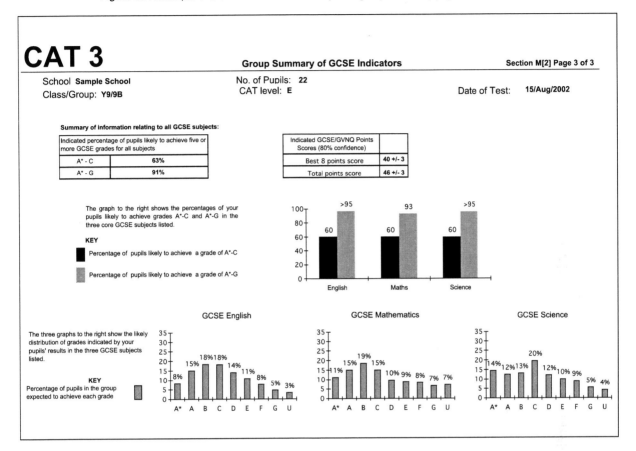

Please note that only English, mathematics and science are included in the summary because these are the only subjects for which nearly all the cohort are entered. These are therefore the only subjects where a group indicator based on the whole cohort is likely to be accurate. For example, if only one third of the cohort take French, then an indicator based on the whole cohort could be misleading. It would be necessary to calculate an indicator for French based *only* on those pupils likely to take the subject.

Note also that this group information is only a 'snapshot'. It gives a very rough estimate of the possible future performance of the group on some key measures for which schools in England are required to set and publish targets. As stated in Chapter 4, if some pupils leave the group and others join, then the summary will no longer be accurate.

We should also remember that these indicators were generated based on the relationship between *CAT* and GCSE/GNVQ as established during the previous year. Even if the group were 100 per cent stable, the relationship between *CAT* scores and GCSE/GNVQ results may have changed by the time these pupils sit public exams. For example, if national GCSE results continue to rise in the *next* five years to the same extent that they have done over the *last* five years, then the group indicator would *underestimate* the likely achievement by the time these pupils take their GCSEs. However, you can still use the *CAT* data to judge whether pupils have achieved better or worse GCSE grades than predicted by their *CAT* scores. The attached CD contains an Excel workbook to help you calculate your 'value added', and this is explained in Chapter 7 (see pages 134 to 147).

Individual Pupil Profile with GCSE indicators

The GCSE indicators can also be added to the Individual Pupil Profile: examples of these were shown in Chapter 3, for example, page 31.

Standard Grade indicator reports

Pupil listing pages and group summary

For each pupil, the report (see Figure 5.8 on page 109) gives the indicated Standard Grade results, either as a whole grade (for example, Grade 1, 2, and so on), or as a split grade where their indicated performance is at a borderline between grades (for example, Grade 1/2, 2/3, etc.). Summary outcomes for each pupil are also given, specifically:

- the percentage probability of achieving five or more passes at Grades 1 or 2;
- the percentage probability of achieving five or more passes at Grades 1 to 4;
- the percentage probability of achieving five or more passes at Grades 1 to 6;
- the grade point average (GPA), which is the mean grade across all subjects taken.

For example, **Richard Glewer** has indicated grades of 3/4 in Accounting and Finance, 2/3 in Administration, 2/3 in Art and Design, and so on. He has a 26 per cent probability of achieving five or more passes at Grade 1 or 2, a 93 per cent probability of achieving five or more passes at Grades 1 to 4 and is almost certain to achieve five or more passes at Grades 1 to 6. His indicated grade point average is 2.9.

Figure 5.8: Example of a Standard Grade pupil listing and group summary

CAT 3

COMBINED SUMMARY OF STANDARD GRADE INDICATORS   Section CSG Page 2 of 3

School: **Dummy School**
Class/Group: **Y9/ALL**
No. of Pupils: **44**   CAT level: **E**   Date of Test: **15/Aug/2002**

Name Of Pupil	CAT Verbal SAS	CAT Mean SAS	Accounting & Finance	Administration	Art & Design	Biology	Business Management	Chemistry	Computing Studies	Craft & Design	Drama	English	French	Geography	German	Graphic Communication	History	Home Economics	Maths	Modern Studies	Music	PE	Physics	Science	SVS	Technical Studies	%Probability of 5+ 1-2	%Probability of 5+ 1-4	%Probability of 5+ 1-6	Grade Point Average
BAILEY, AMY	90	93	4	3	3	3/4	3	3/4	4	3/4	3	3	3/4	3/4	3/4	3/4	3/4	3	4	3/4	2/3	3	3/4	3/4	3	4	10%	80%	97%	3.4
CAREY, KERRY	113	114	2	1/2	2	1/2	1/2	1/2	2	2	1/2	2	2	2	2	2	1/2	1/2	1/2	1/2	1/2	2	1/2	2/3	1/2	2	82%	99%	100%	1.9
CLARK, TOMMY	80	74	6/7	5	3/4	5/6	5	5/6	5	4/5	4/5	4	4/5	5/6	4	5	5	4/5	5/6	5/6	4	4	5/6	5	4	5/6	1%	22%	70%	4.8
CLERKSON, PHIL	121	125	1	1	1/2	1	1	1	1	1/2	1	1/2	1/2	1	1/2	1	1	1	1	1	1	1	1	1/2	1	1	98%	100%	100%	1.1
CULPER, ASHLEY	90	96	4	3	3	3	3	3/4	3	3	3	3	3/4	3/4	3/4	3	3	3/4	3	3	3/4	2/3	3/4	15%	87%	98%	3.2
DAGNALL, REBEKAH	125	118	1/2	1/2	2	1	1	1/2	1/2	2	1/2	1	1/2	1/2	1/2	1/2	1/2	1	1	1	1/2	1/2	2	1/2	1/2	91%	100%	100%	1.6
DAYTON, NIGEL E	95	104	3	2/3	2/3	2/3	2	2/3	2/3	2/3	2/3	3	3/4	2/3	3	2/3	2/3	2/3	3	2/3	2	2/3	2/3	3	2	2/3	41%	96%	100%	2.6
DENTON, NICOLA	85	92	4/5	3/4	3	3/4	3	3/4	4	3/4	4	3/4	4	3/4	3/4	3	4	3/4	2/3	3	3/4	3/4	3	4	9%	78%	97%	3.5
EWELL, EDWARD	72	70	6/7	5	4	5/6	5/6	5/6	5/6	4/5	5	4	5	5/6	4/5	5	5/6	5	6	5/6	4	4/5	5/6	5	4	6	0%	15%	59%	5.1
FERRER, ALBERT	111	107	2/3	2	2/3	2	2	2	2/3	2/3	2	2	2/3	2/3	2	2/3	2	2	2/3	2	2	2	2/3	3	2	2/3	55%	98%	100%	2.4
FLACKTON, SAMMY	75	80	6	4/5	3/4	5	4/5	5	5	4	4	4	4/5	5	4/5	4/5	4/5	4	5	4/5	3/4	4	5	4/5	3/4	5	2%	38%	83%	4.4
FLECK, ALISON	82	90	4/5	3/4	4	3/4	4	4	4	3/4	3/4	4	4	3/4	3/4	4	4	3	4	3	4	4	3	4	6%	72%	95%	3.6
FROGGATT, WALTER	60-	70	6/7	5	4	5/6	5/6	5/6	5/6	4/5	5	5	5/6	5/6	5/6	5	5/6	5	6	5/6	4	4/5	5/6	5	4	6	0%	15%	59%	5.1
GILBRIDE, RACHAEL	140+	132	1	1	1	1	1	1	1	1	1	1	1	1	1	1	1	1	1	1	1	1	1	1	1	1	100%	100%	100%	1.0
GLEWER, RICHARD R	95	100	3/4	2/3	2/3	2/3	2/3	3	3	3	2/3	3	3/4	3	3	3	2/3	2/3	3/4	2/3	2	2/3	3	3	2/3	3	26%	93%	99%	2.9
GREENWOOD, GEMMA	– ²	80 ¶	6	4/5	3/4	5	4/5	5	5	4	4	4	4/5	5	4	4/5	4/5	4	5	4/5	3/4	4	5	4/5	3/4	5	2%	38%	83%	4.4
GREGSON, DAVID N	140+	140+	1	1	1	1	1	1	1	1	1	1	1	1	1	1	1	1	1	1	1	1	1	1	1	1	100%	100%	100%	1.0
HARRISON, KATIE	140+	137	1	1	1	1	1	1	1	1	1	1	1	1	1	1	1	1	1	1	1	1	1	1	1	1	100%	100%	100%	1.0
HAWKSWELL, SALLY	101	98	3/4	3	2/3	3	2/3	3	3/4	3	2/3	2/3	3	3	3	3	3	3	3/4	3	2/3	2/3	3	3/4	2/3	3/4	20%	90%	99%	3.1
HAZELGROVE, EMMIE	120	112	2	2	2	1/2	1/2	2	2	2	2	2	1/2	1/2	2	1/2	2	2	2	2	1/2	1/2	2	2	2/3	2	2	76%	99%	100%	2.0
HUNTE, LARRY	118	110	2/3	2	2	2	2	2	2	2/3	2	2	2	2	2	2	2	2	2	2	1/2	2	2/3	2	2	68%	99%	100%	2.2
JOHNS, LONNY	– ²	108 ¶	2/3	2	2/3	2	2	2	2/3	2/3	2	2	2/3	2/3	2/3	2	2	2/3	2	2	2	2/3	2	2/3	60%	98%	100%	2.3
JOHNSON, NICOLA	60-	60-	7	6	4/5	6/7	6	6/7	6	5/6	6	5	5/6	6/7	5/6	6	6	6	6/7	6/7	5	5/6	6/7	6	5	6/7	0%	5%	31%	6.0
JONES, EMMA	131	126	1	1	1/2	1	1	1	1	1/2	1	1	1	1	1	1	1	1	1	1	1	1	1/2	1	1	98%	100%	100%	1.0
KITCHENER, DAMIAN	60	64	7	5/6	4	6	6	6	6	5	5/6	5	5/6	6	5/6	5/6	6	5/6	6/7	6	4/5	5	6	5/6	4/5	6/7	0%	8%	42%	5.6
The columns to the right give indicators for the group as a whole.																											46%	72%	88%	3.0

Key: * Letter missing in name.   ? Letter unreadable in name.   ¶ Mean SAS calculations are based on one or two battery scores only.   ² If Verbal SAS is missing indicators for languages are based on the Mean SAS **not** the Verbal SAS.

There is no separate group report for the Standard Grade indicators. Instead, the bottom row on the last page of the report gives the group indicators for the four summary measures (five or more passes at Grades 1 to 2, Grades 1 to 4, Grades 1 to 6 and the GPA respectively). For the group listed above, these figures are 46 per cent, 72 per cent, 88 per cent and 3.0 respectively.

Individual Pupil Profile with Standard Grade indicators

A different approach from that used for GCSE has been taken when presenting the indicated outcomes for Scottish Standard Grades. The Individual Pupil Profile with Standard Grade indicators consists of two separate pages. The first page gives the *CAT* results as shown in the standard Individual Pupil Profile. A separate second sheet gives the Standard Grade indicators in the form of detailed progress chart data.

The figure below shows the Standard Grade Individual Pupil Profile for **Richard Glewer**. This shows the detailed Progress Chart data for Richard in all 24 Standard Grade subjects, based on his verbal and mean *CAT* scores.

Figure 5.9: Example of an Individual Pupil Standard Grade indicator report

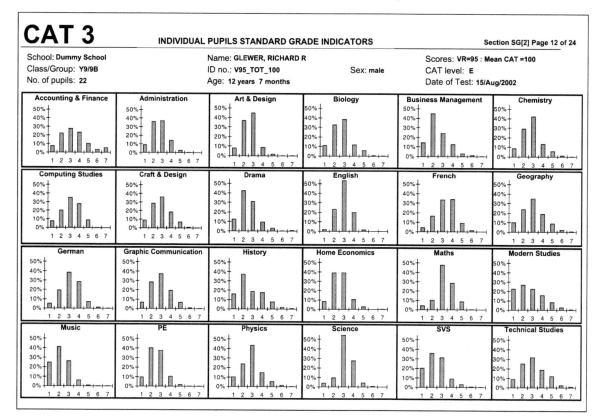

Using the Progress Charts

The Key Stage 3, GCSE and Standard Grade indicators as shown in the previous reports are used by schools in a variety of ways. Given the wide range of positive uses, there are many possible examples that could be given. However, one particularly striking example of good practice is in the use of the Progress Charts for individual pupil target setting. Many schools have found that the Progress Charts are particularly helpful in the process of negotiating challenging yet achievable targets with pupils.

What is a Progress Chart?

The Progress Charts divide *CAT* scores into 12 score bands and show the GCSE grade probabilities for each of these score bands. There are Progress Charts for 30 GCSE subjects and all are included on the attached CD. As an example, we shall use the GCSE Geography Progress Charts, as previously shown in Figure 5.2. However the same principle applies to all other GCSE charts and to the equivalent Key Stage 3 and Standard Grade Progress Charts.

Using the Progress Charts in target setting

Many form tutors, academic counsellors and learning mentors are sharing the Progress Charts with pupils in target-setting discussions. It is clear from the Progress Charts that for each *CAT* score band a *range* of GCSE grades is achieved. Some grades may be more likely than others, but most grades have some (albeit sometimes small) probability of being achieved. By selecting the relevant chart for the pupil's *CAT* score, you can ensure that discussions are focused around challenging yet achievable targets for that pupil.

Consider the chart for mean *CAT3* scores in the range 95 to 99 (see Figure 5.10). Grade C or Grade D are the most likely outcomes for these pupils. Which grade is this particular pupil going to aim for? Since Grade C or above has been achieved by the top 45 per cent of pupils with *CAT* scores in this range, this might represent quite a challenging target. This does not mean that even more aspirational targets should be ruled out: Grades B, A or even A* are also possible, since these are achieved by 10 per cent, 3 per cent and 1 per cent of pupils respectively. The Progress Charts are important in demonstrating to pupils what might be achieved with sufficient motivation and effort, amongst other factors. One message to give your pupils is: 'If you work hard, if we identify the areas where you need support and I provide it, then these levels of performance are achievable.'

Figure 5.10: *CAT3* to GCSE Geography Progress Chart for mean *CAT3* score of 95–99

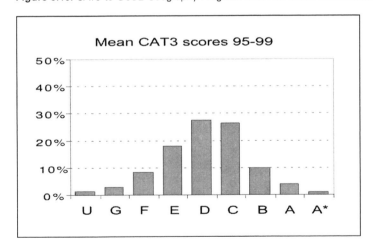

The chart also shows that there is no *guarantee* of a C or D grade for pupils in this *CAT* score band: nearly one fifth (18 per cent) achieved an E, 8 per cent achieved an F, 3 per cent achieved a G and 1 per cent failed. It is important to emphasise this in order to guard against complacency on the part of some pupils who may, if shown the Progress Chart, simply settle for a Grade D. The message you may need to give some pupils is this: 'If you do not put in the effort and work, then you may achieve a Grade E, F, G or even U.'

Consider discussing some of the following questions with your pupils.

- *Targets for attainment*: What grades appear to be easily within your reach? What grades might be achieved with a little more effort and support? What target shall we agree on?
- What aspects of the work in this subject do you find difficult? What aspects do you find relatively easy? Where would you benefit from extra help?
- *Targets for learning*: What are the learning steps to be taken over the next half term if we are to achieve this target? How will we identify the steps? (In English, for example, learning targets might be: to learn to use full stops and other punctuation accurately; to understand the use of metaphor in creative writing, etc.)

Schools' expectations

Schools have sometimes been criticised by the Office for Standards in Education (Ofsted) for having low expectations for pupil attainment. Sometimes, undoubtedly, this criticism has been valid, but it is not easy to quantify expectations and levels of challenge. For example, a Grade C in GCSE English may be unrealistically high for one pupil, appropriately challenging for another but insufficiently stretching for a third. Whilst high expectations are important, it is *realistically* high expectations that count in successful target setting. There is evidence that targets that are unrealistically high are actually demotivating, engendering a sense of helplessness and defeatism. This was commented on by the Chief Inspector of Schools in England (*Times Educational Supplement*, 2003b).

The Progress Charts are useful in allowing staff to gauge the degree or extent of challenge involved in any particular target. For example, we can see from Figure 5.10 that a Grade B is a very challenging target, because less than 15 per cent of pupils in this *CAT* score band actually achieve that grade or better. The rationale for such a target is 'with this particular pupil, given their level of commitment, with the support I will offer, and against the learning steps and forward plan we have agreed, this is the target we will aim for'.

This is exactly how the *CAT* data is used in Earlsheaton School:

> We are using data from nferNelson *CAT* tests that the pupils take in Year 7. We use them to give an indicated level at the end of Key Stage 3. We then do the *CAT* again in Year 9 to confirm what we already think. So then we sit down with the pupil and start to target set. This is new, where teacher and pupil say, 'Look, we have a Grade C/D: which one shall we make your target?' We don't want to set them up to fail. We want to set them up to succeed.
>
> *Chris Brian, Head of Science, Earlsheaton School*

In thinking about *CAT* and target setting, we should make an important distinction between *forecasts* and *targets*. *CAT* scores are helpful in providing *forecasts* for pupils' future attainment at Key Stage 3, GCSE or Standard Grade. These forecasts can provide a starting point for considering *targets* for individual pupils, but they do not necessarily constitute targets in themselves. Targets are more than forecasts, since targets should also include an element of *challenge*. Your wide and detailed knowledge of each individual pupil and of your class/school aspirations are needed if you are to translate these forecasts into challenging yet achievable targets.

This is well summarised in the following quote:

> You can use data and targets with kids as much to lower expectations as to raise them. But I hope we understand that we can use data to know about prior attainment, to show what children *could* achieve – right? – and not to argue for what they *can't* achieve. So I would hope that the use of data is a lively process. It's not about numbers, it's about interpreting children, understanding what kids can do, what capacities they have that maybe they don't know, maybe their parents don't know, maybe their teachers haven't always known and picking up on that and believing in them more than they believe in themselves.
>
> *Richard Martin, Headteacher, Woodlands Community School*

Summary

To summarise, when using the Progress Charts and indicators with staff and parents, and if sharing them with individual pupils, you should follow the established best practice for schools using the results for mentoring purposes by:

■ stressing to pupils that the indicators are a *statistical prediction*, not a prophecy of their actual results;

■ using the Progress Charts for each subject to emphasise to pupils the *range of outcomes* that could be achieved;

■ emphasising the importance of each pupil's *motivation and effort* in determining the grade he or she obtains;

■ identifying any areas in which the pupil requires *greater support from the teacher*;

■ *not using the indicators to label pupils negatively* as actual or potential 'failures';

■ emphasising *the upper limits of the range* shown in the Progress Charts when setting personal targets;

■ considering and setting the indicators *in the context of all other known relevant factors* and assessment information, thus making sure targets are *reasonable and achievable*.

Other uses of the Progress Charts

Identifying borderline performance

The Progress Charts may be used strategically, to identify groups of pupils where performance is at a borderline. For example, from Figure 5.2 it is clear that for pupils with mean *CAT* scores in the range 95 to 99 the probabilities of achieving a D or a C grade in GCSE Geography are evenly balanced. These pupils may therefore be of particular interest when considering target setting. For different subjects, such borderlines will occur at different *CAT* score ranges, so each department should consider the relevant Progress Chart for their subject.

Informing subject choices

Some schools have shared the Progress Charts with pupils and parents to inform subject choices in upper secondary school, but care is needed in the interpretation of the charts. For example, the pupil's interest in any particular subject is vital. The examination indicators may suggest a greater probability of achieving a higher grade in one subject than another, but is this particular individual interested in or motivated by the subject? There is no guarantee that this particular pupil will do better given his or her unique background. Education option choices are complicated decisions and indicators of possible future examination grades are only one piece of information that should be considered.

How do I access the Progress Charts?

Progress Charts for a particular subject

Figure 5.2 (see page 100) showed the Progress Chart for GCSE Geography. There are similar Progress Charts for a total of 30 GCSE subjects, 24 Standard Grade subjects and for English, mathematics and science tests at Key Stage 3. All of these Progress Charts are included as Adobe Acrobat files on the attached CD. Each autumn, updated charts will be available to download at no charge from the *CAT* website (www.nfer-nelson.co.uk/cat). You will need to download these updates annually.

Progress Charts for a particular pupil

Using the Progress Charts in the form described above works well where target setting occurs within subject departments, or is based on discussions between pupils and their subject teachers. In such cases, the geography teacher uses the geography Progress Charts, the English teacher uses the English Progress Charts, and so on. However, in some schools, target setting is negotiated with form tutors or with learning mentors who may wish to discuss with pupils their targets across a wide range of subjects. In these cases, it is more helpful to have all the relevant Progress Charts for the pupil on a single sheet of paper.

Schools selecting Standard Grade indicators get such a report covering 24 Standard Grade subjects (see Figure 5.9). Schools choosing GCSE indicators do not currently have access to such a report. However, the attached CD includes a Microsoft Excel workbook, which will allow you to print all the relevant Progress Charts for a pupil in 24 key GCSE subjects at one go, on a single page of A4. If you enter the pupil's *CAT3* verbal reasoning score and his or her mean *CAT3* score in the top right of the worksheet, the Progress Charts for 24 key GCSE subjects will be automatically updated. You can choose to print this sheet, or save the worksheet for future reference. An example of an individual pupil GCSE Progress Chart report is shown in Figure 5.11.

Figure 5.11: Individual pupil GCSE Progress Chart report

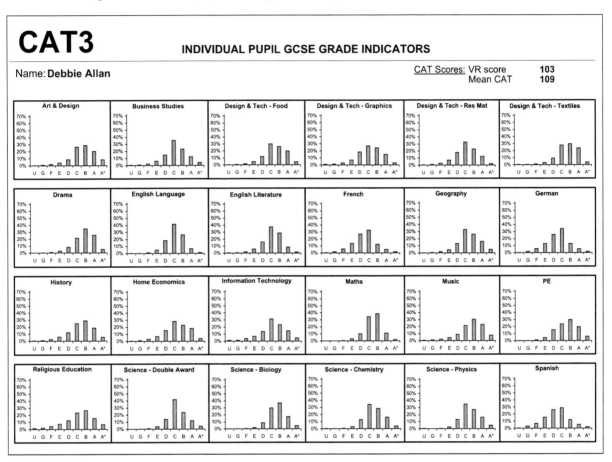

Using the summary indicator tables

Any school selecting one of the indicator options receives a copy of the relevant summary indicator table along with the *CAT* Computer Scoring and Analysis Service reports. The CD contains copies of the summary indicator tables for each of the Key Stage 3, GCSE and Standard Grade indicators. An extract from the *CAT3* to GCSE summary indicator table is shown in Table 5.2 on page 116. This shows that, for example, a pupil with a mean *CAT3* score of 107 would:

- have an indicated total GCSE/GNVQ Best 8 points score of 43;
- have a 79 per cent chance of achieving five or more GCSEs at Grades A* to C;
- be almost certain to achieve five or more GCSEs at Grade A* to G;
- have indicated grades of B/C in English Literature, C in French, C in Geography, B/C in Mathematics, etc.

Some schools use these data to inform their target-setting strategies. For example, the data indicate that pupils with a mean *CAT3* score of 98 have a greater than 50 per cent chance of achieving five or more A* to C grades. Schools can then estimate their cohort targets for five or more GCSEs at Grades A* to C by calculating the percentage of the cohort with a mean *CAT3* score of 98 or above. There are clear limitations to this approach: for example, it is not clear in *which subjects* the pupil is targeted to achieve an A* to C grade, and the cohort targets are not linked to departmental or subject targets. However, some schools have found this approach useful.

Table 5.2: An extract from the *CAT3* to GCSE summary indicators table, Autumn 2003

CAT3 score	GCSE/GNVQ Best 8 points score	Probability of 5+ A*C grades	Probability of 5+ A*-G (including English & maths)	English Language	English Literature	French	Geography	History	Information Technology	Mathematics	Religious Education	Science - Double Award
91	30	25%	93%	D	D	D/E	D/E	D/E	D/E	D/E	D/E	D/E
92	31	28%	94%	D	C/D	D/E	D/E	D/E	D	D/E	D/E	D/E
93	32	31%	95%	C/D	C/D	D/E	D/E	D/E	D	D/E	D/E	D
94	32	34%	96%	C/D	C/D	D/E	D	D	D	D	D/E	D
95	33	37%	96%	C/D	C/D	D	D	D	D	D	D	D
96	34	40%	97%	C/D	C/D	D	D	D	D	D	D	D
97	35	44%	97%	C/D	C/D	D	D	D	D	D	D	D
98	36	48%	97%	C/D	C	D	C/D	D	C/D	D	D	C/D
99	37	51%	98%	C	C	D	C/D	C/D	C/D	C/D	D	C/D
100	37	55%	98%	C	C	D	C/D	C/D	C/D	C/D	C/D	C/D
101	38	59%	98%	C	C	C/D	C/D	C/D	C/D	C/D	C/D	C/D
102	39	63%	99%	C	C	C/D	C/D	C/D	C/D	C/D	C/D	C/D
103	40	66%	99%	C	C	C/D	C	C	C/D	C	C/D	C/D
104	41	70%	99%	C	C	C/D	C	C	C	C	C/D	C
105	41	73%	99%	C	B/C	C/D	C	C	C	C	C	C
106	42	76%	99%	B/C	B/C	C/D	C	C	C	C	C	C
107	43	79%	99%	B/C	B/C	C	C	C	C	B/C	C	C
108	44	82%	99%	B/C	B/C	C	B/C	B/C	C	B/C	C	C
109	44	84%	100%	B/C	B/C	C	B/C	B/C	C	B/C	C	B/C

Review

After reading this chapter you should understand that:

■ *CAT* scores can provide *indicated outcomes* for pupils in future *national tests* at the end of Key Stage 2, Key Stage 3, or in GCSE or Scottish Standard Grade public examinations: you request the indicators when submitting your answer sheets for scoring;

■ *indicated outcomes should never be used to limit aspirations*: the indicator gives the most frequent outcome, but *there is a wide range of outcomes achieved* for any particular *CAT* score, as shown by the Progress Charts;

■ *indicated outcomes are not fixed ceilings*: where pupils are motivated and try hard, and in schools/departments that add a lot of value, pupils are more likely to *exceed* their indicated levels;

■ the CD accompanying this guide contains a unique *Microsoft Excel workbook* that allows you to collate and print all the relevant Progress Charts in 24 GCSE subjects for any particular pupil, on a single A4 sheet; these reports are not available from the *CAT* Computer Scoring and Analysis Service.

6 Pupil tracking and progress monitoring

AIMS

This chapter will:

■ explain the *importance of monitoring and feedback*;

■ provide *case studies demonstrating successful practice* in whole-school pupil tracking and progress monitoring.

The importance of monitoring and feedback

Setting targets is an important step on the way to improving performance. However, unless pupils' progress against their targets is monitored and evaluated, the full benefits of the process may not be realised. Research suggests that the combination of target setting *and* feedback on performance is substantially more effective than either alone. This may be because feedback directs pupils' attention to their performance, providing focus and motivation, and because it helps them to gauge their success. In addition, where problems may be occurring, monitoring and feedback allow pupils to be identified early enough for intervention to occur. For example, if a pupil's performance is dipping well below target during Year 10, there is still time to identify and address any underlying issues. If exam targets are set but then only referred to *after* the exams have been completed, an important part of the process will have been missed.

Case study: St Philip Howard Catholic High School

An example of effective practice in this area is illustrated by a case study from St Philip Howard Catholic High School in West Sussex (see Figure 6.1 on the next page). The case study demonstrates how the school has built the *CAT* indicators into an ongoing pupil tracking and monitoring system. It describes the background to the development and use of the system at Key Stage 3, Key Stage 4 and in the sixth form.

Figure 6.1: St Philip Howard Catholic High School – case study

St Philip Howard Catholic High School

School context

St Philip Howard is a Roman Catholic 11 to 18 comprehensive school situated in a semi-rural catchment area, east of Chichester, along the coastal strip of West Sussex. The school is heavily over-subscribed, having returned to five-form entry in 1996. Pupil numbers have risen from 650 to 820 in 2002. Target setting has grown to become an integral part of assessment, marking and reporting. In 1998, the decision was taken to share individual targets with parents and pupils. The period 1998 to 2002 saw many developments in target setting. In October 2002 the Ofsted [Office for Standards in Education] inspection report stated, 'This is a good school with a strong, warm and caring ethos … a school that knows itself, and is constantly seeking to improve.'

Introduction

For many years, teachers have felt uneasy about sharing with parents their perceptions about possible future Key Stage 3, GCSE or A level performance, fearing that pupils of low ability may be discouraged by the revelation of a comparatively modest target level or grade. We have taken the view that if the pupil is convinced of the inherent challenge in the target level or grade, this need not happen.

Parents have the right to know how their children are doing, and how best they can be encouraged to grow. With this knowledge comes a sense of ownership and responsibility. Individual target setting at St Philip Howard aims to share this responsibility with all partners in the education process. We decided to set challenging yet realistic performance targets for each individual pupil – based on an objective measurement of potential. We also decided, wherever possible, to share these targets openly with parents and pupils at the outset of Years 7, 10 and 12.

Beginnings

We started using *CAT* with Year 7 and Year 9 pupils in 1997. Initially the data was shared with the SENCO, heads of department and subject teachers. At this time, the school had also begun setting whole-school and departmental targets following national and local requirements. It became apparent that individual target setting would become the foundation for future whole-school target setting. For over a year, the Senior Management Team (SMT) examined ways in which this could be achieved. At GCSE, we recognised that *CAT* produced a result which, although accurately standardised, was slightly conservative in the context of our performance, so we incorporated the necessary degree of challenge for each pupil by taking the *CAT* indicated grade and 'adding a grade'. The principle of '*CAT* plus one grade' became the method for establishing a challenging target grade.

Led by the SMT, the principles of pupil target setting were presented formally to all teaching staff on two consecutive INSET [in-service training] days. *CAT* data was imported into SIMS Assessment Manager, which was used to generate user-friendly data sheets specific to subjects for use by heads of department and subject teachers. Assessment Manager was also used to generate the Individual Profile of Potential and Performance (IPPP), which was later distributed to parents and pupils. The SMT decided to share this information with parents of pupils in Key Stage 4, initially with Year 11 and then Year 10. Parents and pupils were invited to a presentation, led by the SMT. This explained, in jargon-free terms, the standardised ways in which potential had been tested and how the results had been used to establish challenging target grades for each individual.

Results

Feedback on the principle of target setting from parents and pupils has been encouraging. All concerned were intrigued to see – on their IPPP – the juxtaposition between *CAT* predicted grade, challenging target grade and most recent performance/examination grade (see Figure 6.2, on page 123, for an example). The differentiation between the three gave food for thought and provided a sharp focus for individual action planning. Subject teachers are now working with pupils to develop strategies for individual support. A Year 11 mentoring service has been established to offer support to small groups of pupils leading up to their examinations. Parents have welcomed the openness that this development has created. The new approach to individual target setting has fostered a fresh impetus for raising standards and expectations.

Individual target setting was extended to Key Stage 3 core subjects in 1999, and non-core subjects in 2000. The SMT led presentations to Key Stage 3 parents and pupils. For non-core subjects in Key Stage 3, the SIMS Assessment Manager was used to correlate Year 9 teacher assessments at the end of the key stage with the pupil's mean *CAT* score. From this it was possible to identify expectations for pupils within Key Stage 3 in lower years, indirectly from school-based judgements. It was clear that *CAT* offered a good objective predictor in English, mathematics and science.

Attendance at presentation evenings increased from 48 per cent at the first Year 11 target-setting evening in 1998 to an average of 85 per cent on subsequent evenings. Pupils usually accompanied their parents. Each parent was provided with his or her child's IPPP. A support pack for parents was produced, suggesting practical measures they could adopt to support their children. At GCSE the pack included a curriculum and coursework guide for parents. At Key Stage 3 a curriculum guide was issued.

Conclusion

Sharing targets at Key Stage 3, Key Stage 4 and in the sixth form has raised awareness of national standards and increased understanding of what needs to be done to improve pupil performance. At all management levels within the school there is discussion about pupils' knowledge, understanding, skills and attitudes to work. Underachievement and low expectations have been brought into finer focus. Dialogue between colleagues, pupils and parents has encouraged a collective understanding and appreciation of standards and the need for support – including, in some cases, closer monitoring.

We are learning to tap a natural resource and, for many pupils, the rich seams of potential still lie deep within. Whilst many fulfil their potential with little intervention or support, others drift along achieving reasonable standards against a background of self-satisfaction. There are also those who underachieve and, despite best intentions, little space remains for improvement. At St Philip Howard times are changing to the benefit of individual pupils as well as whole-school performance figures.

John McGuinness, formerly Assistant Headteacher (Assessment/Performance)

Pupil tracking at Key Stage 4

The key aspects of the St Philip Howard tracking system as used in Key Stage 4 are:

- all pupils are set *target GCSE grades* in every subject they study, based on *CAT scores from Year 9* (July);
- a high degree of challenge is included in the target grades by *adding a full grade to the CAT indicated grade*; for example, a *CAT* indicated Grade C in History would become a target Grade B;
- judgements of pupils' *current performance* are made by subject teachers on a *termly* basis;

- the *current performance* judgements are made against GCSE standards in the form of a *GCSE grade*;
- *subject teachers* enter their assessments of current performance into a database; their entries are transferred directly from their laptop computers to the *SIMS Assessment Manager* using a wireless network;
- at the agreed termly reporting deadline, the Assistant Headteacher uses SIMS Assessment Manager to update and print an *Individual Profile of Potential and Performance (IPPP)* for each pupil, which is sent to parents;
- subject teachers, heads of department, heads of year and form tutors also receive the IPPP; the information is used to *celebrate success*, to *identify pupils who are underachieving* against their target grades and to *develop support strategies* for improvement;
- *form tutors analyse the termly IPPP* and make contact with subject teachers, heads of department, heads of year, the SENCO and parents to discuss any pupil making insufficient progress;
- heads of department are responsible for ensuring that the termly review and subsequent action points are *effectively implemented within departments*;
- departmental and cohort *targets* are aggregated directly from the IPPPs;
- these targets, together with current performance data, are *monitored* by heads of department, the Assistant Head (Assessment/Performance) and the Senior Management Team (SMT);
- the SMT arranges and leads *presentation evenings* for parents and pupils on individual target setting, offering support and advice on ways parents can support their child to fulfil his or her potential.

Assessing current levels of performance

Clarity in making the judgement of 'current performance' is crucial to the success of the monitoring system. This judgement:

- *is an estimate of the pupil's current level of performance* as assessed against *GCSE standards*;
- is *not* a judgement of the grade the pupil would receive if he or she were to be entered for the examination *now*: the pupil will have covered only a limited proportion of the syllabus and coursework, so would most likely achieve a very low grade;
- is *not* the grade predicted for the pupil when he or she sits the examination: on the basis of previous experience, you might believe that the pupil may cram furiously in the three months before the exam and may just achieve a Grade C, but this would not be an accurate reflection of current performance.

The current level of performance may be gauged readily by experienced subject teachers with extensive experience of GCSE coursework assessment and marking, moderation procedures and a sound knowledge of national standards. However, the St Philip Howard school has found it valuable to use tasks from coursework or previous examination questions that have GCSE mark schemes attached, thus allowing GCSE grades to be directly estimated. For example, in science these tasks could include projects or essays on rocks, pollution, chemical elements and so on. This has proved useful, not just in supporting newly qualified teachers (NQTs), but in building across a department a shared understanding of standards and relevant evidence.

Using ICT for management and report generation

ICT is used effectively to manage the process, both in data collection (using laptops and a wireless network to directly enter the data to SIMS Assessment Manager) and in the reporting process (by using SIMS Assessment Manager to automatically generate pupil, department and year group reports). The analysis and reports produced at the individual pupil, department and whole-year group levels are considered below.

Reports generated at Key Stage 4

Pupil level

Figures 6.2 and 6.3 provide examples of the IPPPs generated by the St Philip Howard school during Key Stage 4. These examples help to illuminate the underlying strengths of the data.

■ *Luke* (see Figure 6.2) is performing below his target grade in all subjects. In most subjects, he is also performing below his *CAT* indicated grade. Luke's science teacher is concerned that Luke is currently achieving a Grade C against his A target grade. His form tutor believes that Luke's consistent pattern of underperformance relative to his targets suggests more global difficulties. Are there wider issues of disaffection, emotional problems, lack of effort? His science teacher still feels that he has a responsibility to try and improve Luke's engagement with, and performance in, the subject; however, it is useful to be aware of the wider context in which Luke's performance needs to be interpreted. Formative assessment – identifying how Luke can improve his performance – will be powerful here. This example profile shows only the results for the first assessment of current performance (February, Year 10). If a similar pattern were to be repeated in the next assessment (June, Year 10) this would represent a significant cause for concern.

■ *Philippa* (see Figure 6.3 on page 124) is performing at a very high level, with current performance at or above her target grades in all subjects. Should we be concerned as to whether Philippa will be able to sustain this level of performance? What level of effort is she expending to achieve these grades and is there a risk that she will 'burn out' before the end of Year 11? Is she the sort of pupil who will look at the string of A* and A grades for current performance, but notice only the 'C' for Modern Foreign Language (MFL)? Alternatively, were her *CAT* scores atypically low, maybe affected by an emotional upset on the days of the test? Some triangulation with other information sources will be important here. What about the Grade C in MFL, which is below not only the target grade but also below the *CAT* indicator? Is there an issue for the form tutor to raise? How is Philippa getting on with her French teacher? Are there any problems or clashes?

Figure 6.2: St Philip Howard Catholic High School – Luke's IPPP

| Luke | Spring Term | Year 10 |

The aim of this Individual Profile of Potential and Performance (IPPP) is to set challenging GCSE target grades based upon performance indicators, which can then be shared with pupils, parents and teachers. The *Cognitive Abilities Test* (*CAT*), completed by your son/daughter at the end of Year 9, forms the foundation of target setting at St Philip Howard, supported by his/her Year 9 national curriculum test results. There is a strong correlation between *CAT* scores and subsequent GCSE performance. From our school-based analysis, and more recently that of the County, we believe *CAT* grades are a mid-range and somewhat 'conservative' estimate of future performance. We consider, therefore, that a realistic yet challenging target grade is *CAT* plus one. An example would be English *CAT* Grade C, which becomes a target Grade B. It should be stressed that these target grades reflect a pupil's measured potential based on prior performance and are not predicted grades.

It is our intention to share this information with pupils, parents and teachers in order to encourage, support and motivate pupils to realise their talents and potential, and to make the very most of the period ahead – moving closer to, or even exceeding their personal target grades by the end of Year 11.

Subject	*CAT* grade	Target grade	Current performance			
			Feb Year 10	June Year 10	Nov Year 11	Jan Year 11
English Language	C	B	D			
Maths	B/C	A/B	C/D			
Science	B	A	C			
Religious Studies	C	B	C			
Modern Foreign Language	B/C	A/B	C			
Geography	B/C					
History	B/C	A/B	D			
Technology	C	B	F			
Business Studies	C					

Please note that subjects without a target grade are not being studied by your son/daughter.

Figure 6.3: St Philip Howard Catholic High School – Philippa's IPPP

Philippa   **Spring Term**   **Year 10**

The aim of this Individual Profile of Potential and Performance (IPPP) is to set challenging GCSE target grades based upon performance indicators, which can then be shared with pupils, parents and teachers. The *Cognitive Abilities Test* (*CAT*), completed by your son/daughter at the end of Year 9, forms the foundation of target setting at St Philip Howard, supported by his/her Year 9 national curriculum test results. There is a strong correlation between *CAT* scores and subsequent GCSE performance. From our school-based analysis, and more recently that of the County, we believe *CAT* grades are a mid-range and somewhat 'conservative' estimate of future performance. We consider, therefore, that a realistic yet challenging target grade is *CAT* plus one. An example would be English *CAT* Grade C, which becomes a target Grade B. It should be stressed that these target grades reflect a pupil's measured potential based on prior performance and are not predicted grades.

It is our intention to share this information with pupils, parents and teachers in order to encourage, support and motivate pupils to realise their talents and potential, and to make the very most of the period ahead – moving closer to, or even exceeding their personal target grades by the end of Year 11.

Subject	*CAT* grade	Target grade	Current performance			
			Feb Year 10	June Year 10	Nov Year 11	Jan Year 11
English Language	C	B	A*			
Maths	B/C	A/B	B			
Science	B	A	A			
Religious Studies	C	B	A			
Modern Foreign Language	B/C	A/B	C			
Geography	B/C	A/B	A/B			
History	B/C	A/B	A			
Technology	C	B	A			
Business Studies	B					

Please note that subjects without a target grade are not being studied by your son/daughter.

Department level

Once targets have been set for each individual pupil, these are simply aggregated to generate the target for the department as a whole, or indeed for each teaching group within the department. The target proportion of A* to C grades, A* to G grades and the average points score are directly calculated for the subject or teaching group. Looking at these three performance levels (*high* [A* to C], *average* [average points score] and *floor* [A* to G]) provides an important balance against short-sightedness and a fixation on the single A* to C measure. The targets for any group are not an abstraction: they directly result from (and are dynamically tied to) the targets for each individual pupil. At the simplest level, this demonstrates the internal consistency and integrity of the target-setting process. At a more practical level, issues of pupil mobility or turbulence are accounted for, since group targets are automatically rebased to account for changes in group membership.

Whole cohort level

An example cohort report is shown in Figure 6.4. The report shows all instances where a pupil is two or more grades adrift from his or her target grade; otherwise the relevant cell remains blank. The selection in Figure 6.4 shows the results for the first 30 pupils in a whole Year 10 cohort.

Figure 6.4: St Philip Howard Catholic High School – sample Year 10 cohort report

St Philip Howard - Year 10 - Whole-School analysis for possible underachievement / intervention

The following are students who are two or more GCSE grades adrift from their subject target grade

Pupil	KS3 En Y9	KS3 Ma Y9	KS3 Sc Y9	CAT Verbal	CAT Mean	EN	MA	SC	GY	HY	RS	MFL	TE	BS	Total
Charlotte	A	A	A	70	79										
Lisa	5	5	4	93	104			-2	-2		-2	-3		-2	-11
Amy	5	4	4	90	87						-2				-2
Tamsin	6	5	5	99	99										
David	4	4	5	86	89		-2					-2			-4
Hannah	6	6	5	106	109					-2	-2				-4
Lucy	8	7	6												
Tara	W	3	3	70	70							-2			-2
Charlotte	5	6	6	88	103										
Rachel	6	6	6	103	101	-2									-2
Phillipa	7	7	7	107	113										
Robert	6	6	7	112	111										
Luke	5	6	6	106	113	-2	-2	-2		-2			-3		-11
Julia	7	7	6	122	125						-2				-2
Andrew	3	A	A	73	80						-4	-3	-3		-10
Danny	3	4	4	80	80						-3				-3
Neil	5	5	5	93	93										
Emma	A	A	A												
Shaun	5	3	4	80	76										
Katie	4	4	4	89	87							-2			-2
Phillip	5	5	5	101	105			-3				-3	-2		-8
Karl	4	5	5	89	94	-2				-2	-2	-2			-8
Paul	4	5	5	85	95										
Nicholas	5	6	6	103	103										
Christopher	4	4	5	90	95						-2	-2			-4
Jason	4	5	6	102	106	-3	-2	-3				-2	-2		-12
Sean	4	4	3	80	85						-4				-4
Phillipe	W	3	3	70	71	-2	-2				-2				-6
Carol	4	3	3	71	74										
William	6	7	7	117	117										

Such a report provides powerful information to the head of year, form tutors and heads of department, in two distinct ways.

- The *rows* represent *individual pupils*. We can see from the final column for each individual pupil their *total number of grades adrift from target*. For example, we can see how extreme Luke's current level of performance is. Of the 30 pupils listed, only four are 10 or more grades adrift, including Luke at a total of 11 grades below target. Interestingly, three of the four pupils listed are boys. Is this finding replicated across the entire cohort, with boys predominating? Is there a linking factor? For example, do these pupils perhaps represent a social or peer group?

- The *columns* represent *separate subjects*. Note that many negative figures are recorded for Religious Studies (RS) and Modern Foreign Languages (MFL). Have the departments identified this as an issue? If so, what action has been suggested or taken? It is notable that only seven pupils are adrift in a single subject, and for five of these the subject is RS. Maybe this is because RS is a compulsory subject in this school?

The report has been set up to identify pupils whose performance is a concern because they are underachieving against their potential as indicated by *CAT*. However, there is no reason why a similar report could not be written to show only those results where a pupil's current performance was one or more grades *above* target. We frequently identify concerns; we are sometimes less inclined to celebrate success.

Pupil tracking at Key Stage 3

A similar tracking and monitoring system exists for Key Stage 3 (see Figure 6.1). The system operates on similar principles as for Key Stage 4, with the following exceptions.

- End of Key Stage 3 targets are set on the basis of *CAT* scores gathered at the start of Year 7.

- For the core subjects of English, mathematics and science, the *CAT* indicated level is taken as the target.

- For non-core subjects, *CAT* indicators are not available; this is because there are no national datasets recording pupil level performance in non-core subjects and also because the consistency of teacher assessment in non-core subjects across schools is sometimes questioned. However, in o rder to set targets, St Philip Howard school has analysed the relationship between Year 7 mean *CAT* scores and end of Key Stage 3 teacher assessment for its own pupils in previous years. A regression analysis is completed so that predicted Key Stage 3 levels are generated from the pupils' mean *CAT* score in Year 7. This analysis is completed each year, and the dataset giving the highest predictions is used to set targets for the current Year 7. Essentially, annual targets are set in relation to the school's previous best performance. The school's mean *CAT* score to Key Stage 3 target level table appears in Figure 6.5.

Figure 6.5: St Philip Howard Catholic High School – mean *CAT2E* score to Key Stage 3 target level table

St Philip Howard High School - End of KS3 Target Levels

Correlations based upon progression lines (Mean CAT2E score Y7 vs. Teacher Assessment Y9 July 2000)
To apply to all pupils in KS3 2000/01 related to each individual's mean CAT2E score

NC Subject	1/2	3	3/4	4	4/5	5	5/6	6	6/7	7	8	Correlation coefficent	No. pupils
English (Published CAT indicator used)		70	71-73	74-80	81-93	94-98	99-113	114-118	119-125	126-127	128-130+	0.70	144
Maths (Published CAT indicator used)				70-75	76-85	86-93	94-106	107-113	114-118	119-125	126-130+	0.80	143
Science (Published CAT indicator used)				70	71-85	86-93	94-108	109-116	117-124	125-127	128-130+	0.78	140
Geography					70-74	75-83	84-100	101-108	109-117	118-126	127-130+	0.70	144
History			70-76	77-83	84-94	95-99	100-112	113-116	117-123	124-127	128-130+	0.77	142
French	70-76	77-86	87-97	98-104	105-114	115-119	120-127	128-130+				0.70	143
German		70-75	76-95	96-106	107-127	128-130+						0.44	92
Classics					70-86	87-95	96-115	116-124	125-130+			0.58	142
Religious Studies		70-73	74-83	84-88	89-99	100-105	106-116	117-123	124-127	128-130+		0.59	139
Technology					70-88	89-101	102-124	125-130+				0.50	139
Art						70-80	81-115	116-130+				0.43	144
Music				70-73	74-85	86-97	98-123	124-130+				0.44	143
PE n/a												0.19	144

Progression lines. Correlation coefficent

Date 22/02/01
To be reviewed annually

Please note that the above are intended to be broad target level boundaries based upon the progression lines.
In Modern Foreign Languages the expectation is that at the end of KS3 pupils will on average achieve one level below that in other subjects.

Other correlations:

Mean CAT Y7 vs. Mean CAT Y9 = 0.93   Mean CAT score Y9 vs. Ma NC Test (Y9) = 0.88

CAT RK Y7 vs. PH RK Y7 = 0.85   Mean CAT score Y9 vs. Sc NCTest (Y9) = 0.79

- Current performance in all subjects during Key Stage 3 is recorded using sub-levels indicating whether a pupil has *just attained a particular level* (for example, 5–), is *solidly within the level* (for example, 5) or is *bordering on the next level up* (for example, 5+). This provides sufficient differentiation to record progress.
- *Portfolios of work* and *exemplar material* form an important part of the moderation process within and across departments, providing clarity about the levels of performance necessary to achieve each level, especially in the non-core subjects.

With these exceptions, the process of collating the data, generating reports and monitoring the results is identical to the system described for Key Stage 4.

Summary

The system in place at St Philip Howard school is straightforward: many schools may have similar systems, although not all are as clearly related to measures of pupils' potential or record current performance in quite the same way. The school ascribes a substantial part of its success to the system. Parental attendance at presentation evenings has increased from 45 to over 85 per cent. Over 80 per cent of pupils achieve their *CAT* indicated grade or above, which represents an increase of 10 per cent over a two-year period. About 50 per cent of pupils achieve their target grade or above, which represents an increase of 6 per cent over two years.

Other schools using *CAT* to monitor progress

The focus on *CAT* as a measure of potential is shared by other improving schools. The following quotes are from *Narrowing the Achievement Gap* (DfEE, 2002), which is a guide to good practice in school improvement.

> When I first arrived here in 1998, one of the first targets we had as a management team was to establish a sound basis for assessing pupil potential. For that we used the *Cognitive Abilities Test*, and SATs from Key Stage 2, from which we formed an impression of what a pupil should be able to achieve, and we mapped their day-to-day performance and their half-term performance against that potential. We found that very useful because it gives us a framework in which to operate whereas before you didn't know what a pupil's potential really was.
>
> *Paul Levy, Headteacher, Earlsheaton High School, Dewsbury*

When I first came to the school we just taught the national curriculum. Now ... we apply the pupils' Key Stage 2 data and their *CAT* scores to the work they're doing. If they're an able pupil, we'd look at how we can push them on and fulfil their potential. Also with the lower ability, we look at what things they're weak at, what things they're strong at and actually target them to improve what they're doing.

Tim Nash, ICT Coordinator, Woodlands Community School

We use the *CAT* with all pupils in the second week of term when they come into Year 7. We then have monitoring within departments and the target-setting strategy, which is monitored by the deputy in conjunction with heads of department. All staff are given expected targets, using specific formulae. All staff have a folder of expected targets for every pupil that they teach. It is in the mark book, it is in the grade book, so those targets are a constant reminder of where those pupils should be at as they are going through the year.

Mark Stenton, Assistant Headteacher (Improvement), Kingsdown High School

Review

After reading the last two chapters, you should understand that targets are most likely to be met where:

■ they are informed by a measure of *pupils' potential* and so are realistic but challenging;

■ pupils are actively engaged in *setting* and *owning* the target;

■ there are clear criteria for judgements of *current performance*;

■ the pupil's progress against the target is *monitored and reviewed* on a regular basis;

■ appropriate *intervention* is provided;

■ the target-setting and monitoring processes are *integrated at pupil, subject department and whole-school level.*

7   Measuring and evaluating value added

> **AIMS**
>
> This chapter will:
>
> ■ explain how you can *calculate a measure of the 'value added'* for your class, subject, department or school, by comparing pupils' actual national test or public examination results against the indicators provided by the *CAT*;
>
> ■ provide a Microsoft Excel workbook to support such analyses;
>
> ■ consider some of the detailed questions that can arise from an evaluation of value-added data.

What is 'value added'?

Since 1992, comparative tables of English secondary schools' results in GCSE and A/AS level examinations have been published by the Government (www.dfes.gov.uk/performancetables/). The intention of these initiatives, as outlined in the Parents' Charter (DES, 1991) is to promote greater accountability of the education service and, specifically, to aid parents in their choice of school for their children.

However, the school performance tables have been widely criticised for failing to provide a measure of schools' effectiveness (for example, Strand 1997, 1998 and 1999). Variations in the examination or test results of schools may not accurately reflect their effectiveness, since they substantially reflect factors such as the cognitive ability of the pupils and other factors related to the school's intake. Measures of the educational progress made by pupils in a particular school, relative to that made by *similar* pupils in *other schools*, have come to be called 'value added'. Value-added analyses are fairer and potentially more informative for all intended audiences, including parents and schools themselves.

In 2002, the secondary school performance tables in England for the first time included value-added measures of progress between Key Stage 2 and Key Stage 3, and between Key Stage 3 and GCSE. However, these still fail to provide a measure of pupils' progress over the full five years of secondary education. Value-added analyses using *CAT* enable schools to take account of these factors, as this chapter will explain.

Case study: Ringmer Community College

The Ringmer Community College case study (see Figure 7.1) provides a compelling example of the importance of assessing a school's examination results in relation to the *cognitive ability* or *prior attainment* of the intake. The Principal describes very cogently the misleading picture of the effectiveness of the school provided by 'raw' examination results as published in the school performance tables.

Figure 7.1: Ringmer Community College – case study

Ringmer Community College

School context

Ringmer Community College is an 11 to 16 mixed comprehensive school in Lewes, East Sussex. The total pupil roll in 2002 was 925 pupils, 3 per cent of whom had statements and 15 per cent of whom had non-statemented special educational needs. The school is a designated technology college under the specialist schools programme.

Introduction

Two years ago, Ringmer Community College in East Sussex was awarded an Ofsted 'Oscar' as one of a handful of outstandingly successful comprehensive schools in Chris Woodhead's celebration of excellence. Two weeks ago I was fending off media enquiries about our 'improvement' index of minus 24 points, one of Britain's 'worst performing' schools.

Commentary

I suppose it is possible to plummet from a centre of excellence to worst performing school in three years, but you would have to be pretty determined to do it – good teachers tend to get in the way. And yet it is true that the number of pupils gaining five Grades A* to C has shown a sharp decline from 67 per cent in 1994 to 43 per cent in 1997. Does this signal a collapse in academic standards or the disciplined ethos of the school? Or are there other possible causes?

There are no visible changes to the social composition. No major new housing estates, no sudden migration to independent schools or other local comprehensives, no large factory closure or opening.

It seems the change is simply due to variation in the natural ability of pupils composing a year group. Since we started to relate GCSE success to *Cognitive Ability Test* (*CAT*) scores, we have found the link to be remarkably strong. In 1994, these tests showed that nearly 70 per cent of our pupils were of average ability or above.

That year, we achieved 67 per cent with five Grades A* to C and were seen as one of the best schools in the country. This year, only 45 per cent of pupils were of average ability or better and we achieved 43 per cent Grades A* to C. The link with ability test scores has been equally strong in other years as you can see from the following graph. [See Figure 7.2.]

Disappointingly, there is no sign of consistent improvement and yet over the past 10 years (let alone five) staff have worked hard at improvement strategies – curriculum development, appraisal, Investors in People, homework clubs, extra-curricular activities, mentoring borderline pupils, records of achievement, careers action plans, etc. A cynic might say if the college is to improve, the key task is to improve the intellectual quality of the intake.

If I were tempted to pursue such a policy, I would never get away with it – thank goodness. I feel confident I can be committed to every pupil and still command the support and appreciation of my local community, whatever the league tables suggest.

Figure 7.2: Ringmer Community College – link between *CAT* scores and GCSE results, 1993/97

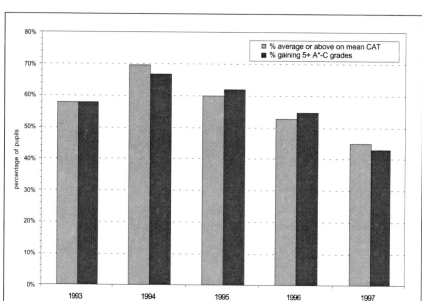

The new requirement to set targets poses interesting dilemmas. If I had been required to set them for each year group over the past five years, I wonder how I would have explained a declining series of targets. The reality is that the intellectual potential of different year groups in the college continues to vary but does not decline. I can be much more optimistic (but not complacent) about next year's results.

But if I adopt an approach on the experience of the past five years, I will be setting targets that go up and down. How do I justify such apparently strange variations to parents and pupils? Do I say: 'Look, you are not such a good year group as last year's Year 11, so I have to set you a lower target?' Year groups are all too easily labelled good or bad without the Head leading the process. And if these targets are met, they will suggest wild swings in 'improvement' on the Government's new indicator. It clearly measures nothing worthwhile at all.

We have to move away from comparisons of performance based on five Grades A* to C. It is the worst possible indicator. We must move rapidly to value-added measures – however inadequate our basis might be. League tables based on five Grades A* to C must be consigned to the dustbin before they do even more damage to our educational system.

Perhaps the best way forward for a government committed to inclusive schools is a national programme of cognitive ability testing at ages nine and 14 years as a basis for measuring school effectiveness.

John Wakely, Principal, Ringmer Community College.
(Times Educational Supplement, 1997)

Understanding outcomes and setting realistic targets

Three key points arise from the Ringmer Community College case study:

■ If we wish to understand variation in outcomes such as public examination results, then we need to interpret the results *in relation to pupils' cognitive ability or prior attainment*.

■ Expectations of annual incremental improvement do not accord well with reality. As those who work in and with schools know, there is *considerable year-on-year variation* between cohorts.

■ If we are to set targets, these must be related to the cognitive *ability or prior attainment of the cohort* for whom the targets are being set. Year groups can differ markedly in their ability and attainment. It is therefore nonsensical to base targets simply on 'last year's results plus x per cent'. Targets must relate to the ability of the cohort for whom they are set.

You may be interested to know that the Principal's optimism in 1997 about future GCSE results at the College, based on the *CAT* scores of the lower year groups, was well placed. Results at Ringmer Community College have returned to the high levels seen in the mid-1990s, with 62 per cent, 72 per cent and 65 per cent of pupils achieving five or more GCSE Grades A* to C grades in 2000, 2001 and 2002 respectively.

Using the *CAT3* Excel workbook to assess your school's value added

Introduction

The graph presented in the Ringmer Community College case study (see Figure 7.2) is a crude example of the value-added principle. It shows that, at an aggregate level, there is an association between the mean *CAT* score of a cohort and the average GCSE results the cohort subsequently achieves. However, professionals in this area of research emphasise that it is vital to complete value-added analyses using *individual pupil level* data. The Microsoft Excel workbook, provided in the accompanying CD, will allow you to do exactly this.

What analyses are available?

This section explains how you can use the *CAT3*-GCSE Excel workbook to conduct a value-added analysis of the overall GCSE/GNVQ performance of pupils in your school. The value-added analysis compares the progress made by pupils in your school with the progress made by a nationally representative sample of over 100,000 pupils. Progress is measured by comparing the relationship between pupils' *CAT3* scores and subsequent GCSE/GNVQ point scores in your school with the nationally representative dataset.

The CD also contains a similar workbook to support value-added analyses of *CAT3* to Key Stage 3 results. The principles of the analysis are exactly the same as described here for GCSE. Specific instructions in using the Key Stage 3 workbook are included in the first sheet of the workbook.

These workbooks are based on *CAT3* data. You cannot use these workbooks with *CAT2E* scores. However, you can download similar workbooks for *CAT2E* from the nferNelson *CAT* website (see www.nfer-nelson.co.uk/cat).

Introducing the value-added workbook

In Microsoft Excel, the term 'workbook' refers to the entire Excel file. The workbook consists of multiple 'worksheets', each identified by name at the bottom of the screen. In this case, the various worksheets provide tables and charts for use in your value-added analysis. The workbook is suitable for use with pupils who have completed *CAT3* assessments at any point prior to GCSE, although in the majority of cases the *CAT* will have been completed in either Year 7 or Year 9.

Making a start

To begin using the workbook:

■ *enter your pupils' data* in columns A to E of the sheet labelled 'PupilData' (*do not* enter any data in columns F to R);

■ use *one row for each pupil*, as shown in Table 7.1.

Table 7.1: Entering your pupils' data in the Excel worksheet labelled 'PupilData'

Pupil ID	Plot label	Mean *CAT3* score	GCSE/GNVQ Total points score	GCSE/GNVQ Best 8 points score
123	Ben	120	46	42
667	Alison	90	35	30

Please note that the analysis is limited to a maximum entry of 500 pupils. The three scores you need to enter are:

Mean *CAT3* score

The value-added analysis here is limited to *CAT3* scores of between 70 and 130. This is because the limited numbers of pupils scoring above or below these figures make the analysis in these extremes of the distribution unreliable. In order to ensure that pupils with scores outside this range are included, ensure that you *recode scores below 70 to 70* and *scores above 130 to 130.*

Total GCSE/GNVQ points score

For GCSE *full courses*, grades are converted to points using the following scale: A*=8, A=7, B=6, C=5, D=4, E=3, F=2, G=1 U/X=0. For GCSE *short courses*, each grade is assigned *half* the number of points of the *full course* grade. For example, a Grade C in a GCSE Geography short course would be assigned 2.5 points.

For GNVQ, the points awarded depend on whether the qualification is a *Full or Part One course*, whether it is at *Intermediate or Foundation level*, and whether it was graded *Distinction, Merit or Pass*. Full details on all the points score equivalencies are contained in the technical annexe to the performance tables (www.dfes.gov.uk/performancetables). The total points score is the sum of all the points gained by the pupil.

GCSE/GNVQ Best 8 points score

Calculate the Best 8 points score by summing the points scores for the best eight subjects taken by the pupil. Again, see the Secondary School Performance Tables for details on completing the calculation.

What scores are generated?

Once you have entered your pupils' data, the following scores will be generated:

■ *expected GCSE/GNVQ points scores*, based on the national dataset, will be calculated in the tables;

■ points representing your pupils' *CAT scores* and their *GCSE/GNVQ points scores* will be plotted in the charts.

There are two separate charts, which plot the relationships with:

■ GCSE/GNVQ total points score (**CAT3_TPS**);

■ GCSE/GNVQ Best 8 points score (**CAT3_Best8**).

The tables show *actual* and *expected* results, for each pupil and for the group. They also show *differences* between actual and expected results, flagging up those pupils whose actual scores are *above* or *below* the level expected from their *CAT* scores. These 'difference scores' can be taken as a measure of the value-added for the pupil.

Adding pupils' names to the charts

To add pupils' names to the charts you will need to download some software. This software, *XY Chart Labeller*, is available from www.appspro.com; you should find a link to this site from the *CAT* website (www.nfer-nelson.co.uk/cat). Once you are on the appspro.com site, you should:

■ click on 'Free Utilities';

■ select the chart labeller;

■ download the .exe file to your hard disk;

■ run the .exe file from your disk;

■ open Microsoft Excel, and go to Tools/Add-ins;

■ select the XY Labeller option.

XY Chart Labeller should now be installed. To add labels in each chart, you will need to:

▓ click on the **CAT3_TPS** or **CAT3_Best8** tab, or anywhere within these worksheets;

▓ select Tools/XY Chart Labels/Add Chart Labels;

▓ in the window which pops up:
  – under 'Select a Data Series to Label', select Pupils;
  – under 'Select a Label Range', type =Pupildata!$B$4:$B$500
  – select OK.

How do I interpret the results?

1. The quartile charts

The lines in the quartile charts show the relationship between pupils' *CAT* scores and GCSE/GNVQ points scores in the national sample. The thick red middle line on each graph is the median line. The median line splits the data set in half and so shows the GCSE scores achieved by pupils in the middle of the distribution for any given mean *CAT* score:

▓ the upper line (upper quartile) shows the GCSE scores achieved by pupils at the top 25 per cent of the distribution;

▓ the lower line (lower quartile) shows the results achieved by pupils at the bottom 25 per cent of the distribution.

Half the pupils, or 50 per cent of the national sample, fall on or between the upper and lower quartile lines. For example, for a mean *CAT* score of 100:

▓ 50 per cent of pupils achieved a GCSE/GNVQ Best 8 points score of between 32 and 43;

▓ 25 per cent of pupils achieved Best 8 points scores below 32, and 25 per cent achieved Best 8 points scores of more than 43.

By comparing the position of the points representing your pupils' scores with the national lines, you can identify those pupils who have made above average, average or below average progress compared to other pupils of the same age and ability nationally (see Figure 7.3 for an example):

▓ pupils falling *on or between* the upper and lower quartile lines can be said to be making the *progress expected* of their age and ability;

▓ pupils falling *above the upper quartile line* can be said to be making *above average progress* given their age and ability;

▓ pupils falling *below the lower quartile line* can be said to be making *below average progress* given their age and ability.

Figure 7.3: Best 8 quartile chart for an example group

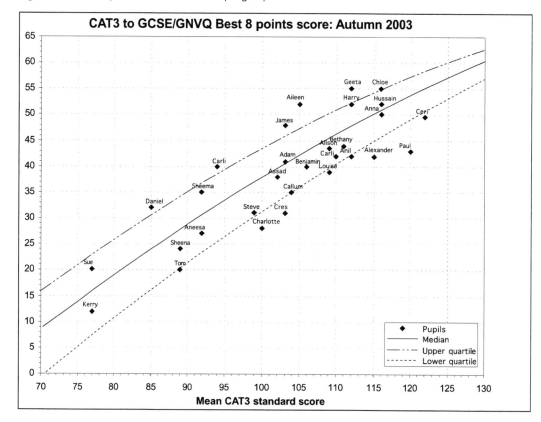

Figure 7.3 shows that Daniel and Geeta achieved very different levels of success in GCSE/GNVQ. For example, Daniel achieved the equivalent of eight GCSEs at Grade D, while Geeta achieved the equivalent of eight A grades. However, both pupils achieved significantly higher points scores than were achieved by pupils of similar cognitive ability in the national sample. At the other extreme, Paul's performance was disappointingly below the lower quartile line. More would have been expected of Paul based on his high mean *CAT* score of 120.

2. The pupil listing

It can be difficult to interpret the quartile charts where the results of a large group of pupils, such as a whole cohort, are being plotted. For example, if data are being plotted for a six-form entry school with a cohort of 180 pupils, multiple pupils may have the same *CAT* and GCSE/GNVQ points scores. It will not be possible to tell if a particular point represents one or more than one pupil. The graph may also be too 'crowded' to read easily.

The information for each pupil is therefore given in a different format in the calculated columns of the 'PupilData' worksheet. Three values are calculated for each pupil:

■ The *expected* points score – This is based on the pupil's mean *CAT3* score and is calculated using the relationship between *CAT* scores and GCSE/GNVQ point scores established by the national dataset.

- The *difference* between the actual score and the expected score – This will be *positive* where the pupil's actual points score is *higher* than their expected score, and *negative* where the actual points score is *lower* than the expected score.
- The *quartiles* flag – This indicates whether the pupil's GCSE score is falling *above* the upper quartile (U) or *below* the lower quartile (L). The results are shown as:
  - U = attainment above the national upper quartile line;
  - L = attainment below the national lower quartile line;
  - Blank = attainment as expected: on or between the upper and lower quartiles.

Figure 7.4 shows the results for the example group whose results were displayed in the quartile graph shown in Figure 7.3. For clarity, these results have been sorted by the size of the difference between actual and expected Best 8 points score. Similar results are shown: Daniel and Geeta are among a group of five pupils with much higher points scores than expected, while Paul's Best 8 points score is over 10 points lower than expected.

Figure 7.4: Example of the pupil listing for the group

Pupil ID	Plot label	Mean CAT3 score	GCSE/GNVQ total points score (TPS)	GCSE/GNVQ Best 8 points score (Best 8)	Total points score	Best 8 points score	Actual - Expected: TPS	Actual - Expected: Best 8	Upper (U)/ Lower (L) Quartile: TPS	Upper (U)/ Lower (L) Quartile: Best 8
545408	Paul	120	52	43	65.3	53.7	-13.3	-10.7	L	L
545321	Charlotte	100	33	28	43.2	37.7	-10.2	-9.7	L	L
545292	Cres	103	37	31	46.5	40.3	-9.5	-9.3	L	L
545315	Alexander	115	48	42	59.8	50.2	-11.8	-8.2	L	L
545240	Tom	89	20	20	31.0	27.7	-11.0	-7.7	L	L
545363	Louise	109	43	39	53.2	45.3	-10.2	-6.3	L	L
545300	Callum	104	41	35	47.6	41.1	-6.6	-6.1		
545302	Steve	99	36	31	42.1	36.8	-6.1	-5.8		
545389	Anil	112	50	42	56.5	47.8	-6.5	-5.8		L
545268	Ceri	122	57	50	67.6	54.8	-10.6	-5.3	L	L
545205	Carli	110	47	42	54.3	46.1	-7.3	-4.1		
545288	Kerry	77	12	12	17.8	16.0	-5.8	-4.0		
545355	Sheena	89	24	24	31.0	27.7	-7.0	-3.7		
545310	Aneesa	92	30	27	34.4	30.5	-4.4	-3.5		
545358	Bethany	111	50	44	55.4	47.0	-5.4	-3.0		
545353	Benjamin	106	46	40	49.9	42.8	-3.9	-2.8		
545361	Alison	109	56	44	53.2	45.3	2.8	-1.8		
545224	Assad	102	43	38	45.4	39.4	-2.4	-1.4		
545193	Anna	116	55	50	60.9	51.0	-5.9	-1.0		
545327	Adam	103	46	41	46.5	40.3	-0.5	0.7		
545187	Hussain	116	57	52	60.9	51.0	-3.9	1.0		
545237	Sue	77	20	20	17.8	16.0	2.2	4.0		
545179	Chloe	116	60	55	60.9	51.0	-0.9	4.0		
545215	Harry	112	58	52	56.5	47.8	1.5	4.2		
545325	Sheema	92	38	35	34.4	30.5	3.6	4.5		
545341	Geeta	112	68	55	56.5	47.8	11.5	7.2	U	U
545229	Carli	94	46	40	36.6	32.3	8.9	7.7	U	U
545287	James	103	61	48	46.5	40.3	14.0	7.7	U	U
545331	Daniel	85	35	32	26.6	23.9	8.4	8.1	U	U
545303	Aileen	105	62	52	48.7	42.0	13.3	10.0	U	U

3. Group summary

The last section of the worksheet presents a summary of the value-added performance of the group. An example of the summary for the example group is presented in Figure 7.5 and described below.

■ The table above the graph gives the group statistics (mean, standard deviation and sample size) for mean CAT3 score, actual GCSE/GNVQ points scores, expected GCSE/GNVQ points scores and the difference or 'value-added' scores. For the example group, pupils on average achieved a total points score around 2.6 points lower than expected from their CAT3 scores, and a Best 8 points score around 1.4 points lower than expected from their CAT3 scores.

Figure 7.5: Summary of value added for the group

GROUP SUMMARY REPORT

Mean, Standard Deviation and number of pupils	Actual	Expected	Difference
Mean CAT score	103.3		
Standard Deviation	12.0		
Number of pupils	30		
Total points score	44.3	46.9	-2.6
Standard Deviation	13.8	13.2	7.7
Number of pupils	30	30	30
Best 8 points score	38.8	40.1	-1.4
Standard Deviation	11.1	10.5	6.0
Number of pupils	30	30	30

Mean Difference with 95% Confidence Bands

Pupils in quartile bands: TPS	Actual	Expected	Difference
Upper quartile	17%	25%	-8%
Average	60%	50%	10%
Lower quartile	23%	25%	-2%
Total number of pupils	30		

Pupils in quartile bands: Best 8	Actual	Expected	Difference
Upper quartile	17%	25%	-8%
Average	57%	50%	7%
Lower quartile	27%	25%	2%
Total number of pupils	30		

■ The graph displays the mean of the difference scores (the average value added) for total points score and for Best 8 points score. As explained in Chapter 4 (page 74) we need to place a confidence band around mean scores to reflect the sample size and the spread of scores within the group. Therefore 95 per cent confidence bands are also shown around the mean scores. Where these confidence bands overlap with the 'zero' line, the mean score for the group is not *significantly* different from the expected score, given the number of pupils and the spread of scores in the group. For the example group, the GCSE/GNVQ points scores are lower than expected given the *CAT3* scores of the pupils, but not to a statistically significant level.

■ The bottom tables report the percentage of pupils in the group whose GCSE/GNVQ points scores fall above the upper quartile line, on or between the quartile lines, or below the lower quartile line for total points score and for Best 8 points score respectively. The expected percentages (25:50:25) and the variation from the expected percentages (difference) are also shown. For the example group, in relation to Best 8 points score, 17 per cent of pupils performed above the upper quartile, or 8 per cent less than the expected proportion, while 27 per cent performed below the lower quartile, or 2 per cent more than the expected proportion.

Further analysis of the results

Subjects and departments

The above analyses allow an assessment of pupils' overall progress in relation to their prior *CAT* reasoning scores. Taking account of prior reasoning scores is an important factor in evaluating how well a school has helped its pupils to make progress. However, because these analyses are based on GCSE/GNVQ total or Best 8 points scores, they may obscure significant differences between subjects or departments. There may be very large positive effects for some subjects, but very large negative effects for others. As the subject differences may cancel each other out, they may be masked in the overall analyses.

School effectiveness research from the early 1980s onwards strongly suggests that only a minority of schools perform consistently across subjects. In the vast majority of schools, performance in one department is only weakly linked to performance in another. You can have a good mathematics department and a poor science department, a competent English department and a poor French one – and of course all the numerous combinations in between (Sammons, Thomas and Mortimore, 1997).

CALCULATING THE VALUE ADDED FOR SUBJECTS AND DEPARTMENTS
You can, of course, complete further analyses for individual subjects or departments.

■ First, convert the *CAT* indicated grades into *indicated points scores*. For GCSE employ the usual system of A*=8, A=7, B=6, C=5 ... (see page 137). Where the indicator is a *split grade*, this should be allocated a score *between* the two relevant grades (for example, A/B=6.5; B/C= 5.5; C/D=4.5, and so on). For Scottish Standard Grade the system is simplified, since the outcomes are already expressed in numeric form. You will, however, need to convert split grades using the same principle as explained for GCSE (for example, '1/2'=1.5, '2/3'=2.5 and so on).

■ Second, for each pupil calculate the difference between their *indicated* grade (as a points score) and their *actual* grade (as a points score). Technically, this difference is called the *'residual'*.

■ Third, sum these residuals for all the pupils taking a subject to get an average residual for the subject. We will call this the *'subject residual'* to distinguish it from the pupil-level residuals calculated in the step above.

The analysis controls for variations in examination grades associated with pupils' cognitive ability, and the question evaluated becomes: 'How well have pupils in my subject achieved, *compared to pupils of the same ability taking the same subject in other schools?'* An example for a Scottish secondary school is shown in Figure 7.6.

The school entered pupils for a total of 23 Standard Grade subjects. For each subject, the graph shows the number of pupils entered and the average residual (the average difference between the indicated and actual grades):

■ where the *residual* for a subject is *zero*, then pupils have on average achieved exactly the grades expected from their *CAT* indicators;

■ where the *residual* is *positive* (greater than zero), then on average pupils have achieved *above* their *CAT* indicated grades;

Figure 7.6: Value-added analysis for individual subjects within an example school

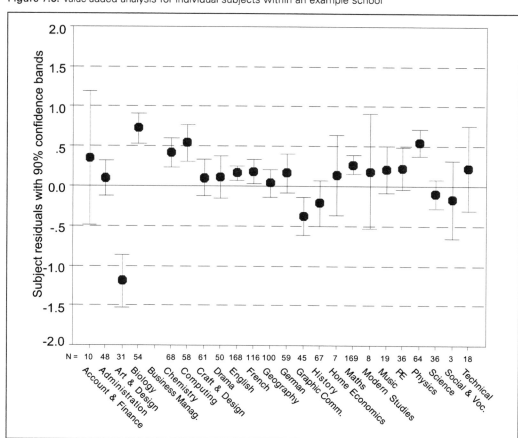

▪ where the *residual* is *negative*, then on average pupils have achieved *below* their *CAT* indicated grades.[1]

Thus we can see the results for Biology are very strong, with pupils achieving nearly three-quarters (0.75) of a grade higher than pupils of similar ability in other schools. Conversely, results in Art and Design are relatively weak, as pupils are achieving on average over a whole grade lower than pupils of the same ability in other schools.

In interpreting the results, it is important to place confidence bands around the subject residuals. The lower the number of pupils taking the subject, and the greater the variation in the pupil-level residuals within the subject (as measured by the standard deviation), the more likely it is that any variation in the subject residual is due to chance factors alone.

The question is, to what extent is the subject residual indicative of a genuine effect, rather than random variation? Ninety per cent confidence intervals have therefore been placed around the residuals for each subject. These can be calculated as summarised in Figure 4.5, described in detail on pages 77 to 79 of Chapter 4, and shown in the 'Compare' workbook. Where these confidence bands cross the average 'zero' line, then performance is not significantly different from expected. Where the entire confidence band is above the zero line then performance is significantly better than expected. Where the entire confidence band is below the zero line, then performance is significantly below the expected level.

For this school, performance is particularly strong in the sciences such as Biology, Chemistry and Physics, and also in Computing Studies, mathematics and French. Performance is below expected levels in Art and Design and Graphic Communication.

Teaching groups

Figure 7.7 on page 144 shows the value-added analysis of results for GCSE Business Studies in a particular school. Pupils were taught in three teaching groups, so the report contains four sets of 'indicated versus actual' bars: one for each class and a fourth for the department total. The overall results for the department are positive, showing a subject residual of 0.43, indicating that, on average, pupils achieve almost half a grade higher than the *CAT* indicated grade.

However, it is interesting to look at the results for *each teaching group*, set according to ability, as can be seen by the difference in the indicated points score for each class:

▪ the *upper* (11.1) and *middle* (11.2) ability sets show positive value added, with residuals of 0.20 and 0.75 respectively;

▪ the *lower* set (11.3) does not appear to have performed so well, having a negative residual of –0.25.

---

[1] In Standard Grade, the highest level of attainment is scored 1 and the lowest level of attainment is scored 7. We have therefore calculated the pupil-level residuals as (**Indicated grade–Actual grade**), so that a higher-than-indicated grade has a positive value. For GCSE the highest level of attainment is scored 8 and the lowest is scored 0. The method of calculating the pupil-level residuals is therefore reversed (**Actual grade–Indicated grade**) in order to maintain a positive value for a better-than-indicated grade.

Figure 7.7: Example of a GCSE department value-added analysis using *CAT3* indicated points score

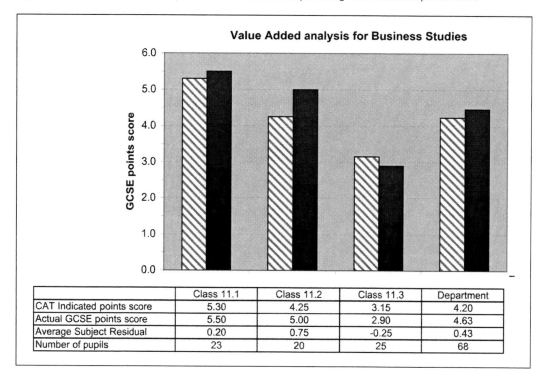

	Class 11.1	Class 11.2	Class 11.3	Department
CAT Indicated points score	5.30	4.25	3.15	4.20
Actual GCSE points score	5.50	5.00	2.90	4.63
Average Subject Residual	0.20	0.75	-0.25	0.43
Number of pupils	23	20	25	68

There may be particular issues for this department to address in relation to setting. Where are the most effective teachers deployed? What attention is paid to the self-esteem of pupils in the lower set? How can the performance of the lower set be improved?

Relating *CAT* scores to performance in individual subjects provides powerful information about the effectiveness of each department because one of the major sources of variation between departments, the ability of the pupils taking the subject, has been controlled.

However, it is important not to ignore other relevant data sources, particularly where these are easily accessible. For example, in analysing departmental effectiveness, schools in England also have access to the relative performance indicators (RPI) from the Additional Information section of Ofsted's Performance and Assessment reports (PANDA). This data, contained in Table S6 and its associated chart, are a further means for considering how each department may be contributing to the school's overall level of success. As with all assessment and data analysis, multiple sources of evidence are an important strength in seeking to understand performance fully.

Only schools have access to their PANDA reports: however, other readers will find an anonymised version on the Ofsted website (www.ofsted.gov.uk).

Groups of pupils

Just as the GCSE/GNVQ points score analysis may obscure differences between subjects or departments, averages calculated for all pupils may also mask differences between the progress of particular groups of pupils: for example, girls and boys.

The quartiles column in the tables of the 'Quartile' workbook may help identify particular groups with different patterns of results:

- Are pupils above the upper quartile (U), or below the lower quartile (L), more often drawn from particular groups (for example, different levels of ability, different teaching groups or sets, gender groups, stage of fluency in English or with special educational needs)?

- Plot the results for different groups using different colours or symbols. Do any patterns emerge?

Many people plot the results for different groups onto separate overhead transparencies, so that they can be overlaid. Some groups may be flagged up as particular successes for the school, or as being in need of particular attention and support in the future.

Another approach, within a subject or department, is to plot the actual grades achieved in a subject against the *CAT* indicated grades. Figures 7.8 and 7.9 show examples for the geography department of the school shown in Figure 7.6.

Figure 7.8: Comparison of actual versus indicated Standard Grade results for Geography

Geography Department - Scottish Standard Grade

number students = 100

Actual grade achieved	1	1/2	2	2/3	3	3/4	4	4/5	5	5/6
7										
6						2		1	3	1
5				1	1	5	3	4		
4		1		1	1	4	5	3	1	1
3			3	3	7	5	2			
2		1	9	9	6	2				
1	2	1	6	1	4		1			

CAT indicated grade

Pupils in the shaded cells of Figure 7.8 have achieved the indicated grades. Pupils in the cells above have achieved somewhat lower than indicated grades, while those in the cells below have achieved better-than-indicated grades. Again, are there any communalities amongst the pupils with below expected or above expected performance?

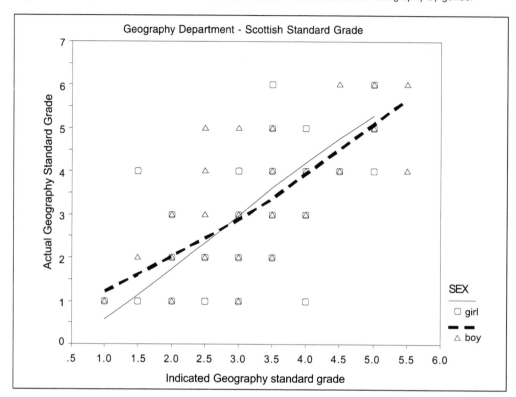

Figure 7.9: Comparison of actual versus indicated Standard Grade results for Geography by gender

Figure 7.9 shows the same data expressed as a graph, plotting the actual Geography grade against the indicated grade and calculating the mean scores separately for boys and girls. This appears to show lower levels of attainment for the more able boys taking the subject, relative to girls of the same ability. This may simply reflect the small number of pupils achieving the higher grades, but is an example of the type of question that is worthy of further exploration.

The above examples are ways of seeing clearly the pupils who have made greater or less progress than is expected. The following is a useful checklist of questions to ask of such data (QCA, 2002).

If some pupils are making significantly more or less progress than the majority, are they:

- boys?
- girls?
- pupils who have joined the school recently?
- pupils of different ability levels?
- pupils with special educational needs?
- pupils for whom English is an additional language?
- pupils who are entitled to free school meals?
- pupils who miss particular classes regularly or miss long periods of schooling?
- pupils from a minority ethnic group?

Alternatively, are they pupils:

- with a particular teacher?
- in a particular set?
- who have had extra support?
- who were supported by booster classes or targeted literacy/numeracy support?
- who followed a particular scheme of work?
- whose teachers used different teaching practices?

If there are classes or groups in which the majority of pupils make better-than-average progress, were strategies implemented that may have made the difference? Such strategies could include:

- careful monitoring;
- effective assessment practice (with clear learning objectives and feedback related to the objectives);
- precisely targeted work;
- breakfast or homework clubs;
- support links for pupils to the school ICT network;
- particular in-service training [INSET] for the teachers;
- better resources, such as accommodation?

Review

This chapter has covered a range of issues related to value-added assessment. The following are a few selected points to remember:

- value-added analyses are essential if you wish to obtain an indication of the effectiveness of your class, subject, department or school in national test or public examination terms; Microsoft Excel workbooks are included on the CD to support you in calculating the *overall value added for groups or cohorts* at your school in Key Stage 3 tests or GCSE examinations;
- schools are rarely uniformly effective, or uniformly ineffective, across all subjects or departments; typically, *schools contain a mixture of strong and weak departments*;
- schools' effectiveness may differ with *different pupil groups, sets or classes*; you should consider further diagnostic analysis of your value-added results;
- for maximum flexibility, always *request the scoring service data disk option* so that you receive the *CAT* scores and indicators in electronic format: the data can then be read into your school's management information system or analysed directly in databases or spreadsheets.

8

CAT in a wider context

AIMS

The aims of this chapter are to:

■ discuss some common misconceptions about reasoning ability, the relationship between *CAT* and thinking skills, and whether reasoning abilities can be taught;

■ discuss the relationship between *CAT* and end of Key Stage 2 tests, and how the results can be combined in target setting for Key Stage 3 or GCSE;

■ discuss different methods of reporting to parents, including examples of school practice;

■ consider some recent developments in the *CAT*, specifically the levels for older pupils and the development of online testing.

CAT and thinking skills

Is reasoning ability innate?

As explained in Chapter 1 (see page 4), *CAT* measures *developed* abilities. A common misunderstanding is that reasoning tests (including *CAT*) measure *innate* abilities, independent of motivation, experience or education. A related assumption is that achievement or attainment tests measure only the knowledge and skills acquired through schooling.

These assumptions may be associated with the historical use of group reasoning tests in the UK between the 1950s and early 1970s to determine entry to selective secondary schools (grammar schools) at age 11. To support their use for selection, it was necessary to assume that reasoning tests were measures of innate ability, a fixed invariant capacity of the pupil, stable over time and relatively impervious to teaching. However, we should remember that selection was primarily a political rather than an educational issue and that these assumptions were heavily contested, even at that time (for example, Kamin, 1974).

Modern interpretations view reasoning tests as assessing developed abilities, arising from the interaction of biology and experience. From this perspective, reasoning abilities reflect the pupils' experiences up to the time of testing, rather than providing an indication of fixed potential (Whetton, 1995).

Ability and achievement and physical skills: an analogy

A useful means of understanding the relationship between ability and achievement (taken from Lohman and Hagen, 2001, page 24) is through an analogy to physical skills.

Let us consider the general reasoning abilities assessed through *CAT* as being similar to general physical fitness. Let us also assume that the knowledge and skills that pupils develop in different areas of study is like proficiency in particular sports (such as football, swimming or tennis). Physical fitness is an aptitude for learning different sports: a pupil's likely performance in a range of sports might broadly be related to his or her level of physical fitness. The pupil who is more physically fit might find it easier to learn physically demanding activities across a wide range of sports including football, tennis, track events etc.

However, this is too simple a conception. Physical fitness is also an outcome of participation in physically demanding activities. Pupils who are active football players not only become better footballers, they also increase their aerobic capacity and improve their overall level of physical fitness. Similarly, pupils who learn how to prove theorems in a geometry class, to solve applied problems in a mathematics class or evaluate source documents in a history class also learn to reason in more sophisticated ways.

With this analogy in mind, it is possible to see the fallacy of characterising reasoning ability as innate: it is like saying that a good measure of physical fitness should somehow be independent of every sport or physical activity in which the pupil has ever engaged. It would be impossible to devise such a measure. All abilities – physical and cognitive – are developed through exercise and experience. This has important implications for teaching, which are discussed further below.

CAT as an indicator of potential

The fact that reasoning is a developed ability does not negate the usefulness of *CAT* as an indicator of potential. The strength of *CAT* is that it assesses reasoning abilities in a decontextualised, or at least context-reduced, setting. There is a fair amount of agreement amongst teachers on what characterises outstanding performance. Examples include:

- seeing patterns in data;
- making links with other topics or areas;
- generalising (and exploring exceptions);
- seeing different viewpoints;
- solving problems;
- checking and refining solutions, etc.

To assess these skills in context requires a tremendous amount of content or subject knowledge, and would be extremely time consuming if the assessment were to be reliable. For example, consider a history class examining the causes of World War I.

Outstanding performance will require the pupil to know about the history and decay of the Austro-Hungarian empire, economic theory, the process of industrialisation and the rise of an urban working class, the interconnected nature of the royal families of Europe at the time and the personality of the Kaiser. Assessment within a subject is context laden. Someone with limited knowledge will be disadvantaged.

In contrast, *CAT* assesses general transferable skills by keeping the stimulus material simple, clear and familiar with minimal specialised content or knowledge. By reducing the knowledge demands to simple words and sentences, numbers and basic number operations, or even simple shapes and figures, *CAT* attempts to assess pupils' reasoning abilities without the requirement of a wide and detailed knowledge base.

Assessing the building blocks of learning

The reasoning abilities assessed by *CAT* may therefore be viewed as basic building blocks of learning. The ability to recognise similarities, analogies, patterns and relationships are fundamental to understanding and assimilating new information and ideas. They enable pupils to make sense of new information and relate it to what they already know. They are used wherever and whenever pupils learn – for example, in:

- learning associations between speech sounds and their written representations;
- recognising similarities between words when learning to read and spell;
- identifying number patterns;
- seeing an analogy between instructions for building a model and recipes for cooking or even between scenes in a film and paragraphs in text.

As a consequence, scores on reasoning tests give an indication of how easily pupils will acquire new concepts and master new material in a wide range of school subjects, based on their current levels of functioning. Reasoning scores are therefore strongly related to success in a whole range of school outcomes.

Using *CAT* to plan learning

As we saw in Chapter 5, a strong relationship exists between *CAT* scores and pupils' performance in national tests and examinations across a wide range of subjects. Even where a pupil's current levels of academic performance may be low, the indicators show levels of performance that can reasonably be expected of the pupil. In this sense, *CAT* provides a useful measure of a pupil's potential level of achievement.

However, *CAT* scores should not be used to constrain expectations for a pupil's performance: see Chapter 5 (pages 111 to 113) and 'Reporting *CAT* results to parents' (page 157).

Can reasoning ability be taught?

The answer to this question is yes, but it depends on the teaching or intervention adopted. Superficial interventions, such as teaching to the test, may increase *CAT* scores in the short term, but the resulting changes are often transient and unlikely to lead to significant long-term improvement in underlying abilities. However, sustained and high-quality teaching *will* improve pupils' reasoning abilities. This follows directly from the conception of reasoning as a developed ability, as discussed above.

Teaching to the test

There may be a temptation, especially with low-scoring pupils, to give pupils specific instruction in tasks similar to those employed in *CAT*. However, the decontextualised nature of the *CAT* tasks, which is a strength for assessment purposes, makes them inappropriate as a focus for teaching. A narrow focus, such as teaching tasks very similar to the nine *CAT* subtests, is likely to lead to surface and context-specific learning. Pupils may become adept at the few tasks taught, but are not necessarily able to transfer these skills to other types of reasoning tasks. Similar types of tasks sometimes occur naturally in the curriculum: for example, classification exercises, which arise naturally in science or other subject contexts. When such tasks are embedded into normal classroom activity, and if low-scoring pupils are given more time and practice on them, they may be effective. In general, however, teaching to the test is not a good idea.

Teaching thinking skills

The way to develop reasoning abilities is through good teaching and challenging learning activities. The national curriculum in England (DfEE, 1999) explicitly refers to five thinking skills:

- information processing;
- reasoning;
- enquiry;
- creative thinking;
- evaluation.

The very description of these as 'skills' implies a taught or learnable component. This is not to suggest that pupils are passive recipients in the process of skill acquisition: developmental psychology emphasises the importance of the active role of pupils in constructing and developing their own thinking (for example, Adey and Shayer, 1994).

Reports from the DfES (2002c) suggest that, where thinking skills are taught well, the lessons:

- provide open and challenging tasks that encourage pupils to think through a problem or issue that may have no single correct answer;
- encourage pupils to use and build on what they already know in order to make sense of new information;
- use problems, and require pupils to make decisions, that are relevant to their 'real-life' experiences;
- offer opportunities for work in collaborative groups with high-quality talk;

- involve intervening, when necessary, by asking questions that support or extend pupils' thinking;
- develop pupils' metacognitive thinking – the ability to monitor, reflect, evaluate and regulate their own thinking processes;
- help pupils to make connections between the thinking involved in the lesson and other contexts (bridging activities) to encourage the transfer of reasoning skills and to consolidate their use.

QUESTIONING AND 'WAIT TIME'

Questions are the most common form of interaction between teacher and pupils in whole-class lessons, as well as in group and individual work. Questioning is a key method of altering the level of challenge provided and determining the progress made in lessons. Many authors consider questioning an essential prerequisite to better thinking. However, research suggests that the average 'wait time' between a teacher asking a question and either receiving a response, asking another question or answering their own question, is 0.9 seconds (Rowe, 1974).

If we want pupils to think about a question, we must allow time for a thoughtful response and develop an atmosphere in which everyone is expected to think. If the wait-time is increased to a mere three seconds, there can be a huge increase in the number of pupils responding, the depth of the answers given and the range of language used. Similarly, research has suggested that less than 1 per cent of teachers' questions elicit more than a literal response (Goodlad, 1984). There is huge potential in using questioning to encourage analysis, evaluation and justification in order to extend and develop thinking – rather than asking questions simply to test for knowledge or factual understanding.

TEACHING MATERIALS AVAILABLE

It is beyond the remit of this book to examine effective teaching strategies in any great detail. However, excellent resource material does exist for the teaching of thinking skills. There are at least three intervention programmes that have been tested and validated in terms of their impact on pupils' thinking skills:

- The *Cognitive Acceleration through Science (CASE)* and *Cognitive Acceleration through Mathematics (CAME)* programmes provide prepared resources as interventions to be delivered over a two-year period within these specific subjects; nferNelson publishes a range of materials by the same authors (Philip Adey and his team at King's College), with the series title *Let's Think!* (see Adey *et al.*, 2003);
- *Philosophy in the Classroom* (Lipman, Sharp and Oscanyan, 1980) is also delivered through a subject-specific route, this time the English or social studies curriculum;
- *A Guide to Better Thinking* (Kite, 2000) is a stand-alone programme for 10 to 12 year olds, designed to be implemented over one term with two or three weekly sessions.

Helping pupils to become better learners

A more generalised source of materials is the Key Stage 3 Strategy training materials for the foundation subjects (DfES, 2002c). These contain 14 detailed staff development training modules, focusing on themes designed to expand teachers' repertoire of strategies and skills. The modules include:

- assessment for learning in everyday lessons;
- the effective use of questioning to promote thinking;
- explaining as a teaching skill;
- modelling as a teaching strategy;
- providing challenging learning opportunities;
- the principles for teaching thinking;
- the use of starters and plenary sessions;
- promoting pupils' engagement in learning;
- talk as a tool for thinking and learning;
- the importance of reflection, a discussion of metacognition;
- identifying principal concepts and skills in foundation subjects.

The materials are available free from the DfES website at www.standards.dfes.gov.uk/keystage3/publications/

Pupils' self perceptions: motivation and esteem

It is also important to address pupils' own theories of ability and their perceptions of themselves as learners. If pupils attribute poor performance in schoolwork to a lack of ability ('I don't succeed at school because I'm not clever'), they are likely to avoid investing effort in learning: they may try to build their self-esteem in other ways, which are possibly less constructive.

Teaching will work most effectively when pupils *believe that they can become better learners*. Teachers are influential and authoritative sources: their views on the nature of ability and their expectations for their pupils have a significant impact on the way pupils view themselves and their capacity to learn. Teachers can provide a positive model by making their feedback to pupils formative and task focused, emphasising what needs to be done to improve and the importance of effort. Making summative judgements may foster comparison with other pupils and a focus on a general concept of 'ability'. Further material on formative assessment in relation to motivation and self-esteem is available in *Working Inside the Black Box* (Black *et al.*, 2002) and on the King's College website (www.kcl.ac.uk/).

To summarise ...

CAT scores are not a measure of innate ability. The *CAT* assesses abilities that develop as a result of the interaction of biology, experience and education. By reducing the role of specialised and subject-specific knowledge, *CAT* can provide a measure of potential that may not be seen in attainment or achievement test scores. Finally, reasoning abilities can be developed through sustained, high-quality teaching and challenging learning activities, which can raise the performance of all pupils.

Using *CAT* and the Key Stage 2 test results

Which is the best indicator?

Schools in England are required to administer national tests as follows:

■ in English and mathematics at the end of Key Stage 1 (age seven);

■ in English, mathematics and science at the end of Key Stage 2 (age 11);

■ in English, mathematics and science at the end of Key Stage 3 (age 14).

Secondary schools receive the Key Stage 2 test results for every pupil direct from the pupil's primary school. They often, therefore, receive both the national Key Stage 2 test results *and* their own directly-administered *CAT* scores. When considering targets for the future attainment of their pupils, secondary schools often ask which is the 'best' indicator: *CAT* or the Key Stage 2 tests?

There is no straightforward answer to this question. On the one hand, some schools remain sceptical about the reliability and validity of the national tests. They point to ever-rising Key Stage 2 test results for their intake, and contrast this with relatively stable *CAT* scores. Some evidence has been reported that increasing Key Stage 2 English test scores are not reflected in improvements in broader domains such as verbal reasoning (TES, 2002b; Hopkins and Davis, 2003); cynics assert that pupils are just becoming increasingly well prepared to take Key Stage 2 tests.

On the other hand, some schools observe that the provision of Key Stage 2 results from primary schools has improved markedly in terms of speed and completeness, and that their LEAs base their discussions about Key Stage 3 targets exclusively on the Key Stage 2 test results. They therefore feel that *CAT* scores are superfluous for their needs.

Measuring curricular attainment and general ability

While recognising that external pressures exist over which test outcomes should be given greater prominence, a strong case can be made that the best information comes from a *combination of both* the Key Stage 2 tests *and CAT*. Each set of tests has its own strengths:

▌ The *Key Stage 2 tests* assess attainment in some core areas of the curriculum, and reflect how well pupils have acquired and retained specific knowledge in these areas. They are 'high stakes' for primary schools, since they are published in national performance tables.

▌ *CAT* assesses more general, transferable learning abilities, and can provide a measure of potential. It is a 'low stakes' test, used primarily for management purposes within the school.

It is apparent, therefore, that they are assessing somewhat different domains. While there is a reasonably high correlation between *CAT* and Key Stage 2 tests, using both would only be unnecessary if they were measuring exactly the same thing. If both tests are used, teachers have access to measures of pupils' general, transferable abilities as well as their attainment in core areas of the curriculum.

Combining *CAT* and Key Stage 2 tests in target setting

Are there differences between *CAT* and Key Stage 2 tests in the strength of their relationship with pupils' subsequent performance? When pupils' Key Stage 2 and Year 7 *CAT* scores were compared with their subsequent Key Stage 3 outcomes for a sample of 17,500 pupils (Strand, 2001):

▌ the Key Stage 2 average points score and the *CAT* standard age scores both gave high correlations with Key Stage 3 test outcomes;

▌ across the Key Stage 3 outcomes, correlation coefficients ranged from *0.70* (*CAT* Verbal Battery and Key Stage 3 English points score) to *0.85* (mean *CAT* score and Key Stage 3 average points score);

▌ in all cases, *CAT* gave a slightly higher correlation with Key Stage 3 outcomes than did the Key Stage 2 points scores; however, the differences between these were not large and in statistical terms both are strong enough to provide reliable Key Stage 3 predictions.

Nevertheless, the Key Stage 3 outcomes predicted from *CAT* and from Key Stage 2 tests are not always a perfect match. Some pupils may be expected to gain a certain outcome by one measure but not by another. One way of making sense of this potentially conflicting information is to plot the various predictions as a Venn diagram, as suggested in a recent DfES publication (DfES, 2002b) and shown in Figure 8.1 on the next page.

Figure 8.1: Venn diagram combining predictions from *CAT* scores, Key Stage 2 test results and current teacher assessment in target setting for Key Stage 3

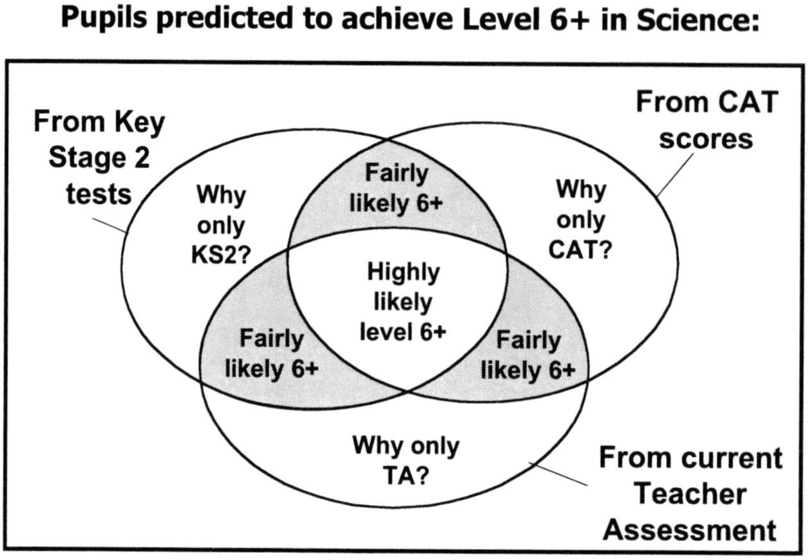

Pupils predicted to achieve Level 6+ in Science:

If the name of each pupil predicted to achieve Level 6+ in the Key Stage 3 science test were plotted in each hoop of the Venn diagram shown in Figure 8.1:

■ pupils whose name appears in only *one* hoop are predicted to attain Level 6+ by only *one* measure;

■ pupils whose name appears in *two* hoops are predicted to gain Level 6+ by *two* measures;

■ pupils whose name appears in all *three* hoops are predicted to gain Level 6+ by all three measures and are *most likely to be successful*.

Target setting for individual pupils

The completed Venn diagram can be a useful prompt to further questions about individual pupils:

■ Are some pupils predicted to achieve Level 6+ by test results, but not by their teachers? Are these pupils underachieving in their classroom performance? Are there social issues or behaviour problems?

■ Are some pupils are predicted to achieve Level 6+ by teacher assessment alone? If so, are these predictions secure? Are the teachers experienced and clear about the standards expected? Do the pupils require further experience to build their confidence – for example, in working under test or examination conditions, or in the effective use of time?

■ Are some pupils predicted to achieve Level 6 by Key Stage 2 test score but not by the *CAT*? What is the teacher assessment for these pupils? Are the pupils all from a particular primary school? If so, are Key Stage 2 results generally high for this primary school? Check the integrity of the *CAT* scores for these pupils (see Chapter 2). Could the *CAT* scores have been affected by poor performance on the test day/s? What are the pupils' profiles across the three *CAT* batteries? A Level 6+ target may be more challenging, relatively, if the pupil has a V– or N+ profile rather than a V+ or N– profile.

■ Are some pupils expected to achieve Level 6+ by *CAT* but not by Key Stage 2 tests? Again, what is the teacher assessment for these pupils? Have there been extended or regular periods of absence from school or from particular subjects? Does the pupil show poor attention, rushed or incomplete work, poor motivation or poor organisational skills? Are there significant gaps in subject knowledge or understanding? Is written work poorly presented in terms of neatness, handwriting, headings and layout, or does the pupil tend to leave work unfinished or superficial?

Target setting for the cohort

The results of the Venn diagram and subsequent discussions can be used to estimate a range of Key Stage 3 targets for the whole cohort:

■ the *least challenging* target for the school to attain is that which includes only those pupils encompassed by *all three* hoops;

■ the *most challenging* target would include any pupil encompassed by *at least one* hoop.

What is the range across these possible targets? How do they relate to current performance?

To summarise ...

CAT can offer the following supplements to Key Stage 2 results alone:

■ a measure of reasoning abilities to contrast with attainment test scores or other measures of school achievement;

■ the potential to identify pupils who may be underachieving;

■ the opportunity to triangulate between national test results and other measures;

■ a basis from which to assess the viability of school targets based on Key Stage 2 results alone;

■ information on pupils' cognitive strengths and weaknesses to inform teaching and learning (see Chapter 3);

■ a baseline administered in a consistent fashion for pupils from all feeder primary schools.

Reporting the *CAT* results to parents

Many schools are concerned about how they should share the results of *CAT* with parents. All schools provide the results if parents request them. However, many schools are unsure as to how best to report on the results as a matter of course and, as a consequence, relatively few do so.

Examples of practice

There is no 'right' or 'wrong' method for reporting to parents. Each school must choose the method that is best in the light of its own history and current context. However, some suggestions can be given based on the practice observed in a number of schools. There are three main approaches.

1. Sharing the *CAT* Individual Pupil Profile

Some schools share the *CAT* Individual Pupil Profile with parents. They talk about and interpret the profile much as suggested for each profile type in Chapter 3 (pages 35 to 61). They look for and emphasise the range of strengths and weaknesses across the three batteries. If indicated outcomes are included on the profile, they also discuss these. You have the opportunity on the group header sheet to decide whether or not you want to include any indicators you have selected on the Individual Pupil Profiles. It is therefore possible to select the indicated outcomes and have them *included* in the pupil listings, group summary reports and data disk, but *excluded* from the Individual Pupil Profiles.

The *CAT* profile is discussed as one piece of information, along with effort and attainment data in individual school subjects. There is discussion of practical activities and strategies that parents can use to support their child's learning (see pages 159 to 162 for some examples).

2. Reporting on stanines and comparative performance across batteries

Some schools argue that most parents want to know the answer to the following basic questions:

- How is my child doing?
- Is my child's performance below average, average or above average?
- What can I do to support my child's learning (particularly if it is below average)?

These schools believe that standard age scores are unnecessarily complicated for parents and potentially confusing to them. The broad descriptions of stanines 1 to 3 as 'below average', 4 to 6 as 'average' and 7 to 9 as 'above average' are seen as sufficient. Where performance varies across the batteries, this is noted and commented on.

A major focus is on the *activities* parents can engage in to support their child's development. These concentrate on literacy, numeracy and visual–spatial activities that can be built on common experiences in the home or wider social environment (see pages 159 to 162 for some examples).

3. Focusing on the *CAT* indicated outcomes

Some schools prefer not to report the *CAT* scores at all. Instead they focus on the *CAT* indicated outcomes such as the indicated Key Stage 3 levels or GCSE grades. These are often combined with the target levels or grades set by the school to generate a discussion on target setting and pupil progress.

A classic example of this approach is seen in the St Philip Howard case study reported on pages 118 to 120. The advantage here is that Key Stage 3 levels or GCSE grades are widely understood by parents, so the language of reporting is familiar. The report promotes a three-way discussion between teacher, parent and pupil – focused directly on the pupil's performance and engaging parents in the target-setting process.

Common threads

In the three approaches described above, there are some common threads:

- The *CAT* results are not presented in isolation. Instead, they are combined with reports on attainment in specific subjects studied, and with feedback on the engagement, motivation and effort made by the pupil.

- The nature and purposes of *CAT* are discussed and any misconceptions of *CAT* as a measure of fixed ability are addressed. Sometimes it is helpful to use the analogy of physical skills discussed earlier in this chapter (see page 149).

- Low *CAT* scores are never used to put a ceiling on expectations of pupil achievement, particularly if the pupil comes from an economically or socially disadvantaged background. Rather they are used as the basis for planning activities and a learning programme aimed at improving the pupils' reasoning abilities as well as key literacy and numeracy skills.

- There is a focus on what the parent can do to assist the progress of their child. As well as emphasising generic support (such as approaches to rewards and motivation, checking homework diaries, supporting out-of-hours classes and activities, facilitating access to computers or the internet, either at home or through library visits etc.) there are also suggestions of specific activities that can be built into everyday circumstances (see below).

Parent activities to support learning

For pupils with less well-developed reasoning abilities, parental activities might focus on building a greater store of verbal and numerical concepts. For other pupils, parental activities might emphasise flexibility in thinking: for example, seeing how ideas apply in different situations. As a result, there is a wide range of activities that parents can be involved in that will support the development of their children's reasoning abilities.

For younger pupils

The DfES provides an excellent source of resources for use by parents with their Key Stage 2 children: the *Help Your Child Discover* guides are available free via the DfES website (www.dfes.gov.uk/parents/discover). These cover a wide range of topics such as settlements, electricity, light and sound, materials etc. They give ideas on how parents can help a child find out more about the topic, suggest activities they can carry out at home and recommend where to go to for more information. While they are aimed primarily at the upper end of Key Stage 2, the guides can still be useful in Year 7, particularly for pupils whose reasoning abilities may need further development. For example, the guide on electricity includes a range of useful activities such as:

■ Think about a world without electricity, what would it be like?

■ When is it useful to have a battery rather than mains electricity?

■ What are the advantages of battery and mains electricity?

The guide suggests that parents ask the child to read the electricity meter, translating dial reading to digits, and see how the numbers on the meter match the units on the bill. It also suggests games to play at home, on a walk or car journey to build concepts – such as 'finding circuits' in the home, 'circuit snap', and so on.

For older pupils

For older pupils, both subject-specific content and independent study skills become a more important focus for homework. The role of parents in supporting their children's development tends to move from direct parental *instruction* to more general parental *support for* learning. However, the best homework will use real-life experiences and materials to help children remember what they have learnt at school and to connect the learning to their everyday life.

Parents can take an active part in homework tasks involving:

■ investigations;

■ interviews;

■ simple experiments;

■ projects;

■ public library visits;

■ essay writing;

■ drafting;

■ report writing;

■ reading;

■ designing;

■ making models;

■ drawing;

■ word processing;

■ desktop publishing;

■ internet searches.

HOMEWORK ACTIVITIES RELATED TO VERBAL REASONING

Homework tasks that emphasise expanding word knowledge or improving verbal skills will help develop verbal reasoning ability. You could, for example, ask parents and children together to make up and play a range of word games:

■ Play 'odd one out' word games, using abstract as well as concrete concepts.

■ On a car journey, make up words from the letter component of car number plates: who can make the longest word?

■ Find out who can generate the longest list of words with similar meanings to a target word. (For example, words related to the word 'witchlike' might include: *sinister, brooding, malevolent, evil, inhuman.*)

■ Play word prefix and suffix games, for example: how many words beginning with 'bi' can you name? (Answers might include: *biennial, bilateral, bikini, bicycle, bitter.*) What, if anything, is common to the words? Are there any exceptions?

■ Play the game '20 questions' to guess a chosen character, object, concept or word.

Other ideas to recommend to parents include:

■ encourage your child to complete word searches and crosswords in magazines;

■ suggest they design their own searches or crosswords (a much more complex activity);

■ if you are reading with your child, encourage guessing and prediction: ask 'What happens next?' and ask your child to justify their answers with evidence;

■ make up limericks, raps or poems together as a means for memorising rules or just playing with words;

■ build vocabulary by consulting a dictionary together and provide help with key spellings;

■ encourage your child to write his or her own instruction sheets on a favourite activity (for example, how to construct a model or to play a computer game); this will build sequencing skills and the ability to analyse and explain a process.

HOMEWORK ACTIVITIES RELATED TO QUANTITATIVE REASONING

Homework tasks in this area might emphasise estimation and mental mathematics. The National Numeracy Strategy Parents' booklets (DfEE, 2001c) contain helpful advice and activities to help parents support their child's mathematical development. For example:

■ Work out what the 'takeaway' bill will be? How much money would a 15 per cent tip come to?

■ If you are painting a wall, ask your child to estimate the area and how much paint you will need. If you are tiling, how many tiles? If you are laying a laminate floor, how many packs?

■ At the supermarket, ask your child to keep a running total of the bill in their head. How many pieces of fruit will you get if you want 2lb of apples?

■ In the kitchen, ask your child how much pasta you will need for the family meal if each person eats 75g? How much should you estimate for younger children? How much will you need if grandparents are also coming to the meal?

■ Ask your child to use timetables to plan a rail or bus journey, work out connection times between services and estimate journey times.

■ Encourage computer games that involve logical or mathematical reasoning (e.g. Microsoft Minesweeper).

■ Encourage work with spreadsheets to solve practical problems (for example, analysing football league tables or managing your money).

HOMEWORK ACTIVITIES RELATED TO NON-VERBAL REASONING

Activities that build visual–spatial awareness are appropriate for all pupils, but may be of particular benefit if non-verbal reasoning scores are low. Some suggestions for parents are listed below (further ideas are discussed in Clausen-May and Smith, 1998):

- Encourage your child to explore your local environment and ask him or her to construct maps of their immediate surroundings. For example, ask for: a diagram to show how the rooms in your home are linked together; a map to show the journey from home to school; a floor plan of the school.

- Help your child to develop an awareness of his or her surroundings and a knowledge of some specialised vocabulary. For example, use the local-built environment to name and describe the basic shapes of architecture – *planes, curves, arches, squares, rectangles, circles, cones, cylinders, pyramids, domes, towers, spirals, slabs* and *blocks.*

- Encourage model making, which can develop visual analysis, spatial judgement and manual dexterity. On a small scale, this could mean using building blocks or construction kits; on a larger scale, it might involve carpentry, metalwork, brick building and so on.

- Support computer games that require players to navigate from one area to another using grid references, distances or directions.

- On a family journey, encourage reading and using maps. What direction are we travelling in? How many miles are we from the next town? How do you work out the distance along a curved route? If 2cm represents 1km, and 1.25 inches represents 1 mile, what is the ratio between the different scales?

- Encourage sketching and drawing, which develop the ability to estimate lengths, heights, angles and relative proportions.

These are only a small selection of very general activities that might be suggested to parents. Remember that reasoning abilities are best developed through challenging learning activities centred on subject content. More specific activities, directly related to the topics and areas of work the pupil is currently engaged in, will be most relevant and powerful.

Recent *CAT* developments

CAT Levels G and H

From autumn 2003, two further levels for older pupils, Level G and Level H, are added to *CAT*. This takes the upper age range of *CAT* to 17 years and above. Levels G and H will benefit all secondary schools, making it possible to assess new entrants to the school during Key Stage 4. This will ensure that secondary schools have totally comprehensive coverage of the reasoning abilities of their cohort and GCSE indicators for all pupils throughout the period of statutory school education.

Levels G and H are of specific interest to:

- secondary schools with mobile pupil populations, which experience a high level of transfer or turbulence during the last two years of secondary education;

- secondary schools wishing to assess their value added over a relatively short time period, for example, from the start of Year 10 or Year 11 through to GCSE or Standard Grade examinations;
- schools and colleges seeking additional information to guide vocational and modular course choices at age 14 or post 16;
- school sixth forms, sixth form colleges and further education (FE) colleges seeking a further baseline measure, in addition to GCSE results, as an independent assessment of pupils' abilities;
- teachers wishing to identify those pupils who may have high ability, but who may not have demonstrated this in their examinations attainment to date;
- teachers wishing to identify 'gifted and talented' pupils and those whose ambitions and attainment lag behind their potential;
- teachers seeking a measure of potential that is not reliant on language skills and minimises the role of prior school experience (for example, to give indicators of the potential of pupils who have entered the school/college with English as an additional language);
- post-16 teachers and lecturers seeking information on the learning styles and preferences of their pupils, as provided by the *CAT* Individual Pupil Profiles (see Chapter 3).

In addition, AS, A2, GNVQ and Scottish Higher Grade indicators are being developed for use with *CAT3* Levels G and H.

CAT online

CAT3 can also be administered online through nferNelson's *TestWise* digital assessment engine. This option gives you increased flexibility as to how your pupils take the test. You may decide that it is most practical to continue to assess the majority of your pupils using pencil and paper, particularly if you are a large school. However, the online option can be particularly appropriate for some groups of pupils. The computer-based tasks can be more motivating, both through the intrinsic interest of the medium itself and through providing rapid feedback. The online version can also be particularly useful if a small number of pupils were absent when the tests were originally administered. The online version allows you to gain full and complete data on these pupils without needing to repeat the formal *CAT* administration yourself, which will save you considerable time. The online version also provides the benefit of instant scoring, rapid turnaround of results and compatibility with SIMS, the leading schools management information system. For further details on taking *CAT3* online, see the *CAT* website (www.nfer-nelson.co.uk/cat).

Review

The main points to remember from this chapter are:

■ *CAT* scores are *not* a measure of *innate ability or fixed capacity*: there is *a reciprocal relationship* between *reasoning ability* and *achievement in school subjects*;

■ *CAT* can provide a *measure of potential attainment* in a range of subjects through an assessment that *reduces the role of content- and subject-specific knowledge*;

■ reasoning abilities and thinking skills can be developed through *sustained, high-quality teaching* and *challenging learning activities*;

■ *CAT scores, Key Stage 2 test results* and *teacher predictions combined* provide the most solid foundation for Key Stage 3 and GCSE target setting;

■ Consider the three methods of reporting to parents, described on pages 157 to 159. Would using any of these methods improve your current practice?

Appendix 1

Summary of contents of the CD

There are two types of resources contained on the CD. These are:

■ **Indicators**: ADOBE Acrobat copies of the summary indicators and Progress Charts for national end of Key Stage 3 tests in England, GCSE public examinations and Scottish Standard Grade public examinations, and;
■ **EXCEL Workbooks:** copies of the EXCEL workbooks as referred to in the guide.

1. Indicators

The following specific resources are included:

End of Key Stage 3 (KS3) tests – Autumn 2003

■ CAT3-KS3 indicators summary table
■ CAT3 Progress Charts for end of KS3 English
■ CAT3 Progress Charts for end of KS3 maths
■ CAT3 Progress Charts for end of KS3 science

GCSE public examinations – Autumn 2003

■ CAT3-GCSE indicators summary table
■ CAT3 Progress Charts for Art & Design
■ CAT3 Progress Charts for Business Studies
■ CAT3 Progress Charts for Design & Technology – Electronics
■ CAT3 Progress Charts for Design & Technology – Food
■ CAT3 Progress Charts for Design & Technology – Graphics
■ CAT3 Progress Charts for Design & Technology – Resistant materials
■ CAT3 Progress Charts for Design & Technology – Systems Control
■ CAT3 Progress Charts for Design & Technology – Textiles
■ CAT3 Progress Charts for Drama
■ CAT3 Progress Charts for English Language
■ CAT3 Progress Charts for English Literature
■ CAT3 Progress Charts for French
■ CAT3 Progress Charts for Geography
■ CAT3 Progress Charts for German
■ CAT3 Progress Charts for History
■ CAT3 Progress Charts for Home Economics

- CAT3 Progress Charts for Information Technology
- CAT3 Progress Charts for Mathematics
- CAT3 Progress Charts for Media
- CAT3 Progress Charts for Music
- CAT3 Progress Charts for Physical Education
- CAT3 Progress Charts for Religious Education
- CAT3 Progress Charts for Science (Double Award)
- CAT3 Progress Charts for Science (Single Award)
- CAT3 Progress Charts for Biology
- CAT3 Progress Charts for Chemistry
- CAT3 Progress Charts for Physics
- CAT3 Progress Charts for Sociology
- CAT3 Progress Charts for Spanish
- CAT3 Progress Charts for Statistics

Scottish Standard Grade Public Examinations — Autumn 2003

- CAT3 Scottish Standard Grade indicators summary table
- CAT3 Progress Charts for Standard Grade Accounting & Finance
- CAT3 Progress Charts for Standard Grade Administration
- CAT3 Progress Charts for Standard Grade Art & Design
- CAT3 Progress Charts for Standard Grade Biology
- CAT3 Progress Charts for Standard Grade Business Management
- CAT3 Progress Charts for Standard Grade Chemistry
- CAT3 Progress Charts for Standard Grade Computing Studies
- CAT3 Progress Charts for Standard Grade Craft & Design
- CAT3 Progress Charts for Standard Grade Drama
- CAT3 Progress Charts for Standard Grade English
- CAT3 Progress Charts for Standard Grade French
- CAT3 Progress Charts for Standard Grade Geography
- CAT3 Progress Charts for Standard Grade German
- CAT3 Progress Charts for Standard Grade Graphic Communication
- CAT3 Progress Charts for Standard Grade History
- CAT3 Progress Charts for Standard Grade Home Economics
- CAT3 Progress Charts for Standard Grade Mathematics
- CAT3 Progress Charts for Standard Grade Modern Studies
- CAT3 Progress Charts for Standard Grade Music
- CAT3 Progress Charts for Standard Grade PE
- CAT3 Progress Charts for Standard Grade Physics
- CAT3 Progress Charts for Standard Grade Science

■ CAT3 Progress Charts for Standard Grade Social & Vocational Studies
■ CAT3 Progress Charts for Standard Grade Technical Studies

2. EXCEL Workbooks

Filename	Description	Page cited on
Dataset1.csv	Example data file, used to illustrate the analysis of pupil's results in Chapter 2.	Chapter 2, p. 21
Dataset2.xls	Example data file, used to demonstrate the analysis of group differences in Chapter 4.	Chapter 4, p. 77
Compare_Blank.xls	Used to compare the significance of score differences between groups. Used in Chapter 4 for multiple comparisons.	Chapter 4, p. 74
Compare_Dataset2.xls	Example of a completed COMPARE worksheet for the data contained in Dataset2.	Chapter 4, p. 79
Scatter_Blank.xls	Template for completing the group visual–verbal learning profile.	Chapter 4, p. 86
CAT2-CAT3.xls	CAT2-CAT3 conversion workbook.	Chapter 4, p. 91
Pupil_GCSE_Profile.xls	The user enters the pupil's CAT3 verbal reasoning and mean CAT3 standard age scores. The workbook produces a graph of the pupil's indicated grades in 24 key GCSE subjects, based on their CAT3 scores.	Chapter 5, p. 114
KS3_Quartiles.xls	CAT3-KS3 Quartile graphs. Used to assess value added between CAT in Y7–Y9 and KS3 points scores.	Chapter 7, p. 134
GCSE_Quartiles.xls	CAT3-GCSE Quartile graphs. Used to assess value added between CAT in Y7–Y9 and GCSE points scores.	Chapter 7, p. 134

Appendix 2

Sample pupil answer sheet for *CAT3*, Level D

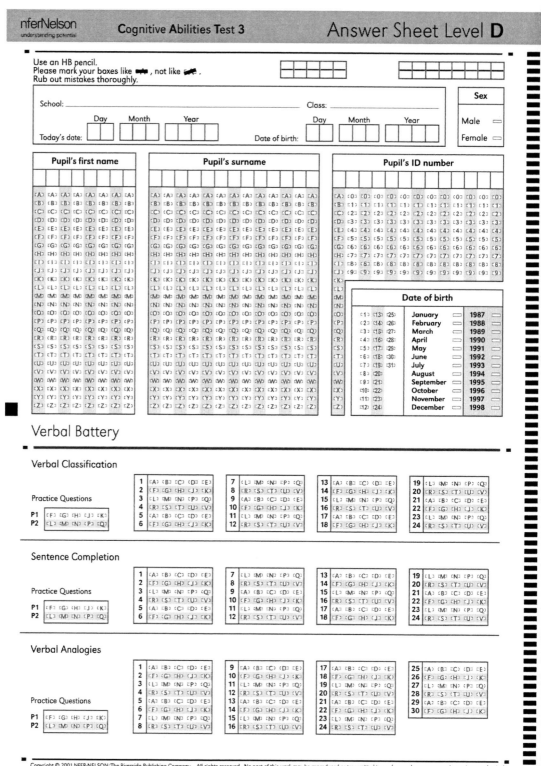

Cognitive Abilities Test 3

Answer Sheet Level D

Quantitative Battery

Number Analogies

Practice Questions

P1 ⊂F⊃ ⊂G⊃ ⊂H⊃ ⊂J⊃ ⊂K⊃
P2 ⊂L⊃ ⊂M⊃ ⊂N⊃ ⊂P⊃ ⊂Q⊃
P3 ⊂R⊃ ⊂S⊃ ⊂T⊃ ⊂U⊃ ⊂V⊃

1 ⊂A⊃ ⊂B⊃ ⊂C⊃ ⊂D⊃ ⊂E⊃
2 ⊂F⊃ ⊂G⊃ ⊂H⊃ ⊂J⊃ ⊂K⊃
3 ⊂L⊃ ⊂M⊃ ⊂N⊃ ⊂P⊃ ⊂Q⊃
4 ⊂R⊃ ⊂S⊃ ⊂T⊃ ⊂U⊃ ⊂V⊃
5 ⊂A⊃ ⊂B⊃ ⊂C⊃ ⊂D⊃ ⊂E⊃

6 ⊂F⊃ ⊂G⊃ ⊂H⊃ ⊂J⊃ ⊂K⊃
7 ⊂L⊃ ⊂M⊃ ⊂N⊃ ⊂P⊃ ⊂Q⊃
8 ⊂R⊃ ⊂S⊃ ⊂T⊃ ⊂U⊃ ⊂V⊃
9 ⊂A⊃ ⊂B⊃ ⊂C⊃ ⊂D⊃ ⊂E⊃
10 ⊂F⊃ ⊂G⊃ ⊂H⊃ ⊂J⊃ ⊂K⊃

11 ⊂L⊃ ⊂M⊃ ⊂N⊃ ⊂P⊃ ⊂Q⊃
12 ⊂R⊃ ⊂S⊃ ⊂T⊃ ⊂U⊃ ⊂V⊃
13 ⊂A⊃ ⊂B⊃ ⊂C⊃ ⊂D⊃ ⊂E⊃
14 ⊂F⊃ ⊂G⊃ ⊂H⊃ ⊂J⊃ ⊂K⊃
15 ⊂L⊃ ⊂M⊃ ⊂N⊃ ⊂P⊃ ⊂Q⊃

16 ⊂R⊃ ⊂S⊃ ⊂T⊃ ⊂U⊃ ⊂V⊃
17 ⊂A⊃ ⊂B⊃ ⊂C⊃ ⊂D⊃ ⊂E⊃
18 ⊂F⊃ ⊂G⊃ ⊂H⊃ ⊂J⊃ ⊂K⊃
19 ⊂L⊃ ⊂M⊃ ⊂N⊃ ⊂P⊃ ⊂Q⊃
20 ⊂R⊃ ⊂S⊃ ⊂T⊃ ⊂U⊃ ⊂V⊃

Number Series

Practice Questions

P1 ⊂F⊃ ⊂G⊃ ⊂H⊃ ⊂J⊃ ⊂K⊃
P2 ⊂L⊃ ⊂M⊃ ⊂N⊃ ⊂P⊃ ⊂Q⊃

1 ⊂A⊃ ⊂B⊃ ⊂C⊃ ⊂D⊃ ⊂E⊃
2 ⊂F⊃ ⊂G⊃ ⊂H⊃ ⊂J⊃ ⊂K⊃
3 ⊂L⊃ ⊂M⊃ ⊂N⊃ ⊂P⊃ ⊂Q⊃
4 ⊂R⊃ ⊂S⊃ ⊂T⊃ ⊂U⊃ ⊂V⊃
5 ⊂A⊃ ⊂B⊃ ⊂C⊃ ⊂D⊃ ⊂E⊃

6 ⊂F⊃ ⊂G⊃ ⊂H⊃ ⊂J⊃ ⊂K⊃
7 ⊂L⊃ ⊂M⊃ ⊂N⊃ ⊂P⊃ ⊂Q⊃
8 ⊂R⊃ ⊂S⊃ ⊂T⊃ ⊂U⊃ ⊂V⊃
9 ⊂A⊃ ⊂B⊃ ⊂C⊃ ⊂D⊃ ⊂E⊃
10 ⊂F⊃ ⊂G⊃ ⊂H⊃ ⊂J⊃ ⊂K⊃

11 ⊂L⊃ ⊂M⊃ ⊂N⊃ ⊂P⊃ ⊂Q⊃
12 ⊂R⊃ ⊂S⊃ ⊂T⊃ ⊂U⊃ ⊂V⊃
13 ⊂A⊃ ⊂B⊃ ⊂C⊃ ⊂D⊃ ⊂E⊃
14 ⊂F⊃ ⊂G⊃ ⊂H⊃ ⊂J⊃ ⊂K⊃
15 ⊂L⊃ ⊂M⊃ ⊂N⊃ ⊂P⊃ ⊂Q⊃

16 ⊂R⊃ ⊂S⊃ ⊂T⊃ ⊂U⊃ ⊂V⊃
17 ⊂A⊃ ⊂B⊃ ⊂C⊃ ⊂D⊃ ⊂E⊃
18 ⊂F⊃ ⊂G⊃ ⊂H⊃ ⊂J⊃ ⊂K⊃
19 ⊂L⊃ ⊂M⊃ ⊂N⊃ ⊂P⊃ ⊂Q⊃
20 ⊂R⊃ ⊂S⊃ ⊂T⊃ ⊂U⊃ ⊂V⊃

Equation Building

Practice Questions

P1 ⊂F⊃ ⊂G⊃ ⊂H⊃ ⊂J⊃ ⊂K⊃
P2 ⊂L⊃ ⊂M⊃ ⊂N⊃ ⊂P⊃ ⊂Q⊃
P3 ⊂R⊃ ⊂S⊃ ⊂T⊃ ⊂U⊃ ⊂V⊃

1 ⊂A⊃ ⊂B⊃ ⊂C⊃ ⊂D⊃ ⊂E⊃
2 ⊂F⊃ ⊂G⊃ ⊂H⊃ ⊂J⊃ ⊂K⊃
3 ⊂L⊃ ⊂M⊃ ⊂N⊃ ⊂P⊃ ⊂Q⊃
4 ⊂R⊃ ⊂S⊃ ⊂T⊃ ⊂U⊃ ⊂V⊃
5 ⊂A⊃ ⊂B⊃ ⊂C⊃ ⊂D⊃ ⊂E⊃

6 ⊂F⊃ ⊂G⊃ ⊂H⊃ ⊂J⊃ ⊂K⊃
7 ⊂L⊃ ⊂M⊃ ⊂N⊃ ⊂P⊃ ⊂Q⊃
8 ⊂R⊃ ⊂S⊃ ⊂T⊃ ⊂U⊃ ⊂V⊃
9 ⊂A⊃ ⊂B⊃ ⊂C⊃ ⊂D⊃ ⊂E⊃
10 ⊂F⊃ ⊂G⊃ ⊂H⊃ ⊂J⊃ ⊂K⊃

11 ⊂L⊃ ⊂M⊃ ⊂N⊃ ⊂P⊃ ⊂Q⊃
12 ⊂R⊃ ⊂S⊃ ⊂T⊃ ⊂U⊃ ⊂V⊃
13 ⊂A⊃ ⊂B⊃ ⊂C⊃ ⊂D⊃ ⊂E⊃
14 ⊂F⊃ ⊂G⊃ ⊂H⊃ ⊂J⊃ ⊂K⊃
15 ⊂L⊃ ⊂M⊃ ⊂N⊃ ⊂P⊃ ⊂Q⊃

16 ⊂R⊃ ⊂S⊃ ⊂T⊃ ⊂U⊃ ⊂V⊃
17 ⊂A⊃ ⊂B⊃ ⊂C⊃ ⊂D⊃ ⊂E⊃
18 ⊂F⊃ ⊂G⊃ ⊂H⊃ ⊂J⊃ ⊂K⊃

Non-verbal Battery

Figure Classification

Practice Questions

P1 ⊂F⊃ ⊂G⊃ ⊂H⊃ ⊂J⊃ ⊂K⊃
P2 ⊂L⊃ ⊂M⊃ ⊂N⊃ ⊂P⊃ ⊂Q⊃

1 ⊂A⊃ ⊂B⊃ ⊂C⊃ ⊂D⊃ ⊂E⊃
2 ⊂F⊃ ⊂G⊃ ⊂H⊃ ⊂J⊃ ⊂K⊃
3 ⊂L⊃ ⊂M⊃ ⊂N⊃ ⊂P⊃ ⊂Q⊃
4 ⊂R⊃ ⊂S⊃ ⊂T⊃ ⊂U⊃ ⊂V⊃
5 ⊂A⊃ ⊂B⊃ ⊂C⊃ ⊂D⊃ ⊂E⊃
6 ⊂F⊃ ⊂G⊃ ⊂H⊃ ⊂J⊃ ⊂K⊃

7 ⊂L⊃ ⊂M⊃ ⊂N⊃ ⊂P⊃ ⊂Q⊃
8 ⊂R⊃ ⊂S⊃ ⊂T⊃ ⊂U⊃ ⊂V⊃
9 ⊂A⊃ ⊂B⊃ ⊂C⊃ ⊂D⊃ ⊂E⊃
10 ⊂F⊃ ⊂G⊃ ⊂H⊃ ⊂J⊃ ⊂K⊃
11 ⊂L⊃ ⊂M⊃ ⊂N⊃ ⊂P⊃ ⊂Q⊃
12 ⊂R⊃ ⊂S⊃ ⊂T⊃ ⊂U⊃ ⊂V⊃

13 ⊂A⊃ ⊂B⊃ ⊂C⊃ ⊂D⊃ ⊂E⊃
14 ⊂F⊃ ⊂G⊃ ⊂H⊃ ⊂J⊃ ⊂K⊃
15 ⊂L⊃ ⊂M⊃ ⊂N⊃ ⊂P⊃ ⊂Q⊃
16 ⊂R⊃ ⊂S⊃ ⊂T⊃ ⊂U⊃ ⊂V⊃
17 ⊂A⊃ ⊂B⊃ ⊂C⊃ ⊂D⊃ ⊂E⊃
18 ⊂F⊃ ⊂G⊃ ⊂H⊃ ⊂J⊃ ⊂K⊃

19 ⊂L⊃ ⊂M⊃ ⊂N⊃ ⊂P⊃ ⊂Q⊃
20 ⊂R⊃ ⊂S⊃ ⊂T⊃ ⊂U⊃ ⊂V⊃
21 ⊂A⊃ ⊂B⊃ ⊂C⊃ ⊂D⊃ ⊂E⊃
22 ⊂F⊃ ⊂G⊃ ⊂H⊃ ⊂J⊃ ⊂K⊃
23 ⊂L⊃ ⊂M⊃ ⊂N⊃ ⊂P⊃ ⊂Q⊃
24 ⊂R⊃ ⊂S⊃ ⊂T⊃ ⊂U⊃ ⊂V⊃

Figure Analogies

Practice Questions

P1 ⊂F⊃ ⊂G⊃ ⊂H⊃ ⊂J⊃ ⊂K⊃
P2 ⊂L⊃ ⊂M⊃ ⊂N⊃ ⊂P⊃ ⊂Q⊃

1 ⊂A⊃ ⊂B⊃ ⊂C⊃ ⊂D⊃ ⊂E⊃
2 ⊂F⊃ ⊂G⊃ ⊂H⊃ ⊂J⊃ ⊂K⊃
3 ⊂L⊃ ⊂M⊃ ⊂N⊃ ⊂P⊃ ⊂Q⊃
4 ⊂R⊃ ⊂S⊃ ⊂T⊃ ⊂U⊃ ⊂V⊃
5 ⊂A⊃ ⊂B⊃ ⊂C⊃ ⊂D⊃ ⊂E⊃
6 ⊂F⊃ ⊂G⊃ ⊂H⊃ ⊂J⊃ ⊂K⊃

7 ⊂L⊃ ⊂M⊃ ⊂N⊃ ⊂P⊃ ⊂Q⊃
8 ⊂R⊃ ⊂S⊃ ⊂T⊃ ⊂U⊃ ⊂V⊃
9 ⊂A⊃ ⊂B⊃ ⊂C⊃ ⊂D⊃ ⊂E⊃
10 ⊂F⊃ ⊂G⊃ ⊂H⊃ ⊂J⊃ ⊂K⊃
11 ⊂L⊃ ⊂M⊃ ⊂N⊃ ⊂P⊃ ⊂Q⊃
12 ⊂R⊃ ⊂S⊃ ⊂T⊃ ⊂U⊃ ⊂V⊃

13 ⊂A⊃ ⊂B⊃ ⊂C⊃ ⊂D⊃ ⊂E⊃
14 ⊂F⊃ ⊂G⊃ ⊂H⊃ ⊂J⊃ ⊂K⊃
15 ⊂L⊃ ⊂M⊃ ⊂N⊃ ⊂P⊃ ⊂Q⊃
16 ⊂R⊃ ⊂S⊃ ⊂T⊃ ⊂U⊃ ⊂V⊃
17 ⊂A⊃ ⊂B⊃ ⊂C⊃ ⊂D⊃ ⊂E⊃
18 ⊂F⊃ ⊂G⊃ ⊂H⊃ ⊂J⊃ ⊂K⊃

19 ⊂L⊃ ⊂M⊃ ⊂N⊃ ⊂P⊃ ⊂Q⊃
20 ⊂R⊃ ⊂S⊃ ⊂T⊃ ⊂U⊃ ⊂V⊃
21 ⊂A⊃ ⊂B⊃ ⊂C⊃ ⊂D⊃ ⊂E⊃
22 ⊂F⊃ ⊂G⊃ ⊂H⊃ ⊂J⊃ ⊂K⊃
23 ⊂L⊃ ⊂M⊃ ⊂N⊃ ⊂P⊃ ⊂Q⊃
24 ⊂R⊃ ⊂S⊃ ⊂T⊃ ⊂U⊃ ⊂V⊃

Figure Analysis

Practice Questions

P1 ⊂F⊃ ⊂G⊃ ⊂H⊃ ⊂J⊃ ⊂K⊃
P2 ⊂L⊃ ⊂M⊃ ⊂N⊃ ⊂P⊃ ⊂Q⊃

1 ⊂A⊃ ⊂B⊃ ⊂C⊃ ⊂D⊃ ⊂E⊃
2 ⊂F⊃ ⊂G⊃ ⊂H⊃ ⊂J⊃ ⊂K⊃
3 ⊂L⊃ ⊂M⊃ ⊂N⊃ ⊂P⊃ ⊂Q⊃
4 ⊂R⊃ ⊂S⊃ ⊂T⊃ ⊂U⊃ ⊂V⊃
5 ⊂A⊃ ⊂B⊃ ⊂C⊃ ⊂D⊃ ⊂E⊃

6 ⊂F⊃ ⊂G⊃ ⊂H⊃ ⊂J⊃ ⊂K⊃
7 ⊂L⊃ ⊂M⊃ ⊂N⊃ ⊂P⊃ ⊂Q⊃
8 ⊂R⊃ ⊂S⊃ ⊂T⊃ ⊂U⊃ ⊂V⊃
9 ⊂A⊃ ⊂B⊃ ⊂C⊃ ⊂D⊃ ⊂E⊃
10 ⊂F⊃ ⊂G⊃ ⊂H⊃ ⊂J⊃ ⊂K⊃

11 ⊂L⊃ ⊂M⊃ ⊂N⊃ ⊂P⊃ ⊂Q⊃
12 ⊂R⊃ ⊂S⊃ ⊂T⊃ ⊂U⊃ ⊂V⊃
13 ⊂A⊃ ⊂B⊃ ⊂C⊃ ⊂D⊃ ⊂E⊃
14 ⊂F⊃ ⊂G⊃ ⊂H⊃ ⊂J⊃ ⊂K⊃
15 ⊂L⊃ ⊂M⊃ ⊂N⊃ ⊂P⊃ ⊂Q⊃

16 ⊂R⊃ ⊂S⊃ ⊂T⊃ ⊂U⊃ ⊂V⊃
17 ⊂A⊃ ⊂B⊃ ⊂C⊃ ⊂D⊃ ⊂E⊃
18 ⊂F⊃ ⊂G⊃ ⊂H⊃ ⊂J⊃ ⊂K⊃

Appendix 3

Sample group header sheet for *CAT3*

---

nferNelson
understanding potential

Cognitive Abilities Test 3

Group header sheet

Please see opposite for instructions on how to complete this sheet.
Use an HB PENCIL - do not use ink or biro.

Please mark your boxes like ▬▬ NOT like ▬ . Rub out mistakes thoroughly.

1. Name and address of school/college, with a contact name

Contact person:

School/college name:

Address:

Postcode:

Email:

Telephone:

Fax:

School no. | LEA | School

2. Date of testing

Day			Month		Year	
⊏1⊐	⊏13⊐	⊏25⊐	January	⊏⊐	2003	⊏⊐
⊏2⊐	⊏14⊐	⊏26⊐	February	⊏⊐	2004	⊏⊐
⊏3⊐	⊏15⊐	⊏27⊐	March	⊏⊐	2005	⊏⊐
⊏4⊐	⊏16⊐	⊏28⊐	April	⊏⊐	2006	⊏⊐
⊏5⊐	⊏17⊐	⊏29⊐	May	⊏⊐	2007	⊏⊐
⊏6⊐	⊏18⊐	⊏30⊐	June	⊏⊐	2008	⊏⊐
⊏7⊐	⊏19⊐	⊏31⊐	July	⊏⊐	2009	⊏⊐
⊏8⊐	⊏20⊐		August	⊏⊐	2010	⊏⊐
⊏9⊐	⊏21⊐		September	⊏⊐	2011	⊏⊐
⊏10⊐	⊏22⊐		October	⊏⊐	2012	⊏⊐
⊏11⊐	⊏23⊐		November	⊏⊐	2013	⊏⊐
⊏12⊐	⊏24⊐		December	⊏⊐	2014	⊏⊐

3. Test level administered

A   B   C   D   E   F   G   H

4. Year group

Age	England & Wales	Scotland	Northern Ireland
7-8+ years	Y3	P4	Y4 (P4)
8-9+	Y4	P5	Y5 (P5)
9-10+	Y5	P6	Y6 (P6)
10-11+	Y6	P7	Y7 (P7)
11-12+	Y7	S1	Y8 (F1)
12-13+	Y8	S2	Y9 (F2)
13-14+	Y9	S3	Y10 (F3)
14-15+	Y10	S4	Y11 (F4)
15-16+	Y11	S5	Y12 (F5)
16-17	Y12	S6	L6
17+	Y13		U6

5. Class/group name

Class/group identifier (mark no more than ONE letter)

⊏0⊐ ⊏A⊐ ⊏K⊐ ⊏U⊐ ⊏0⊐
⊏1⊐ ⊏B⊐ ⊏L⊐ ⊏V⊐ ⊏1⊐
⊏2⊐ ⊏C⊐ ⊏M⊐ ⊏W⊐ ⊏2⊐
⊏3⊐ ⊏D⊐ ⊏N⊐ ⊏X⊐ ⊏3⊐
⊏4⊐ ⊏E⊐ ⊏O⊐ ⊏Y⊐ ⊏4⊐
⊏5⊐ ⊏F⊐ ⊏P⊐ ⊏Z⊐ ⊏5⊐
⊏6⊐ ⊏G⊐ ⊏Q⊐ ⊏6⊐
⊏7⊐ ⊏H⊐ ⊏R⊐ ⊏7⊐
⊏8⊐ ⊏I⊐ ⊏S⊐ ⊏8⊐
⊏9⊐ ⊏J⊐ ⊏T⊐ ⊏9⊐

6. Number of pupil answer sheets included

⊏0⊐ ⊏0⊐ ⊏0⊐ ⊏0⊐
⊏1⊐ ⊏1⊐ ⊏1⊐ ⊏1⊐
⊏2⊐ ⊏2⊐ ⊏2⊐ ⊏2⊐
⊏3⊐ ⊏3⊐ ⊏3⊐ ⊏3⊐
⊏4⊐ ⊏4⊐ ⊏4⊐ ⊏4⊐
⊏5⊐ ⊏5⊐ ⊏5⊐ ⊏5⊐
⊏6⊐ ⊏6⊐ ⊏6⊐ ⊏6⊐
⊏7⊐ ⊏7⊐ ⊏7⊐ ⊏7⊐
⊏8⊐ ⊏8⊐ ⊏8⊐ ⊏8⊐
⊏9⊐ ⊏9⊐ ⊏9⊐ ⊏9⊐

7. Options (see page 1 for details)

(a) Report options	Options required	Mark if indicator not required on pupil profile**
Summary of results (merit order)	⊏⊐	
Summary of results by sex	⊏⊐	
Summary of subtest results	⊏⊐	
Indicators		
KS2* (A-C)	⊏⊐	⊏⊐
KS3 (C-F)	⊏⊐	⊏⊐
GCSE (C-H)	⊏⊐	⊏⊐
Scottish standard grade (C-H)	⊏⊐	

*   If you have chosen KS2 as an option, you cannot have KS3, GCSE or SG as additional options.

** By default the indicators you choose are added to the pupil profile. If you do not wish this information added to the profile, please indicate above in the right-hand column.

(b) Other options

Data disk required ⊏⊐

Group rank omitted ⊏⊐

8. Further use of data

I do **not** consent to the further use of my data as specified overleaf ⊏⊐

References

ADEY, P., and SHAYER, M. (1994). *Really Raising Standards: Cognitive intervention and academic achievement.* New York: Routledge.

ADEY, P., SERRET, N., ROBERTSON, A., NAGY, F., and WADSWORTH, P. (2003). *Let's Think through Science!* Windsor: nferNelson.

ANASTASI, A. (1976). *Psychological Testing.* New York: Macmillan.

BLACK, P., HARRISON, C., LEE, C., MARSHALL, B., and WILIAM, D. (2002). *Working Inside the Black Box: Assessment for learning in the classroom.* London: King's College.

BUTTERWORTH, B. (2003). *Dyscalculia Screener.* London: nferNelson.

CLAUSEN-MAY, T., and SMITH, P. (1998). *Spatial Ability: A handbook for teachers.* Slough: National Foundation for Educational Research.

DEPARTMENT OF EDUCATION (1991). *Parents' Charter.* London: HMSO.

DEPARTMENT FOR EDUCATION AND EMPLOYMENT (1999). *The National Curriculum: Handbook for secondary teachers in England.* London: The Stationery Office.

DEPARTMENT FOR EDUCATION AND EMPLOYMENT (2001a). *Framework for Teaching English: Years 7, 8 and 9 (DfEE 0019/2001).* London: DfEE Publications.

DEPARTMENT FOR EDUCATION AND EMPLOYMENT (2001b). *Framework for Teaching Mathematics: Years 7, 8 and 9 (DfEE 0020/2001).* London: DfEE Publications.

DEPARTMENT FOR EDUCATION AND EMPLOYMENT (2001c). *Targets for Pupils – Parents' booklets.* London: DfES publications. Also available on the internet at: http://www.standards.dfes.gov.uk/numeracy/publications/?dwnld_id=869&top_id=0&art_id=4573.

DEPARTMENT FOR EDUCATION AND SKILLS (2002a). *Narrowing the Achievement Gap.* London: DfES Publications.

DEPARTMENT FOR EDUCATION AND SKILLS (2002b). *Releasing Potential, Raising Attainment: Managing data in secondary schools.* London: DfES Publications.

DEPARTMENT FOR EDUCATION AND SKILLS (2002c). *Training Materials for the Foundation Subjects (DfES 0350/2002).* London: DfES Publications.

FREDERICKSON, N., REASON, R., and FRITH, U. (1997). *Phonological Assessment Battery (PhAB).* Windsor: nferNelson.

GALTON, F. (1883). *Inquiries into Human Faculty and its Development.* London: Macmillan.

HOPKINS, D. R., and DAVIS, R. (2003). *An investigation into Key Stage 2 National Test data and consideration of issues affecting Primary/Secondary phase transition within one Local Education Authority.* Unpublished research supported by Teacher Research Scholarships granted by the General Teaching Council of Wales (Professional Development References 151 & 3022).

KAMIN, L. (1974). *The Science and Politics of IQ*. London: Penguin Books.

KITE, A. (2000). *A Guide to Better Thinking*. Windsor: nferNelson.

LIPMAN, M., SHARP. M., and OSCANYAN, F. (1980). *Philosophy in the Classroom*. Philadelphia: Temple University Press.

LOHMAN, D. F., and HAGAN, E. P. (2001). *CogAT Form 6: Interpretive guide for teachers and counsellors*. Itasca, Illinois: Riverside Publishing.

LOHMAN, D. F., THORNDIKE, R. L., and HAGEN, E. P., adapted by SMITH, P., FERNANDES, C., and STRAND, S. (2001). *Cognitive Abilities Test (Third Edition)*. Windsor: nferNelson.

NATIONAL COMMISSION ON EDUCATION (1996). *Success Against the Odds: Effective schools in disadvantaged areas*. London: Routledge.

NAYLOR, S., and KEOGH, B. (2002). 'Concept Cartoons.' *Teaching Thinking*. Autumn 2002, pp. 8–12.

NEALE, M., with WHETTON, C., CASPALL C., and McCULLOCH, K. (1997). *Neale Analysis of Reading Ability (NARA)*. Second Revised British Edition. Windsor: nferNelson.

PARR, A. (2000). 'Magic Squares.' *Times Educational Supplement: Primary Maths and Science Supplement*, October 2000, pp.10–12.

PAIVIO, A. (1971). *Imagery and Verbal Processes*. New York: Rinehart and Winston.

QCA (2002). *Value Added Guide*. Available on the internet at: www.updata.org.uk/q6_value_add_guide.htm.

RICHARDSON, A. (1977). 'Verbalizer-Visualizer: A cognitive style dimension.' *Journal of Mental Imagery*, 1, 1009–125.

ROWE, M. B. (1974). 'Wait time and rewards as instructional variables, their influence on language, logic and fate control.' *Journal of Research in Science Teaching*, 11, 81–94.

SAMMONS, P., THOMAS, S., and MORTIMORE, P. (1997). *Forging Links: Effective schools and effective departments*. London: Paul Chapman.

SHARP, C. (2003). *Playing for Success: An evaluation of the fourth year*. Slough: NFER.

SMITH, P., FERNANDES, C., and STRAND, S. (2001). *Cognitive Abilities Test (Third Edition): Technical Manual*. London: nferNelson.

STRAND, S. (1995). *Wandsworth Assessment Programme: Year 6 test results 1993/94 (REU 40/94)*. Education Department: London Borough of Wandsworth.

STRAND, S. (1997). 'Pupil progress during Key Stage 1: A value added analysis of school effects.' *British Educational Research Journal*, 23, (4), 471–487.

STRAND, S. (1998). 'A value added analysis of the 1996 primary school performance tables.' *Educational Research*, 40, (2), 123–137.

STRAND, S. (1999). 'Ethnic group, sex and economic disadvantage: Associations with pupils' educational progress from Baseline to the end of Key Stage 1.' *British Educational Research Journal*, 25, (2), 179–202.

STRAND, S. (2001). 'Secondary schools' use of reasoning tests: letting the CAT out of the bag'. Paper presented to the Annual Conference of the British Educational Research Association, 13–15 September 2001, Leeds University.

STRAND, S. (2003a). 'Consistency in Reasoning Test Scores over Time'. *British Journal of Educational Psychology*, in press.

STRAND, S. (2003b). 'Sex differences in Cognitive Abilities Test scores: A national picture'. Paper presented to the Annual Conference of the British Educational Research Association, 12–14 September 2003, Heriot-Watt University, Edinburgh.

TIMES EDUCATIONAL SUPPLEMENT (1997). 'A Fall from Grace', 5 December 1997.

TIMES EDUCATIONAL SUPPLEMENT (2002a). *Primary Maths and Science Supplement*, April 2002, pp.17–19.

TIMES EDUCATIONAL SUPPLEMENT (2002b). 'Great results fudge true picture,' 10 May 2002, pp.28–29.

TIMES EDUCATIONAL SUPPLEMENT (2003a). 17 January 2003.

TIMES EDUCATIONAL SUPPLEMENT (2003b).'Hate targets? So does Ofsted.' 28 February 2003, p.17.

WHETTON, C. (1995). Verbal reasoning tests. In: Husen, T., and Postlethwaite, N. (eds) *International Encyclopaedia of Education*. Oxford: Pergamon Press.

WILLIAMS, S., and SUTCLIFFE, R. (2000). *The Philosophy Club*. London: DialogueWorks.